BOOKS BY DARYL HINE

POETRY

In and Out   1989
Academic Festival Overtures   1985
Selected Poems   1981
Daylight Saving   1978
Resident Alien   1975
Minutes   1968
The Wooden Horse   1965
The Devil's Picture Book   1961
The Carnal and the Crane   1957
Five Poems   1954

FICTION

The Prince of Darkness and Co.   1961

TRAVEL

Polish Subtitles   1962

TRANSLATION

Theocritus: Idylls and Epigrams   1982
The Homeric Hymns AND
The Battle of the Frogs and the Mice   1972

IN AND OUT

DARYL HINE

Alfred A. Knopf New York 1989

IN AND OUT

A Confessional Poem

Naturam furca expelles, tamen usque recurret.

HORACE

THIS IS A BORZOI BOOK
PUBLISHED BY ALFRED A. KNOPF, INC.

Library of Congress Cataloging-in-Publication Data

Hine, Daryl.
    In and out.

    Previous ed. has title: In & out.
    I. Title
PR9199.3.H5I5 1988   811'.54   88-45263
ISBN 0-394-57249-1
Manufactured in the United States of America
First Edition

ANTONY MAURICE STERN

AND

LISELOTTE VON BAEYER STERN

Nox perpetua luceat eis

IN AND OUT

Proem

I N AND OUT: the quotation from Horace
I've taken as epigraph, *Naturam*
furca expelles, explains,
tamen usque recurret: "Although
you may drive away nature by means
of a pitchfork, she never the less
will return all the way." An example
of cynical wisdom we ought
to remember, although we have nearly
forgotten who nature was—what
is her nature? An antelapsarian
goddess of kind, *demiourga*,
Great Mother, who framed the *gecyndlimu*
("genitals"), plainly a genial,
cereal soul? A personified
aggregate known in Chinese
as "the ten thousand things"? Or the gentle
Wordsworthian muse? Well, whatever
her beeswax, as we said in childhood,
this fable will not in the main
be about her, although it recounts
her expulsion, or, rather, attempted
expulsion (*expelles*: condition
contrary to fact), from the breast
of a wilful believer, and tells
the perverse psychomachia consequent
on the outrageous attempt,
with the means whereby mischief was nearly
effected, the ablative *furca*,
the pitchfork that proved instrumental
in Nature's repulse and reverse.

But so much I can promise the reader
at least, that anonymous nature
will play in the scenes of the drama
that follow, or rather behind
them, the part of provocative agent
or patient, and wait in the wings
until ultimately we demand
her triumphant and total recall,
the return of the fabled repressed.

An experiment, then, and the method
that we were instructed to use
once in school to describe all experiments,
namely the table of contents.
Hypothesis, first, or our problem,
the thing we are going to prove.
In a narrative poem, or novel
in verse, if the critic prefer,*
this emerges—we hope it emerges—
unforced in the course of the story.
Discreetly, if not unobtrusively,
near the beginning your true
proposition should somewhere be stated,
to give the narrator the chance
to say later, "I told you so, didn't
I? What did I tell you? You see?
Tamen usque recurret, indeed!
Hoc erat demonstrandum! The reader,
thus flattered, can join in the rigged
recognition, and murmur, "Ah ha!"

So a naked hypothesis offers
the best opportunity first
for the solid construction of plot.
But as life is a series of accidents

* It is prudent perhaps to point out
  in parenthesis what should be obvious,
  that this is written in running
  accentual anapaests, three
  to a line, with allowance for word-
  breaks, mutatis mutandis, like so:
  ta-ta-TUM ta-ta-TUM ta-ta-TUM,
  an unbroken, continuous ribbon
  of verse from beginning to end,
  which may look like free verse but is not.

clumsily mimicked by art
as coincidence, next you must mention
your data, particular facts
circumstantially stated, like places
and dates, your material and
apparatus, the furniture of
the laboratory—such as the character
of the protagonist, if
he has got one (in first person narrative
this might be better implied
than described, or suggested throughout
by the tone of the narrator's voice.)

But in general, character—ethos—
belongs with empirical data
unearthed in the course of the story,
developed along with the plot,
which in chemistry would be called Method,
the means or procedure whereby
an experiment may be conducted
successfully: how it is done.
Now the drama, or praxis, or action
deserves the most detailed attention
of all, both in science and art;
it is life that demands "execution,"
the treatment they used to consider
the crowning distinction of craft
and the bulk of a book. Observation,
conclusion the chorus supply
in the classical manner—a chorus
of one. In the end we shall come
if we're lucky, full circle, as nature
was said in our premise—remember?—
to have hypothetically done.

Book One

Presbyterian College

A man may a while
Nature beguile
  By doctrine & lore,
Yet at the end
Will Nature home wend
  There she was before.
ANONYMOUS

IN the Old Presbyterian College,
as gothic an edifice as
had been seen since the late nineteenth century
in or about Montreal,
with its battlements, buttresses, ogival
windows and gargoyles and groining,
the fortress of predestination
had fallen on difficult days
by the midst of the 'fifties: the bulk
of its membership had been seduced
by the Baptists and Methodists and
Congregationalists to combine
in a newfangled national church,
till this bastion of Calvinist doctrine
located conveniently
at McGill on the edge of the campus,
the northwestern corner, attracted,
in place of the youthful elect
who had flocked there before, now the fold
had been pilfered, a different or
an indifferent new clientele,
and the stronghold of Knox was reduced,
like the best theological schools
in that secular decade, to letting
out rooms to the reprobate, medical
students and justified sinners
in Law, Engineering and Arts,
unregenerate Anglicans, Pagans,
and members, too, of the detested,
detestable United Church—
even agents of Rome, not to mention
agnostics, in whose tiny number
(for doubt was not fashionable
in the heyday of Positive Thinking)
I counted myself at the almost
incredible age of eighteen.

I was lying alone on my bed
in the ex-Presbyterian College
one dull afternoon in the winter
that should have been Spring, 'fifty-five.
I had covered my feet with a quilt
which had slipped to the floor; on my stomach
a copy lay, open, face down
and half-read, of the *Poems and Sonnets
of Shakespeare.* Outside it was snowing.
Distracted by boredom and guilt,
I was thinking again of the problem
my life was becoming, a triangle
not too dissimilar to
that depicted, unless I misread
it, in Sonnet one-hundred-and-forty
or one-forty-four. As I counted
my friends on my fingers, I numbered
my loves on my thumbs: they were double,
a man and a woman, of comfort,
respectively, and of despair,
as the poet expressed it. The better—
my angel!—was Mark, who was almost
a man, and teutonically fair.
We were just of an age—what is more,
since our birthdays occurred the same day
(which we thought an amazing coincidence,
seeing how distant our birthplaces
were) we were twins, in a manner
of speaking. We'd met in November,
that year I had come to McGill
as a freshman from British Columbia.
Mark was expecting the day
of his family-sponsored departure
for Europe. Who brought us together?
His mother, a dragon to whom
I'd come armed with a brief introductory
note—she was sprung from a Baltic
baronial family, all
of whose members were dragons. Medea,
she'd followed a journalist lover
called Jason to London, and married
him weeks before Mark had been born;
but thereafter she had immolated

her offspring to other, more up-to-date
interests: fashion photography,
politics, cars. By the time
that I met her, she "did" anthropology.
Somewhere or other, perhaps
in the move from Great Britain to Canada,
Freya mislaid her son's father
whose use had apparently ceased
with conception, though Mark bore his name
while his mother's was different. Meeting
them, then, I was puzzled. My notions
of normal maternal behaviour
were drawn from my own, more conventional
upbringing. Freya and Mark
on acquaintance seemed less like a mother
and son than an oddly matched couple
who'd made a companionate marriage
in spite of their difference of age—
an impression that Mark would examine
in horrified retrospect during
his years of analysis later.
His mother had recently ordered
him out of her house or apartment:
at his age, she said, it was better
for children to live by themselves.
Independence was one of her favourite
virtues. But soon she went further
and ordered him out of the country,
to taste at first hand (as she put
it) in Europe his cultural heritage.
Switzerland had been selected
(I never knew why) as the place
of his exile, an eminent firm
of lithographers somehow persuaded,
in view of his putative talent
in visual matters, to offer
the boy an apprenticeship. Freya,
in this as in everything else
that concerned the career of her son,
after all she had done to neglect
him in childhood and youth, as a baby
abandoning him to the care
of a nursemaid, and later exposing
the delicate shoot to the brutal

conditions of boarding school life,
was implacable in her mistaken
maternal ambition as any
Hyrcanian tigress (a favourite
of all the classical authors
for motherly fierceness and pride).
It was all a mistake, because Mark
as an adult ("Now you are full grown!"
I can hear her abrupt and Germanic
indicative somehow imperative
statement of duty as fact),
or as what she conceived as an adult,
while certainly sweet and goodnatured,
was neither ambitious nor clever,
and Freya must be disappointed
of such intellectual company
as she might hope to obtain
from a son of her powerful bore.

Though I've mentioned our meeting, it's odd
that whereas I am sure that we met
in November, and even remember
the hour and the date, which were late
afternoon and a Sunday, I cannot
recall the location—perhaps
the Museum? a tea room? or Freya's
apartment? The frame is erased
by the forcefulness of the impression
the principals made. They abide
in my memory still like an ivory
diptych of Mother and Son
from Ravenna or Paris or Rome:
hierarchical, marvellous, posed
in relief, paradoxically human,
the mother a masculine woman,
the son an ambiguous youth.

All that autumn the pair were my only
companionship, which may seem strange;
of my neighbours and classmates I never
imagined that one might emerge
from the oddly anonymous mass
as a friend, though I don't understand
why I didn't, except I was shy.

This improbable couple, selected
at random, almost (for the letter
that brought us together was written
by one who himself was a stranger
I'd met on the 'bus from B. C.),
must fulfill all the functions of friends.
While with Freya at least I had something
in common because we considered
ourselves intellectuals, talking
a language not just transatlantic
but spanning the chasm of years
which in my generation we hadn't
begun to consider a gap,
I had little in common with Mark
but our age and our sex—which were better
than nothing, but hardly enough.

What we talked of I cannot recall,
save that Freya would frequently lecture
us both by the hour on a subject
she called anthropology, mainly
a mishmash of Frazer and Freud
with a tincture of even less plausible
theories drawn from a dubious
discipline termed The Occult;
and she liked to conclude such a session
by reading aloud from the Book
of the Dead. "The Collective Unconscious,"
I murmured to Mark as he stifled
a yawn and a giggle, "*c'est nous*."
As one does, I said more than I meant,
for such sessions resembled a course
of remedial sex education,
where Freya, a frustrated pedagogue
sought by exotic example—
subconsciously sought—to awaken
our latency, with some success.

Mark's departure for Switzerland, scheduled
at first for the end of November,
was little by little postponed
inexplicably till after Xmas,
which Freya austerely observed,
but in anthroposophical fashion—

the tree, she declared, was a symbol
of life: even life was a symbol
of something—by reading aloud
not from Dickens but Mme. Blavatsky.

At Christmas time I was the only
inhabitant of Presbyterian
College who didn't go home
for the holidays: nowhere to go.
In the interval I was alone
in the dormitory over a week.
In the daytime the halls and the stairs
and the normally echoing showers
as well as the empty and locked
other rooms, seemed abnormally quiet;
the sunlight and dust had the place
with its several floors to themselves.
But at night-time you might have imagined,
as Mark, who rejoiced in romantic
frissons like a schoolboy, remarked,
that the jolly old college was haunted;
the wind and the snow on the wind
orchestrated the picturesque battlements,
rattled impractical windows,
unnatural noises abounded
within as without. It was cosy
to sit in my room, with a cup
of hot cocoa, just Mark and myself
(for his sensible mother was never
invited to join the debauch
of unreason), and whisper such frightening
stories as either remembered—
for Mark had heard many at school—
or for my part had read or invented.
I almost persuaded myself
once, at three in the morning, I'd seen
for a second as if at the outermost
angle and limit of vision
a spectre descending the stair:
it was brown, like a stain on the air,
insubstantial, transparent, amorphous,
and not very terrible. Chiefly
I think my reaction was triumph.
I'd seen one! But what had I seen?

The authorities, Mark reassured
me, insisted irrational panic
accompany all supernatural
manifestations, however
perspicuous these might appear;
if you're scared, as the saying was, practically
witless, you know you are haunted.

On top of his boyish good humour
and sluggish vitality, Mark's
most egregious characteristic
was evident absence of guilt,
that continuous sense of unworthiness
that undermines the neurotic
and gifted, the private persuasion,
whatever goes wrong, it is somehow
one's fault; but just how he escaped
the original and universal
conviction is open to doubt.
Did his mother's indifference free
him from any reciprocal debt?
(not the debt that we all pay to nature,
but something less natural) or,
had his father's complete disappearance
removed the insane obligation
we all of us feel to Papa?
Did he somehow imbibe by osmosis
the freedom from guilt that is almost
a twentieth-secular credo?
The reasons, as psychoanalysis
teaches, were equally futile
and tedious to disinter:
but if ever an innocent, Adamite
nature existed, that nature
in *esse* and *posse* was his.

His departure again was put off
after New Year's. The weather had set,
the Saint Lawrence was shut for the winter,
as we could observe from the top
of Mount Royal, the scene of our afternoon
walks. Since my classes were all
in the morning, by noon I had nothing
to do, nor had Mark, while awaiting

a date of removal that now
must be further deferred to the Spring.
In those weeks our unique entertainment
was walking where nobody walked
during winter, beneath us the city,
withdrawn into premature twilight,
its windows and chimneys and roofs,
and beyond it the sweep of the river
whose frigid magnificence flashed
in the westering trail of the sun
like a scimitar fashioned of ice,
and beyond that the featureless plain—
could we see it or not?—which extended
from hence to the border; this view,
if we felt we required an excuse
(and my conscience supplied the demand),
was sufficient. Transpicuous groves
of deciduous trees interrupted
by conifers once in a while
made a delicate Japanese screen
or a monochrome picture: the white
or off-white of the snow was like paper,
the branches were sketched or suggested
in sombre but colourless ink.
The ascent of the mountain was steep,
and in places we paused to recapture
our breaths and a glimpse of the view
that emerged as the fruit of our climb
and the ocular crown of our arduous
walk. At the top a deserted
casino awaited us when
we were through; there was also a path
that encircled the brow of Mount Royal
a mile, maybe more, in circumference.
When we protracted our set
promenade, we would visit the graveyards
that filled the far side of the mountain,
the Protestants' spacious and parklike,
still prosperous-looking, with marble,
elaborate, grand mausolea
and angels and urns and inscriptions
in elegant Latin and English
proclaiming the puritan virtues,
Prosperity, Prudence, and Pride;

and the Catholics' nearby, plebeian
in death as in life—proletarian
rather, because of the Pope's
and their priests' prohibition of birth
control: squalid memorials crowded
promiscuously and in hideous
taste to a Protestant eye:
crucifixions, and other events
in the life of Our Lord and Our Lady
(including the Spotless Conception
or Phantom of Fatima) were
represented there, as were the lately
deceased, by their portraits, unflattering
photographs, plastic and glass.

The casino I mentioned, the scene
of imagined encounter and putative
revel, was always abandoned
at three (it grew dark before four):
an extravagant structure intended
for popular use but neglected,
illumined by vast chandeliers.
Each electrical fixture containing
(Mark counted them) dozens of bulbs
was reflected in acres of polished
mosaic; uncountable chairs,
at present unoccupied, stood
underneath them at tables that should
have been gaily and loudly surrounded.
The place was a virtual desert
where silence and vacancy reigned
like an interim government, where
hospitality of the description
dispensed by machinery served
our immediate needs, which were simple
and few: cigarettes, and a species
of fruitcake that came in a cellophane
wrapper, hot chocolate, which
was a favourite drink at eighteen,
though I'm sure I should gag on it now.
In the midst of this splendid and sinister
solitude (which I exaggerate),
Mark and myself were enisled
in the mindless conspiracy most

adolescents pretend is their social
condition; we whispered, although
if we wished there was nothing to keep
us from shouting; our figures repeated
again and again at a distance
in windows that with the arrival
of darkness had turned into mirrors.
We lingered and listened to tunes
on the jukebox, whose hill-billy plangency
suited the hardscrabble food
and our mood of contingency: "Heartbreak
Hotel," with its welcome to loneliness,
struck a discordantly ominous
chord as we plunged down the snow-covered
mountain at nightfall together.

A curious thing: as the day
of his sailing drew nearer, insensibly
I became fonder of Mark.
An agreeable friend, if a dull
one, became, on the eve of estrangement,
unique, irreplaceable, dear.
It is sometimes the case thus; at parting
the heart will awaken, alarmed
into life by the prospect of loss
and provoked to a late recognition
of what it is going to miss;
then the daily companion you'd taken
for granted is changed by departure,
a whiff of mortality, into
a rich and mysterious stranger,
more capable now than before
of exerting a strange fascination,
and, presto! your innermost feelings,
concealed from yourself by *ennui*
and the habit of every day
are unmasked by the threat of removal,
which makes the most commonplace person
appear like a hero or martyr,
transformed by the magical formula
"Must you be going?" to Hector,
Aeneas, or Don Giovanni.
The platform whereon are enacted
the dramas of heartbreak assume

the prestige of the scaffold; the quay
and the waiting-room, these are the stage
on which every lover is Titus,
and even the hitherto boring
belovèd becomes Bérénice.
Thus a 'bus station mimics an opera
house, where the fortunate traveller
catches a last matinée—
mediocre performances mostly,
but acted to standing room only—
of Tristan, Otello, or Faust.

We had come to be friends in the shadow
of such separation, for Mark
had been going as long as I'd known
him; the very first words that his mother,
that subtle diplomatist, speaking
in French, used to bring us together,
were, "*Marc est en train de partir.*"
But the day was so often postponed
that I started to think it would never
occur, and forgot that it could.
On our birthday in late February
he showed me the ticket his mother
had given him: it was One Way.
Thus the date of his sailing was set,
and the ticket provided a warrant
for its execution, or ours.

On the weekend before, he suggested—
I thought he suggested—we go
on a last expedition together.
Though Mark said he hadn't been skiing
since school, that's to say, since the winter
before, he had never forgotten
the pleasures of life on the slopes,
and he wished to initiate me
in their mysteries, at Mont Tremblant,
which I rendered as Trembling Mountain.
I trembled myself, to be frank,
at the prospect: I'd never been skiing,
was scarcely *sportif*—and I stifled
a yawn at the thought of a weekend
alone in a chalet with Mark.

It was different here in the city,
with nothing to do. In addition
to walking and talking, we went
on an average five times a week
to the movies, for those were the days
before telly. Our favourite flics
were, predictably, horror shows, gothic
confections with whimsical titles,
that dealt with such grand fundamental
clichés as the amateur vampire
and Frankenstein's monster's resentment
at being created—the line
that was drawn, as it seemed to us, not
always accurately, between human
and super- and sub-. We concealed
these nocturnal excursions (which often
took place in the daytime) to cinemas
showing not double but triple
attractions, from Freya, who might
after all have approved of their anthropological object, for fear
she express a desire to accompany
us. Our triangular friendship,
diminished since Xmas, had shrunk
to a twosome, and that was exclusive.

But—several days in the country
together! What were we to do?
It was plain I could hardly refuse
this request of an ultimate favour
intended to educate me;
I accepted my friend's invitation
with what, after some hesitation,
I tried to make look like alacrity,
packing my suitcase with every
woolen I owned, and (too young
for a flask) something meaty to read.

We set out on a Saturday morning
at nine, in a Land Rover Mark
had persuaded a friend of his mother's
to lend him, his skiing equipment
attached to the roof. As we quit
the periphery of Montreal

(which was quicker to do in that decade),
I noticed how winter, diminished
and dirty and sad in the suburbs,
existed in primitive rigor
beyond, in the country. The road
to the North was a scene from an ad
for Canadian National Railways:
between the monotonous sombre
and primitive verdure of evergreen
forests, the newly built highway
ascended, it seemed, to the sky,
while on this side and that the horizon
was broken by snow-covered conical
hills, very small, very ancient,
the mountains that form the Canadian
Shield, or Laurentian Chain.

After lunch, which we ate in a diner,
we dawdled along undetermined
upon our direction. We turned
off the highway, the road grew impassable;
Mark was a dangerous driver;
I quickly discovered I didn't
know how to interpret a map;
we were lost, and the car, as if conscious
of our inefficiency, stalled.
There was nothing in such a predicament
for it, but get out and walk.
So we did, in a minute; but first
we were fixed by the silence we heard
in the car now the motor had stopped.
In the midst of the tranquillized landscape
the only impetuous object
was ours; now that we were arrested
in flight, we were less the exception
except for our heartbeats, quite audible
(so I imagined) for miles.
The interior temperature
of our vehicle dropped with the sun,
nonetheless we were slow to get out
as the men on the moon from their module,
so lunar the landscape appeared.

But at last, not so much out of panic
at possibly freezing to death
as embarrassment, we must abandon
our transport impeded by snow.
As we did so, we laughed at the signals
our breath superscribed on the air.
With the snow reaching over the tops
of our boots, in a matter of yards
we were soaked to our socks, paradoxically
sweating and chilled to the bone.
So continued the rest of the short
winter day; as if trying to run
in a nightmare we stumbled and trudged
until nightfall. The sun had retired
prematurely behind a convenient
hill, when we glimpsed in the distance
what might be the lights of a village,
and even more cheerful, the smoke
of its chimneys betokening warmth
and a promise, though not yet the odour,
of food. We were starving, exhausted,
half-frozen and wet to the skin.

Then, suspecting the lights were a fata
morgana, or *ignis fatuus*
misleading the traveler, I
had resolved not to look up again
while I counted to fifty, to see
if the village would get any nearer.
It didn't apparently, yet
when I lifted my eyes in despair
it was suddenly nearly upon
us. The village was, as it turned out,
not a village at all but the very
hotel where we hoped to be spending
the night. We were welcome. They said
they would send for our car in the morning,
but meanwhile we'd better get out
of the clothes we were wearing, though what
(we demanded), our things being all
in the car, were we going to put
on instead? We might do as we pleased.
They provided us both with a toddy
and showed us the way to the cabin,

a few hundred yards from the central
chalet, where a fire had been laid
in an old-fashioned pot-bellied stove.

While we waited for supper we took
off our clothes, which we spread out to dry
by the fire, and enveloped ourselves
in the Hudson's Bay blankets we found
on the beds. I had never seen Mark
with his clothes off before; the occasion
had never arisen between
us. But now as we changed he displayed
with a casual absence of modesty
far from the shyness or shame
that had prompted me first to undress
chastely draped in the blanket, his person,
as naked he stood for a minute
or two, or it may have been longer,
in front of the stove to get warm.
He was very well made, and the firelight
that danced in the stove's mica window
embellished his handsome if perfectly
commonplace body. His shoulders
were broad, unexpectedly so
for a lad of his sedentary habits,
his buttocks were narrow and hard
as an eighteen-year-old could desire.
His immodesty stemmed, in my view
from the fact that he'd been to a boarding-school
where, I imagined, the parts
we are taught to call private were public?
His vigour, more potent than beauty,
transformed my naive curiosity
into obsession, my casual
glance became fixed as a stare,
which a knock on the door interrupted.

The meal that was served in a covered
container was steak-and-potatoes,
a menu that Mark must have ordered
himself, plus a bottle of wine.
In Quebec I had found that, whatever
the law, one could drink at eighteen,
although nobody asked us our age.

So we dined in our improvised togas,
reclining like Romans in front
of the cosily wood-burning stove
and laconically sharing the wine.

After dinner, with nothing to read,
in the absence of cards and all other
distractions, compelled to converse,
we discovered what one might have guessed,
we had little to say to each other.
In such situations the obvious
course—as is also the case
when invention, or "something to say"
is deficient in formalist verse—
was a game: but what sort of a game?
Botticelli was out of the question,
as Mark mightn't know of a single
explorer beginning with B,
let alone of a classical poet
beginning with C, or a modern
composer beginning with A.
Education and intimacy
were in vain: the devices with which
intellectuals try to amuse
themselves weren't available; even
I Spy was abandoned in giggles.

In lieu of a game, we reverted
to riddles and jokes and such poems
as skulk in the oral tradition
and seldom emerge on the page,
bawdy ballads and limericks Mark
as a schoolboy had laid up a lifetime
supply of. Too literate for
my own good, I could hardly compete:
that usurper of memory, print,
had bequeathed me a tame, expurgated
anthology. Having exhausted his storehouse
of lore—the inventive *Young Man
from Lachine*, the contorted *Young Man
from Nantucket*, the polyincestuous
Fellow of Trinity—Mark
next resorted to personal anecdote,
told, I had cause to believe,

(for invention with him was no joke),
with as little embroidery as
seemed consistent with verisimilitude,
yet with a fervour that bordered
on mythopoetical; for
reminiscence already—so soon!—
had begun its mysterious working
whereby our corruptible bodies
are changed into glorious bodies.
The glamour that clung to these stories
or story was focused nostalgically
not on himself, as I might
have predicted, nor yet on a place
(though he often referred to "the farm"),
even less on the mythical innocence
grown-ups attribute to childhood
in retrospect; rather, it highlighted
someone called Hyacinth Star.

I had already gathered that Mark
had been sadly neglected in childhood
for all of the fitful attentions
of Freya, whom he was instructed
emphatically not to call Mother.
It seemed that between his eleventh
and seventeenth years he had spent
every summer with friends of the latter's,
the Stars, on a farm near Quebec.
And these holidays, which were the only
pathetic exceptions to boarding-
school life in his teens, he remembered
as idylls, an album of pastoral
scenes, where the role of the swain
was assumed by the son of the family,
Hyacinth, just of an age
with our own, or a little bit younger.
"You ought to meet Hyacinth, really
you must!" was the theme of his song,
though as Hyacinth's home was in Ottawa
during the winter, it wouldn't
be easy to make his acquaintance
at once; but he might be enrolled
at McGill in the following year,
when no doubt I should meet him. According

to Mark, he must be without parallel,
nothing much less than a model
of everything one should admire
in a person of parts, as ingenious,
generous, wicked, capricious—
all average gifts which to Mark
seemed the birthmarks of genius. Hurt,
I agreed that he must be delightful,
a paragon, plainly, a prince,
the perfection of friendship. Too bad,
I ironically murmured, he wasn't
available. Would he were here
in my place! But, as Mark wasn't listening,
irony plainly was wasted.
The only complaint he would add
to the budget of Hyacinth's virtues
concerned his religion. His father,
a noted psychiatrist, also
a Jew, had converted, a few
years ago, to the Catholic Church,
and had taken his wife and his children
like luggage or hostages with
him, recording the move in a best-selling
book called *The Pillar of Salt*.
Mark confessed he was sometimes embarrassed
by things that the Stars took for granted,
like Grace before Meat, as a first
generation agnostic. (His mother
could not be described as agnostic:
she knew, and her friendship with Hyacinth's
father had suffered a set-back
because of his views, which she thought,
for a witch-doctor, unscientific.)
I granted it must be uncomfortable,
Hyacinth's being so pious.
"Who? Hyacinth? Pi? He's a regular
fellow!"—which signified normally
naughty, immodest, and frank.
For the little that Mark didn't know
about sex, he'd been taught, he averred,
by the life of the farm, and by Hyacinth's
hints: so the handbook of nature
replaced the unnatural manual
practised at school. He related

a church service Hyacinth claimed
he'd attended one Sunday: the sermon
that day was in English, albeit
the parish was French, on account
of the numerous anglophone visitors.
Hyacinth swore, in the gospel according
to Mark, some *curé de campagne*,
understandably nervous because
of this language difference, took
as his topic the practice of that
form of prayer which the textbooks describe
as "ejaculatory": a brief
and spontaneous utterance, pious
in character, such as, "My God!"
"Jesus Christ!" or "Hail Mary!" His thesis,
which wasn't a bad one except
for a choice of expression deriving
as much from linguistic simplicity
as from his clerical innocence,
was, that such prayer, as an excellent
thing, should be practised as often
as feasible. Then he displayed
an acquaintance with everyday life,
or with what he described as "the facts
of the workaday world," that was staggering
in application. He urged
everybody, in view of their limited
time and their rare opportunities,
given their lives, for such acts,
"to be sure to ejaculate often."
The layman, he said, as he warmed
to his theme (and here Mark was inspired
with the words of the preacher verbatim),
"The workman ejaculates when
and wherever he can, on arising
and dressing, while brushing his teeth
or when kissing his wife before breakfast,
while driving to work—at the office—
at lunch—in the 'bus or the subway...
the Christian should ask himself, how
many ejaculations he's had
in the course of a day." This became
quite a byword between the two boys,
who would greet one another thereafter

facetiously, "Did you ejaculate
recently? Oh? and how often?"

I laughed. He expected me to,
and, besides, it was funny; but Mark
who could never, I'm sure, have made up
such a sermon, was silent. This subject
had seldom been mentioned between
us in so many words; the allusion
occasioned a pause, and I saw
that a topic taboo hitherto
was disturbing him not unobtrusively
till he adjusted his blanket.
We finished the wine, he insisting
I tell him a story in turn.
I had nothing to tell; my adventures
were few and inferior, such
as could scarcely divert the susceptible
youth that I took him to be.
My material being so scant,
it was clearly incumbent on me
to invent (but my mind was a blank),
or adapt, which is nearly as hard.
I began with an incident taken
from Burton's *Arabian Nights*.
I had always found art more instructive,
as well as amusing, than life,
and as lies are more likely than truth,
I invented *ad libitum*. Mark,
with his legs folded under the blanket,
was listening with the uncritical
somnolent air of a child,
with the fire like a story-book lion
asleep in the cage of the stove.

I've forgotten the drift of my story,
except that it drifted. Too often
in retrospect I am unable
myself to distinguish the fable
I read or made up from the fabulous
nonsense that actually happened.
My ramshackle narrative ended
at last, though potentially endless,
at random as it had begun,

and its secondhand, fictive existence
concluded unchallenged by Mark,
who remarked as he rose, rearranging
his toga, "Let's call it a night."
An Arabian one, would it also
be rated a night to remember?
A yawn: was it bedtime already?
Though neither was wearing a watch,
I agreed it was time to turn in—
into what? We took turns in the bathroom
and climbed between separate sheets.
In a moment, exhausted as much
by my fictional effort as after
our hike through the snow I had fallen
asleep and was telling the fire
the remarkable exploits of Mark.

I awoke in a fathomless darkness
with no way of telling the hour
save the usual symptoms: like clockwork
my body assumed it was late
while my psyche presumed it was early
and darker, proverbially,
before dawn. I was painfully conscious
of lying alone, in the cold
that pervaded the cabin, the fire
being out, and my loneliness came
as a premature chill of the tomb.
I could tell from his musical breathing
that Mark was asleep. I remembered
as if it were scorched on my retina,
how pornographic he looked
in the lecherous glow of the stove
dimly visible still, like a sword
in the intimate darkness between
us. He stirred, and his breath came abrupt
and irregular now. Then he spoke
in a whisper or what was intended
to pass for a whisper but rang
like an amorous challenge: "Awake?"
"Uh." "It's freezing, I bet that it's twenty
below." "Do you think so?" "Outside."
"If you're cold..." "Yes?" "One way to get warm
would be bunking together." "O.K.,

if you like." With a hop and a skip
across no man's dark, cold, inhospitable
land, I slipped into his bed.

Now the curious reader will wonder—
the candid will frankly demand—
to be told what we did. I don't know.
What does anyone do at eighteen,
without special instruction, the like
of which neither of us had received,
but the age-old instinctual fumble?
The temperature of the room,
had our tastes been more fully developed,
prevented extensive experiment
anyway. First, I suppose,
we pretended to huddle together
for warmth. Opportunity being
the mother of liberties, we
then began to explore our adjacent
erogenous zones. But before
our impersonal parts could occur—
insofar as identical parts
can occur—we were forced to transgress
certain boundaries verbally, such
as, "I'm sorry?" "No, please go ahead."
Homosexual play has to talk
in comparatives. Heterosexuals,
finding themselves in the same
situation, a man and a woman,
would not feel the slightest occasion
for any apology, surely:
desire can be taken for granted
between them. An equally natural
tacit attraction between
individuals of the same sex,
on the other hand, isn't. The love
that is shameless enough to pronounce
its own name has to spell it as well;
so the dubious text is encumbered
with footnotes and scholia, plus
introductions by various hands.
It is nearly impossible after
the fact, to recapture the flavour and
texture of passion. The acts

that are covered by four-letter words
were spontaneous once; and the lover
reflects in the morning as often
as not, "Did we really do that?"

I awoke beside Mark as a wintery
dawn resurrected the room.
Without speaking we rose and in haste
and incurious modesty dressed,
then we trudged to the lodge for a taciturn
breakfast. I asked, had it snowed
overnight? He replied, did I want
any more maple syrup? Immediately
after, he said he was going
to ski. As he didn't suggest
I accompany him, I was hardly
about to suggest it myself.
Overnight some invisible agent
had rescued our Rover as promised,
a decorative icing of snow
on its roof. Mark removed his equipment,
his skis and high boots and the poles
that he needed to steer with. I chose,
among several books I had brought,
the *Confessions* of Augustine. Why,
with so many so much more amusing
to choose from—*A Book of the Winter,
Deciphering Linear B,
The Desire and Pursuit of the Whole*—
I elected the Bishop of Hippo,
I couldn't have told you. Perhaps
if my choice had been otherwise then
all the rest of this story would not
have occurred as it did, or at all?
It is futile to speculate, raising
the spectre of predestination.

I watched inarticulate Mark
as he entered the "white, snowy nunnery"
(Donne, on the Alps) and returned
to our cabin intending to spend
an agreeable day with another
repentant but eloquent sinner.
For lunchtime I waited, absorbed
in my narrative, nearly till two,

when I ate a ham sandwich, the book
on the table in front of me propped
by the water carafe. As for Mark,
insofar as I bothered at all,
he might eat when he pleased. Thus it wasn't
till nightfall, at last, having finished
the first psychological novel,
I started to wonder where he
could have got to, and worry. I waited
a while after dark in the cabin
and smoked an improbable number
of cigarettes; then, about seven,
descended again to the inn
to make inquiries. As I arrived
in the lobby, an ambulance pulled
from the driveway, its sirens lamenting
the human predicament, subject
to accident, illness, and death.
When I asked after Mark at the desk,
I was told I had missed his departure
by seconds, for hospital, he
having broken or twisted an ankle
while skiing alone on the slopes.
I must telephone Freya at once.
When I told her what happened, "An accident?
Nonsense!" There were, she insisted,
no accidents. Nevertheless
she was ready to come to my rescue,
or that of the Land Rover; she
could be there before midnight by train.
And she was. I awaited her guiltily,
much as I fancy the culprit
awaits his omniscient judge
and the swift execution of justice.
But Freya, whatever she thought,
wasn't talking. She'd called at the hospital:
Mark was described as progressing
according to schedule. "And that
means he's resting—they've given him something.
The ankle's not fractured, but cracked,
and no nonsense about it. However,
he ought to be home by tomorrow.
Of course he will be in a cast,"
she explained, not unkindly, while changing

the gears in her capable manner.
The only reproach that she uttered
was, "Pity, you know, you don't drive."
"I can't drive, I can't swim, I can't dance,"
I hysterically added, "or ski!"
She ignored my hysteria. "If
he's in plaster for six or eight weeks,
it appears we shall have to postpone
his departure for Europe again."

It was providence, plainly, unless
you prefer the unconscious, which had
intervened in this singular way
to decide our immediate futures.
While Freya was clearly inclined
to a matter-of-fact explanation—
a mixture of guilt and desire
in an equal proportion explosive,
touched off by his coming departure—
I took the traditional view
as to accidents that were no accident.
Freya's debunking had backfired.
When what we unknowingly wish
unexpectedly happens, we think
it is heaven that grants our desire.
As for Mark, he maintained an amnesiac
silence and seldom referred
to the accident, less to its cause.
But the cast which his leg was encased
in remained, like a cheap reproduction
in quick drying plaster of Paris,
for weeks. It was solid, off-white,
and impressively heavy, impossible,
obviously, to ignore
as it lay on the sofa, a symbol
of something, we couldn't say what.

He returned to his basement apartment
as soon as the plaster had set;
there he hobbled about with the aid
of a cane, and I visited him
as before. Like a poet who masters
a novel and difficult meter,
he learned to manoeuvre his foot

in the cast, yet his silence extended
to cover not only his fall
but the fall that occasioned it, which
was repeated again and again
in the course of the weeks that ensued,
underneath reproductions of Braque
and Picasso, and dubious African
masks, in the shadow, or so
I conjectured, of Freya's indifferent
tolerance. What if she guessed?
But she hardly could help but have known,
since the morning she found us together
in bed when she came, in a fit
of uncharacteristic maternal
concern, with an armful of groceries.
"Sleepyheads!" gruffly she greeted
us, showing no trace of embarrassment;
"Isn't it time you got up?"
Her discretion I came to equate
with her son's; on the sensitive matter
in hand, they were equally mute.

My inferior spirit, I said
when I started to paraphrase Shakespeare
originally, was a woman,
and one, in his words, "coloured ill."
No, not Freya, as one might suppose,
whose complexion and poise a Valkyrie
might envy, in spite of her years,
and who now like Brünnhilde will forthwith
oblige us by going to sleep
until needed again by the story.
This spirit I'll call Theodora,
producing her out of a hat
like the rabbit she rather resembled:
at least half-a-dozen years older
than we, and a doctoral candidate,
so she informed us, in English,
specifically James; her appearance
befitting a serious scholar,
betrayed the pedantic result
of a studious cult of cold water
and soap, and her stern, academic
refusal to make up her face.

Who remembers the hey-day of James,
and of plain, intellectual girls?
I had taken her first (to employ
the invidious language in vogue)
for a fag hag or dyke; she was only
an old-fashioned bluestocking frump.

Theodora, abrasive by nature,
had scraped our acquaintance in one
of those Austro-Hungarian dives
near the gates of the campus dispensing
old Viennese pastries along
with the dregs of espresso. She crouched
at the table adjacent to ours
annotating in pencil a paperback
mercilessly. When I peered
to decipher the title—*The Wings
of the Dove*—in a guttural coo
she demanded I pass the paprika.
Peremptory though her approach,
it provided an opening. Yet
there were depths, we were both to discover,
of feeling behind that façade:
lower depths. I was never to fathom
her motives for so condescending
to two insignificant specimens—
freshmen!—as we must have seemed.
Had it something to do with the crutches
and cast that encumbered my chum,
and the fact that his feet, or his foot
was of clay—or of plaster of Paris?
A whimsical Jamesian pity?
She told me, not very much later
but after our friendship had burgeoned
from something she scraped into something
that should have been nipped in the bud,
that the glum and uncomfortable silence
we sat in had led her to speak.
My relief when she did so reminded
me strangely of what I had felt
in Grade Eight, when a talkative girl
had accosted me as I was walking
one noon with a boy of remarkable
beauty with whom I had nothing

in common except my onesided
attachment, an innocent crush
that fell short of flirtation: bewildered,
good-natured and shy, he accepted
my homage in silence, in which
it was offered, believe it or not,
for the sonnets I'd scribbled, though to
them, were not for his eyes... I felt guilty
but grateful for my liberation,
in spite of myself, from my hopeless
devotion, by means of indifferent
feminine gabble. I always
preferred, with a few sympathetic
exceptions, the garrulous sex
conversationally, and responding
as much to the text Theodora
was busy defacing as to
Theodora herself, I began
to discourse on the novels of James
I had read or attempted to read.
She indulgently smiled: a mere reader,
her attitude seemed to imply,
a rank amateur, missed all those layers
of meaning that James in his terminal
phase had confected to tickle
the critical palate; and in
illustration she bit off a mouthful
of strudel. "*The Turn of the Screw*
is my favourite!" Mark interjected,
ignored hitherto: in reaction
perhaps to his mother's ambivalent
rationalism, he liked
supernatural stories the best.
"And that other one: *Casting the Runes.*"
Theodora looked puzzled till I
in a whisper informed him, "It's not
by the same..." "I imagine *The Portrait*,"
she sneered, "*of a Lady*, or possibly
Dorian Gray is your speed?"
Like the Lady in Comus (remembering
Milton was known as "the lady
of Christ's"), I escaped from my chair
and her knowing, impertinent scrutiny.
Mark with a clumsy attempt

at a bow and a pleasantry (awkward
on crutches), excused himself, too.
As we paid for our coffee and pastries,
however, he grumbled, "What's up?
She was just being friendly, that's all."

I encountered her friendliness later
that week on the steps of the library
clutching an armload of books,
(ambiguity fully intended).
She stopped, though the cold was conducive
to briskness, to ask after Mark,
or "your friend in the cast" as she put
it, or him, and suggested we drop
by her lair (she divulged the address)
for a Nescafé some afternoon.

When I did, unaccompanied (instinct,
or something more conscious, had prompted
me not to convey her polite
invitation to Mark), Theodora
received me with circumflex eyebrows
and open, hospitable arms.
So appropriately over instant,
undrinkable coffee we broached
instantaneous intimacy.
In dissecting the Jamesian heroines,
Isabel, Maisie and Milly,
and Maggie and Fleda and Kate,
Theodora opined that they all
were "repressed," an offhand diagnosis
which Freya was fond of as well.
I objected: such characters seemed
too complex for a complex. "Are you?"
At that age, though not madly red-blooded,
I'd rather be torn limb from limb
than admit it—I'd sooner confess
The Ambassadors bored me to tears.
"Have you ever," she lit a du Maurier,
"slept with a woman?" My speechless
embarrassment told her the truth.
"I suppose, like so many inhibited
sensitive boys nowadays,
you imagine you're queer?" I not only

imagined as much, I'd confirmed
the hypothesis (not quite as often
as I should have liked to) empirically.

"Nonsense. You're just inexperienced!"
Meaning: repressed? Energetic
and brusque as a nurse, she unbuttoned
her blouse, with a clinical wink
reassuring me would-be seductively,
"Come on, this won't hurt a bit."
But it did. Being squeamish, I went
through the time-honoured motions unseeing,
my glasses abandoned on top
of a tower of books by the bedside,
at times sorely tempted to reach
out for something diverting to read.
I assumed that the softness and wetness
I felt, as distinct from the arid
rigidity which I was used
to, formed part of the feminine mystery
Goethe extolled as *Das Ewige
Weibliche*. "Ugh! Is it always
so sticky?" The sheets, when I opened
my eyes, and the relevant parts
of our bodies were dappled with gore.
"But it's not," Theodora cut short
my disgusted, fastidious outcry,
"My time of the month." She inspected
the carnage. "It seems to be yours!
And I thought only feminine virgins...!"
she giggled, unable to finish.
A small laceration I found
on the frenum to blame, or to bless,
for my hair's-breadth escape from *vagina
dentata*. I bandaged the bloody
but miniscule wound in the bathroom
with metres of tissue. Again
fully dressed, I effected a graceless
ungrateful departure, embracing
the chill of the street like a strong
disinfectant. Ingratitude is
a peculiar thing: one is only
aware of it when it is over,
like happiness. Tea and a dollop

of Sympathy—Nescafé rather,
and what? defloration?—were all
Theodora was able to offer.
It wasn't her fault if I found
her prescription unpalatable,
an experiment proving no more
than the obvious. As for the womanly
gesture that won such applause
on the stage, but which bombed in the bedroom,
that generous act might be treated
as child molestation today.

Lately Mark had begun to complain,
though not always in so many words,
of our tacit arrangements, too often
inveighing against the discomfort,
the awkward and painful delays
that his fall had occasioned. The cast,
he declared, was beginning to itch;
and how heavy it was, and how hot!
I began to suspect that the clay,
or the plaster of Paris, that he
felt so onerous, stood, as it were,
in a metaphor hardly unique
for the clay we call mortal, that classical
plaster of Paris, our flesh.
And that flesh, at another remove,
might have stood, if you'll pardon the pun,
for those sins of the flesh that the Bishop
of Hippo subsumed, so I'd noticed,
beneath the more general heading
of habit: the garment of flesh
and the habit of carnal concupiscence
clothing or rather enveloping
Adam and all his descendants:
bad habits, indeed! Whether this
was what Mark had begun to rebel
against, I with my delicate conscience
of wrong-doing, reckoned as much.
And the remedy? Sometimes religion
assumes the most curious forms!
In our age in America there
has developed a mystery cult
of normality, which is enshrined

in the hearts and the minds and the bowels
and armpits of men; and of all
the diversions of men, there is none
which religions exert their tyrannical
empire more utterly over
than pleasure. The normal, whatever
that is, has dictated the rules
of behaviour in sex as in diet,
opinion, and dress. Who respect
this mysterious norm shall be welcome,
but woe unto them that transgress
by the merest iota! Their names
are anathema. Any established
religion derives overwhelming
support not so much from its fervent
promoters, as from its unconscious
adherents: the tepid, in short,
of whom Christ, who appears to have had
the most execrable temper and shocking
bad manners, as well as a terrible
tongue, is supposed to have said
he would vomit them out of his mouth.
As a conscious apostate from normalcy,
normally I should have nothing
but sociological scorn
for convention—which nevertheless
in a pinch I unwittingly worshipped
as negligently as the next one;
for deep in my innermost core
I was somehow or other convinced
that what Mark needed most was a skirt.

I confided as much to the authoress
of our ensuing misfortunes
(I couldn't quite blame her for what
had occurred, which we never discussed),
over tea in a tea shop on Mountain
Street, which in the swift revolution
of time has been changed to la rue
de Montagne, though it owed its original
name to an Anglican bishop
named Mountain: the tea-room today
is a bistro, with *vin ordinaire*
and Pernod in the place of Darjeeling

and Orange Pekoe. Theodora,
in spite or because of a set-back
she needn't acknowledge, succeeded
in making a crowd of our company
quickly enough. I have called
her abrasive: she bored herself into
our lives like a safecracker—not
that they needed much boring—and rifled
my confidence effortlessly.
For I told Theodora, incredible
as it must seem, an approximate
version of what I related
above; as I did so, increasingly
wretched and foolish and guilty
(while thinking it none of her business)
beneath her implacable sympathy,
much, I suppose, as an insect
might feel when it's fixed by the field
entomologist's glass which destroys
what it magnifies. Scrutiny like
Theodora's eventually dries
up the most inexhaustible source.

"I intuited something suspicious
the moment I saw you together,"
she said with an air of posterior
insight that many physicians
affect at the death of a patient.
"You looked so ill-matched and uneasy."
"You noticed?" She did not refer
to her earlier efforts at physical
therapy, giving me up
as a stubborn, intractable problem.
"Poor baby!" she commented, somewhat
ambiguously: was it Mark
or myself whom she saw as an infant
in need of a change? "I can always—
a woman can usually tell.
So confused, and no wonder, poor darling!
One ought to do something. Let's see."
She consulted her watch as if hoping
the dial would tell her her duty.
"He's home, do you think, about now?"
It was quarter to six. I persisted

with what I considered a brilliant
analysis, witty and brief,
of the new situation, to see
Theodora become inattentive,
the frightening force of her womanhood
now focused elsewhere, while she
was beginning to pack up such props
as her notebooks and library books
in an old-fashioned purse like a medical
bag, while she did so emitting
a series of clucks of maternal
distress, like a hen's for an egg:
"O poor child! O poor lamb! O poor innocent!"
leaving me as she departed,
sustained by her mission of pity,
to pay for the tea she had eaten,
the sandwiches, muffins and scones,
absent-mindedly during my lecture.

O nimium loquax! The urge
to deliver a lecture is one
that I then or thereafter could never
resist. The more intimate, awful
the matter, the greater my impulse
to air and expatiate views
that would do a philosopher credit,
a sophist, at least a gymnosophist
vowed to indecent exposure.
As Augustine shows, all confession
entails a confession of faith
necessarily public in nature.
The tongue, an inveterate traitor
that sells out the gates of the city,
betrays for the sake of its news;
indiscreet to a fault, unreliable
always, this maverick member,
(whatever the Doctor may say)
is endowed with peculiar motion,
the least in control of the bodily
organs. I must have been crazy
to wag it in front of a woman.
For women a narrative spun
for the sake of the spinning appears
inconceivable. Matter-of-factly

the sex has no use for the "imagine,"
"for instance," "for argument's sake!,"
but a slavish addiction to truth.
I admit that a lot of my favourite
novels were written by women—
*Persuasion, Orlando, La Princesse
de Clèves, Mister Wrong,* and *The Mill
on the Floss,* for example; their authors
however (the plural of "authoress"
sounds both insulting and clumsy),
have something in common, improbable
as it may seem, with their sob-sisters
printed in *Vogue, Woman's Day*
and *The Ladies' Home Journal,* to judge
by their penchant for uplift and factual
fudge. True to Life is the catchword,
or phrase, to describe the too credible
mixture of sentiment, scandal
and verisimilitude coated
with moral improvement, the female
aesthetic that links Murasaki
to Murdoch. The ladies, god bless
them! imagine that fiction, and life,
have a purpose. To women all art
is didactic; if offered a choice
of Platonic ideals, they'd plump
for the True and abandon the Beautiful,
lock, stock and barrel, to men.

To return to our mutton: it's cold,
in the words of the poet and martyr,
unlike Theodora, for whom
the old adage, to strike while the iron
is hot, had acquired a new urgency.
Mark was the iron in question,
with whom she intended to press
her remedial sexual suit.
For her second attempt in a week
she went armed like a goddess, or a fury,
some thoroughly modern Medea,
to slay the unnatural dragon,
(or put it to sleep), resurrecting
the heterosexual man.
She flew straight to her Mark like an arrow

released from the string; with a "twock!"
she embedded herself in her target,
or with him, to be more exact,
where she found him, not prostrate precisely,
but certainly supine, expecting
no visit and scanning a book
of obscene reproductions of Indian
temple reliefs. She relieved
him of that; though a picture is worth,
so they say, many words, a correct
demonstration is worth any number
of pictures. I learned of this later,
of course; at the time I believed
that I went for a walk in all innocence.
Little I knew! (which should teach
me to talk like a character in
a Victorian novel.) The cast—
not the cast on his foot but the cast
of his character she, willy-nilly,
was eager to change; and at last
she succeeded, I never knew how,
but she had by the time that I saw
them again, when, like anyone else
when the trauma has somewhat abated,
he seemed to be pleased and pathetically
smug. I discovered my loss,
the next evening on paying my usual
visit to Mark. There she was,
there they were, *in flagrante*, as if
in a photograph offered in evidence
for a divorce: unambiguous
proof. They composed a domestic
tableau as I opened the door:
A new Mark, looking sleek, slightly flushed,
in pyjamas and bathrobe, embarrassed
to see me, perhaps, but defiant,
defiantly normal, his foot
in its cast on the table beside
an imperial bottle of brandy;
he held a Havana cigar
in his fingers, although, I observed
as one notices everything on
an occasion like this, with a nightmare-like
clarity, it was unlit.

Theodora was knitting—maternity
garments already? I wondered
sarcastically, though it was plain
from the colour (maroon), and the shape,
(a few inches in either direction)
that the wool was intended for Mark—
as a scarf to pull over his eyes?
They said nothing, of course, not a word
to the foolish; their silence sufficed.
Explanation, apology: neither
was thought of. They simply excluded
me, like a perspicuous wall,
an impervious window, until
I was ready to leave them alone;
which I did, and as soon as I decently
could, still attempting to make
my *adieux au revoirs*—"See you soon?"—
with my hand, which was wiser than I,
on the doorknob. They murmured "So long,"
in the languorous accents of lovers.
But I paused on the sidewalk outside
by the window that stared from the basement
apartment. A gap in the curtains
revealed to the baffled voyeur
the extent of his crime. Theodora
reclined in a butterfly chair
while caressing the cast in her lap,
which was all I could see, all I ever
supposed I should see any more
of my erstwhile *eromenos*, Mark.

I was lying alone on my bed,
as I said at the start of the chapter,
repentant, though not on account
of my sins, but because of my virtuous
impulse in telling, informing,
instructing my enemy, to
my undoing. I've called Theodora
my love for the sake of analogy:
who can distinguish a passionate
hatred from something like lust?
I was wholly obsessed with the pair
of them, and, in regard to the woman,
the other, I felt I'd created

a double who cruelly mimicked
my actions, emotions, and thoughts,
one who slept in my bed and the bed
of my love, and became by that token
a surrogate love—might I never
set eyes on her person again!
As for him: for a while I expected
a telephone call or a visit;
we had in our fashion been friends.
I was sure that, if left to himself...
but he wasn't. Armida, I realized,
couldn't forgive or permit
her Rinaldo a masculine friendship
like ours, nor the echo of one.
When I telephoned once, Theodora,
who answered, abruptly informed
me "Wrong number." In *posse*, it was.
I abandoned all further pursuit
and began to attend to the studious
pastimes, the lectures and reading
I'd lately neglected in favour
of passion. With minor success.
There was little in Latin or Greek
to afford me much comfort—at least
at the age of eighteen. But the effort
involved, which was never extreme,
automatically answered my need
to be busy. I mastered those tongues
in a daze of unhappiness, finding
amusement of sorts in the fact
that while Latin, like English, afforded
but one way of saying "I love,"
namely *amo*, in Greek there are three.
But though Plato took pains to distinguish
philéo, for friendly regard,
from *eráo*, erotic desire,
it was difficult even for Plato
to do so, and harder for me.
Yet *eráo*, my lexicon told
me, could also mean "vomit," or "pour."
Agapáo, the third and by far
the least common, one seldom encounters
in classical literature
in the sense it assumes in the letters

of Paul and the pages of *Time,*
where I guess they pronounced it "agape."
But originally it provided
a nice way of saying Hello.
The Septuagint first employed
(I am cribbing from Liddell & Scott)
this affectionate verb for the feelings
that God may not only inspire
but, reciprocally, feel towards us:
a conception that Platonists such
as Plotinus found blasphemous. Paul
later popularized this idea
with other Egyptian notions.
I noted that, though *agapáo*
is used for *philéo* at times,
it should not be confused with *eráo.*
I knew what the latter two meant
from experience. What of the first?
I would not be the first or the last
to be led to the threshold of faith
by philology. "What," I naively
supposed for the sake of the argument,
"if it were true?" *Agapáo,*
I meant, and all that: what I heard
in the words of the worn Buxtehude
cantata that spun on my portable
turntable still though the music
had ended, since I was too lazy,
discouraged and bored, to get up
and remove the repetitive needle
whose scratchy p.s. underlined
the composer's celestial counterpoint:
Also—not *sprach Zarathustra*
alas! If my musical bent
had been modern instead of baroque,
Buxtehude less winsome than Strauss,
would the rest of this story be different?
Also hatt Gott the cantata
continued, however, *die Welt*—
repetition had rendered the German
transparent—*geliebet.* The text,
so familiar from somewhere, from childhood
no doubt, I looked up in the polyglot
Bible I found in the Old

Presbyterian library. "God,"
it informed me, "so loved"—*agapasen*—
"the world, that He gave it His Only-
Begotten...." This gnostic or neo-
Platonic non sequitur struck
me as moving, mysterious, meaningful.

Since what I called the debacle,
I had taken to sleeping a lot
between classes and meals, and I often
recalled the same dream when I woke.
I was groping my way in a dark
subterranean passage toward
something somehow both faintly familiar
and utterly strange: in the distance
a melody ever more audible,
sung in a language I didn't
believe I could recognize, yet.
But the hymnody quickened my steps.
As the darkness decreased I emerged
in an underground cavern. The chords
were translated to light. In the midst
I beheld on a throne, as the source
of the radiance, shining, an infant
that smiled an ineffable smile.
I was shaken awake by the effort
of somebody's sobbing: my own.
Unrelenting, the ultimate snowflakes
of winter descended, as rare
as the prayers that are answered, outside
of my window. "And if it were so?"
I awoke from my dream a believer
of sorts, or inclined to belief,
and the obvious thing to believe
in appeared the incredible Christian
religion in which I was raised,
not that relative Protestant brand
but the absolute claims that the Catholic
church was still pushing back then,
before Vatican Two, that unhappy
occasion when Rome lost her marbles.
What might I have turned to today?
Christian Science? or Zen? or Vedanta?
In principle faith is a mystery—

otherwise, can it be faith?
The more dark and irrational what
you are asked to believe in, the better.

Atypical silence for late
afternoon in the residence reigned
like a desert: I took it for peace,
or the vacuum the spirit requires
for its action. It might be the somnolent
wood Sleeping Beauty inhabited
once in a dream, everybody
asleep or away but myself,
the imprudent and conscious intruder
who heard or imagined the snore
of the mouse in the wainscot, the breath
of embroidering spiders, and stealthily
heard, like the prince who was destined
to waken these echoes, within,
a directive, to quote Theodora:
"Immediately. Do it now."

At that moment a third proposition
with those I had borrowed from Newman,
myself and my Maker, appeared
to me equally evident; this
was the practical step I must take,
and the Church I must join. I was lucky.
There lived down the hall, I had noticed,
a Catholic student, at least
that was what I presumed him to be
from the crucifix that I'd remarked
on one wall of his room when the door
stood ajar. I knew nothing about
him beyond this, not even his name,
just the pertinent fact of his faith.
Having none but a stranger to turn
to, no wonder the Church always struck
me as strange. With my ear to his door
I deciphered the painfully tentative
taps of a portable typewriter.
Taking my faith in my fingers
and making a fistful, I rapped.
Sudden silence. I knocked once again,
and a masculine voice in a tone

of astonishment said to come in.
I stepped into the tidiest room
I have seen. There was nothing, apart
from the crucifix that I'd observed
and the typewriter that I had heard,
to suggest occupation, not even
a book or an ash-tray. The bed
had been carefully made, on the desk
no innocuous fragment of paper;
not even a waste-paper-basket
disturbed the immaculate order.
The person who'd answered the door
and, I guessed, had created this cosmos,
was standing, six feet and six inches
at least, in his stockings to greet
me, a mixture of friendly surmise
and concern in his welcoming smile.
Looking haggard, I'm sure, and unshaven,
untidy as always, I tried
to effect in a brief introduction
the called-for, complete explanation.
"I am," I informed him, "your neighbour."
"I see," he said gravely. "Sit down."
I inquired if he knew of a priest?
"What's the matter?" he asked me. "I want
to become," I said blithely, "a Catholic."
"Holy Loyola! what for?"
This spontaneous ejaculation
would be typical of the reaction
of most cradle Catholics whom
I encountered; the faith they accounted
a blessing not wholly unmixed
which you either were born with, or not.
The invidious Protestant who
in "invincible ignorance" might
have committed the juiciest sins
with impunity, would be a fool
to insist on enlightenment. Ignorance,
so it persisted, was bliss.
Thus my neighbour, who answered to Mike,
an obedient son of the church,
could not hide his astonishment, seeing
that fortunate, free unbelievers
like me should express a desire,

as I did, to be baptized at once!
"You will need to be given Instruction,"
he pondered. "But where, and by whom?"
I confess that I thought my conversion,
or inner rebirth, should be quite
instantaneous: recognized, sealed,
and made final in one afternoon.
I contained my sublime disappointment
(could anything be so naive?)
at this first of the Church's delays:
brontosauran bureaucracy! Later
I came to regret these as only
too few and too brief. As for Mike,
who rejoiced in the surname O'Toole,
introduced as a *Deus ex machina*
here, what the Greek calls a messenger—
angelos—honest, Hibernian,
nondescript angel, disguised
as a young Engineer: he would never
in future be anything more
than my godfather—which was sufficient.
Good-natured, he might have been graceful
if nature and Grace were not opposites.
What was he like? What is anyone
like who supplies a necessity,
doctor or dentist or priest?
The character under the role
doesn't matter. Does anyone notice
the angel's? Said Michael O'Toole,
"If you're serious, you ought to visit
our Campion Club, talk it over....
I go there for Mass every Sunday;
I'll give you the name of the chaplain."

The Campion Club was the pivot
of Catholic life at McGill
University; every campus
possesses a similar isle
of tridentine belief in a sea
of agnostics and protestants who
in their turn were a drop in that bucket
of Catholic Frenchness, Quebec.
It is worthy of passing remark,
with a few unimportant exceptions

our membership did not include
any young French Canadians, heirs
of the world that surrounded us, theirs
were the names of the churches and suburbs
and streets—Notre Dame, S. Eustache,
Ste. Catherine, Bon Secours, Saint Laurent.
As for us in the Campion Club,
Lithuanian, German, or Scotch
as we some of us were by descent,
but in mass overwhelmingly Irish,
we used a small chapel donated
in memory of the deceased
by the will of a prominent brewer,
O'Brien, and liked to imagine
ourselves as recusants surrounded
by heretics—whom, paradoxically,
we'd more in common with than
our Quebec co-religionists, namely
a language and culture of sorts.
I say "we," for already, remark,
I'd begun to identify with
the exclusive pretentions of Rome.

The next Sunday, no holiday for
the religious, forearmed with a note
to the chaplain, I called at the club.
Father Hapgood—or "Happy"—resembled
the poet and Jesuit G.
Manley Hopkins, I thought, in my need
for familiar assurance: the same
rugged features and mystical eyes,
and the businesslike jawline. The fancied
resemblance abruptly aborted
the moment he opened his mouth.
The apostle (self-styled) of the gentiles
admonishes us, though we speak
with the accents of angels and yet
are deficient in charity: here
was no tinkling of cymbals, no sounding
of brass but the Voice of America,
broadcasting Country and Western,
a hillbilly twang of the sort
that you get accidentally turning
the radio dial in your car

when you're driving across Manitoba.
He greeted me much as a banker
might welcome one eager to open
a savings account, and began
my instruction *ex tempore*, harping
at first overmuch, as I thought,
on such elements not fundamental
to Faith, as the Virgin's Assumption,
Conception and Birth—those details
the least likely to speak to a Protestant,
all on account of his private
devotion to Mary no doubt.
For the rest, he expressed himself satisfied,
even impressed, by my grasp
of the truths of religion—the fruit
of my heterogeneous reading—
impressed, had he known, by a grasp
more like clutching at straws. I was ready,
I frankly confessed, to believe
in whatever the Church in Her Wisdom
required: Virgin Birth? Resurrection?
A trifle. Infallible teaching
in morals and faith *ex cathedra*?
Whatever the dogma, I'd gladly
subscribe to it. "Tell me," I begged,
"what the Council of Trent has proposed
for belief, and, behold, I believe
it. While as for the old Athanasian
Quicumque, however absurd
it may be," (as Tertullian wrongly
is thought to have cried), "I believe
in it too." There seemed nothing I couldn't
believe if I tried. The most difficult
doctrines demanded no effort
at all for my cormorant faith
to digest, or at any rate swallow.
The priest who instructed me didn't
demand understanding as well,
or if that was impossible, given
the limits of our understanding,
expect explanations in lieu
of implausible mental gymnastics
from converts. Though quick to define
propositions, I couldn't have told

him what anything meant. In that decade,
the 'fifties, when faith was in fashion
and many self-styled intellectuals
furthered the fad by converting
to Rome, a conversion like mine,
of a person of some education,
was glorified as "intellectual."
"*Commonweal* Catholics," as
they were stigmatized, bandied
the term, paradoxically: intellect
being the last thing on earth,
or in heaven, involved. If informed
that the Church had condemned the eleven-
times table, as once it pronounced
Galileo in error, I'd quickly
discover the source of the heresy
taught in the secular schools
and submit to whatever the Curia
wanted to put in its place.

At this rate my religious instruction
was over in less than a month
from the middle of March—or of Lent.
In the church I adopted the practice
of dating events by a different
calendar, heading a letter
"The Vigil of Pentecost," "Trinity
Sunday," perhaps, or "Good Friday."
The days of the week, Maundy Thursday,
for instance, Ash Wednesday, as well
as the seasons, had mystical meanings
implicit. I read the liturgical
year like the book that it was,
but I never quite finished it. Open
it anywhere, what do you find?
At a glance you're abreast of the plot,
which while gripping from Christmas to Easter
predictably drags after Pentecost;
Advent attempts to awaken
the flagging communicant, starting
the cycle all over again.
All in vain, in my case, for the calendar
failed, as I say, to compel
my attention right through to the end,

or, the year being circular, up
to the point at which I had come in.

I anticipate, though. Holy Saturday,
once the traditional date
catechumens (or converts) were baptized
and therefore appropriate for
my reception, approached. If my faith
could be counted mere lip-service, born
of an inner, mysterious need
to believe which had nothing to do
with religion, my practice at least
was whole-hearted. Devout from the first,
I frequented the services, such
as they were, at the Campion Club,
or the church of the parish, S. Ronan's,
or at the cathedral downtown
where His Eminence never, I noticed,
presided in person on weekdays.
With missal in hand, a bilingual
guide, I infrequently glanced
at the English, which since—but much worse—
has usurped the position of text.
In the past one "assisted" at Mass,
unobtrusively doing one's bit;
now the phrase has acquired a more literal
meaning, the whole congregation
in unison prompting the celebrant.
Then, while I studied my program
in silence, the others were telling
their beads. In this way I developed
a passion, or rather affection,
rewarded with some understanding,
for liturgy, or for the language
of liturgy—Latin, of course,
I was lucky enough, or old-fashioned
enough, to have learnt. That arcane
and abandoned but beautiful vehicle,
once I could make out the barbarous
clerical accent in *more
Romano*, afforded me more
both of pleasure and sense than the wretched
vernacular ever could offer
of either, since Cranmer and Coverdale

issued their splendid, schismatical
prayerbook, and cornered the tongue.
Did they have any inkling, I wonder,
those Roman panjandrums and pundits
who govern the Catholic Church,
that this question of language would damage
her edifice more than the whole
reformation? The audible proof
that she was, as she said, universal
consists in the language she spoke,
notwithstanding parochial accents
not Roman but Latin. The language
of prayer is the stuff, the material
prop of religion, and when
it's dismantled the structure collapses.
The Church as I knew it, the Church
that I entered and left, I can never
recapture; the door has been fastened
behind me by Vatican Two,
when the vast, immemorial fabric
which weathered the French Revolution,
the cavils of Luther and Calvin,
the onslaughts of Zwingli and Huss,
not to mention its own reputation,
succumbed to reform from within.
Had I wanted, I couldn't go back,
for in place of the house of his father,
the prodigal, on his return,
would discover not even a picturesque
ruin, but only a parking-lot.

Formerly people imagined
that persons of my—shall we call
it persuasion?—converted because
of the Church's artistic attractions,
the candles and chanting and incense
and vestments and polychrome statues
and riches and ritual camp.
Since the era of Beardsley and Corvo,
how many impressionable aesthetes
their dubious tastes have undone!
My reactions, if anything, proved
paradoxical. Any fastidious
tourist who ever inspected

a Catholic church in Quebec
will appreciate my disillusionment.
Really, my dear, the décor!
with its gilding and plaster and paint
like the icing on top of a cake,
and the portraits of excellent persons
in execrable taste, all that mystical
tat! The aesthetic appeal
of the Church, in America anyway,
must be agreed to be minimal;
hardly a further inducement
to Rome, it provides opportunities,
never amiss for a martyr,
for sensual mortification.
The Campion Club, to be sure,
was inclined to the other extreme,
and a Protestant plainness in practice.
The chapel, in spite of O'Brien's
bequest, was quite dowdy compared
to the First Presbyterian Church,
and the service, except for its Latin,
looked forward to later reforms.
Father Happy performed at an altar
that faced the minute congregation—
which often on weekdays consisted
of no one but me—though the standard
position dictated his facing
the wall, in those days; and the altar
itself, which tradition had cluttered
with junk, like a vanity table,
stood empty, except for a book
and the plainest of functional vessels.

Before Easter Saturday I,
in my daily attendance at Mass,
was a spectator merely, the mystery
which I could put into words
with the help of my missal, reserved
for the wordless communicants whom
I observed at a signal approaching
the sacrament. Seen from this distance,
the sacrifice viewed as a spectacle,
drama, or Aristoteleian
action, had all the essentials

of tragedy, *peripeteia*,
beginning and middle and end,
and the trappings of tragedy also,
its grandeur and swank, an heroic
protagonist, *anagnorisis*—
what else would one call Consecration
except recognition, that bread
is the body as wine is the blood
of the victim in whom all the ills
of the world are vicarious? Vain
repetitions? The councils forbid!
Transformation occurred every time,
Father Hapgood assured me. The problems
of time and eternity worried
me less than I sometimes pretended;
symbolic or not, the rehearsal
dramatically palled in the end.
The identical formulae every
morning are boring whatever
their beauty. Alas, as the day
of my baptism drew ever nearer,
I couldn't quite stifle my doubts—
not the solid Victorian quibbles
about the existence of God,
immortality, regeneration,
the literal truth of the scriptures
as seen in the light of the progress
of science and biblical scholarship—
rather, a growing misgiving,
irrational, almost unconscious,
a fit of emotional fidgets
equivalent to the discomfort
experienced trying to hold
any difficult posture for long.
My position I couldn't admit
to be frankly untenable, all
but impossible long to maintain.
I had nothing, I told myself glumly
to worry about. In the tension
between the desire to believe
and the intellect, who can doubt which
will prevail? Father Hapgood pooh-poohed
my misgivings with, "Everyone entertains
doubts on the eve of reception;

the devil delights in such tardy
temptations as at the last minute
bewilder the wavering soul.
Persevere." My discomfort, however,
was not intellectual but
existential. Naively, I didn't
intend my conversion to have
much effect on my daily existence.
Assisting at Mass, if a little
too often (congenital catholics
went once a week as a rule),
comprehending bizarre and improbable
concepts, like learning an alien
language (not Latin), presented
no serious problems compared
to a change of direction or heart,
metanoia, a total conversion
of life. A decision like mine
(if indeed a decision) involves
willy-nilly a thorough estrangement
from previous habits which, taken
together, amount to a self.
"You are never so free," they are fond
of repeating in Catholic circles,
"as when you abandon your freedom."
And this you could do without noticing,
all it required was a single
but fatal original step
(which some martyrs are said to have taken
while holding their heads in their hands)
but, God help me! I'd stumbled already!

But meanwhile I saw Father Hapgood
routinely for our little chats
about dogma, and as he displayed
the historical claims of the Church
I pretended to listen. Alas,
Apostolic Succession escaped me,
as most of his arguments did,
such as whether the Anglicans had
valid sacraments. What if they had?
If you think the good father was leading
me up the proverbial path,
he believed that this path was the path

of the garden whence we were expelled
long ago. As for me, I was grateful
to wander a while in a labyrinth
which I found charming; each turning
had something to offer, some novelty,
something enchanting. The views
that I glimpsed were superb, as I dawdled
along, like a visitor lost
at Versailles. I admired the statues,
les bois, les bassins, les parterres,
and the prospects that suddenly opened
upon my uncritical gaze,
never asking what tyranny built
or what cunning designed such delights,
nor the heartlessness that had enjoyed
or the force that exacted their price.
I grew careless how late it was getting,
the sun slipped behind the *boscages*
and imbued with imperial crimson
bassin and *parterre.* In the dusk
individual flowers were losing
their wonderful colours. Already,
unnoticed the *parc* would be closing;
those picturesque wrought-iron gates
would be locked for the night without warning
surprising the tourist inside.

Like a customer, who is afraid
of affronting the sensitive salesman
who's somehow succeeded in selling
him something that nobody wants,
I refrained from embarrassing questions
while Lent wore away like a dream.
During Passion Week at the cathedral
the statues were muffled in purple
and tension was mounting. Palm Sunday,
a ragged procession provided
with dessicate fronds of some species
of verdure assembled, intoning
the *Vexilla Regis;* the standards
advanced out of step and suggested,
or so an impartial observer
might say, no successful campaign.
Thus in no time the week before Easter,

or Holy Week, as it is called,
was upon us, the crown of the liturgy
with its succession of solemn
events, which I followed with interest
mixed with increasing anxiety,
since the agenda contained
my reception. The washing of feet
Maundy Thursday, performed by the clergy,
produced an effect of humility
limited to the specific
occasion, it's true. But Good Friday
provided the annual climax;
and although there were two days to go
in the weekend, the Passion remained
the most thrilling event in the popular
calendar. Freya had claimed
that the pagan and mystery elements,
plainly preserved under layers
of "rational" dogma, bestowed
on the Church, in Quebec as in Naples,
or Egypt, its primitive magic.
The death of Adonis, Osiris,
or Thammuz or Quetzalcoatl
or Jesus—the name doesn't matter:
a handsome young man has been wounded
and lies in the lap of the Mother,
as shown in our own pietá
and described in Theocritus' *Idyll*
XV, at the great Alexandrian
festival of Aphrodite,
a spectacle yearly enacted,
unaltered in any essential
detail, though more decent, perhaps,
for the faithful today, with processions
and rites all surrounding a flowery
altar or Bower of Repose.
Any wonder if, after an orgy
of mourning like this, Holy Saturday
seemed a distinct anticlimax?
For all that the Church had attempted
to make it a high point, the Vigil
(compared to the Orthodox version)—
for all its elaborate symbols,
the water and fire and the incense,

resembles most Saturday nights
I remember, as being a flop.
(Easter Sunday, the mysteries' climax,
has sunk to a social affair.)

But I'm getting ahead of myself:
On that Saturday night at the Campion
Club, in the presence of Mike
as my sponsor, I gladly renounced
(although not for the last time!) the world
with the flesh and the devil, as well
as the various errors and heresies
I had adhered to unwitting;
conditional baptism followed,
in case I'd been baptised before—
so I was, as a child, but it might
not have taken because of the dubious
nature of Anglican orders—
and Anglican names, for that matter!
The night that I entered the Church
(as the Roman communion, in error
and schism affects to be called),
I adopted a name from her Calendar,
one to be known by in Catholic
circles in heaven, perhaps.
And the name that I chose as appropriate
(why be ashamed to admit
it?) was Thomas. I hoped, as a prig,
to resemble the humanist chancellor
who as a closet Carthusian
refused to subscribe to the Act
of Supremacy, hence was beheaded
by Henry the Eighth, autocephalous
head of the national church.
Absit omen! My namesakes—Aquinas,
à Becket, à Kempis and More—
had been christened in turn after Thomas
called Didymus, one of the dozen
apostles, the doubter, of whom,
when he had been convinced by empirical
evidence, Jesus observed,
"Just because you have seen you believe,
whereas blessed are those who believe

without seeing!" How odd, if I didn't
remember this text at the time!

I was led to the improvised font
by my godfather, Mike. Father Hapgood,
our chaplain, excused himself, pleading
an Easter retreat, a strategic
withdrawal I wistfully envied,
too late! The officiant sent
by the bishop awaited us, Father
O'Fay, a tomato-faced, pot-bellied
clerical Irishman, clutching
the instrument of my salvation,
a basin of water. The practice
of total immersion, when shivering
converts disrobed on the steps
of a sunken piscina, belonged
to the picturesque days of the primitive
church. "Are you ready?" the priest
like a starter impatiently asked.
"Be a man!" at my elbow my virginal
sponsor, whose manhood seemed out
of the question, advised. So virility
flourished, like liberty, best
when surrendered? However prepared,
as a hitherto natural product
(whatever some purists may say),
I recoiled from denying my nature
and maker. Despairing, I gazed
at the Stations, which breathed the deplorable
influence of Eric Gill,
round the walls of the chapel, as if
at a roadmap. "*In nomine patris,*
et filii," Father O'Fay
was intoning indifferently.
With my muscular godfather holding
my face down by force in the basin
as if I were going to vomit,
("*Et spiritus sancti.*") I noticed
the water, though holy and lifegiving,
looked rather dirty. "*Amen!*"
As if drowning, the whole of my reprobate
lifetime unfolded before me.

I felt a few drops on my forehead
and heard the indelible formula,
"*Thoma, ego te baptizo.*"
Discarding my former identity
like a security blanket
along with the world and the flesh.
and the devil, I found that in practice
not even my godfather Mike
could address me as Thomas, except
in inverted and audible commas.
Immune, I presumed, to the mortal
contagion of sin, with the blood
of the Lamb as the sinner's vaccine,
for a moment, but only a moment,
I knew what it was to feel guiltless.
My past had been sponged from the slate
and the innocent future, God willing,
forever a tabula rasa,
could only be better, I thought.

In a future not perfectly sinless,
though blameless compared to the past,
the forgiveness of sins is conditional,
as I found out in the Church,
on repentance, expressed in the form
of confession, the oddest, for me,
of the folkways of faith. To begin
with, you had to admit you had sins
to forgive, which at first isn't easy,
the Protestant conscience insisting
at once on one's natural sinfulness,
and upon something approaching
to personal infallibility.
Then, when you've muttered your *Quia
peccavi*, you have to describe,
I discovered, in detail, specific
peccata, a frankly embarrassing
task at the best, since the failings
that trouble us most are inclined
to be nasty and far from romantic
or flattering. Telling a stranger
your meanest, most secretive actions
and thoughts seems a curious way
of achieving catharsis; however,

the priest merely acts as a vessel.
The end of it all is contrition,
the *sine qua non* of forgiveness,
an humble, sincere and spontaneous
grief and regret at offending
God's goodness and majesty—not
a mere dread of the torments of hell
(although hell could be quite a deterrent),
but pure and disinterested sorrow
for sin and desire to amend,
which, expressed to the priest in the form
"I am heartily sorry" should quickly
induce him to grant absolution,
of course at a price: "You may go,"
—in the words of the gospel, so often
misquoted—"and try not to do
it again." So confession and penance
are one and the same, an apology
offered to God, as a rule
before taking communion, in case
you have anything grave on your conscience.
This sacrament, one of the chief
supernatural channels of grace,
is exacted by means little short
of the methods employed by inquisitors
ancient and modern, determined
to get a confession by hook
or by crook: by suggestions or premises,
threats, innuendos and bribes.
Psychological tortures like these
are inflicted in daunting surroundings,
those boxes I'd noticed in churches,
like gothic or romanesque telephone
booths, where a grille separated
the patient, or penitent, from
the invisible priest who inspires
by his presence a feeling of dread,
which, although in itself claustrophobic,
arises, since truth must be told,
from the knowledge the other may have
up his clerical sleeve an omniscience
practically equal to God's,
in the speak-easy known as confession.

The first time I sought absolution
became very nearly the last.
In the week after I was received,
my interior life had been altered
beyond recognition. The soul
that embarks on a spiritual voyage
had better prepare for a difficult
trip: you may think you are riding
at anchor one moment; the next,
you are sailing along amid icebergs
and, presently, tropical storms.
Now I hadn't been finding it easy,
at that, to be even an everyday
Christian. Heroical virtue
I never considered my style.
With alacrity I could renounce
both the world and the devil; the flesh
was a different kettle of fish.
I unwillingly lived in the world
as it was, to its blandishments, such
as they were, temperamentally deaf,
while the devil, so far as I knew
to the contrary, did not exist—
his existence, at least, unlike God's,
undefined as a matter of faith.
But the flesh didn't lend itself to
an ascesis for which I'd not bargained
when taking the plunge. Biological
urges at my age resisted
denial in ways pretty hard
to ignore. Theodora and Mark,
in the nature of spirits, had vanished,
the latter direct, not to Switzerland
where he'd been sternly dispatched
by his anthroposophical mother,
but rather to Paris and (Freya
declared) instantaneous ruin,
the former more totally still
in a treacherous maze of research
on her thesis. Their whereabouts held,
I insisted, no interest, their absence
inspired only gratitude, since
it assured me a cloistered existence.
(The Old Presbyterian College,

however, appeared an unsuitable
Thebaid.) Even in cloisters,
alas, though in practice the world,
and the devil in theory, may
be excluded, the flesh can be fairly
obtrusive. The average anchorite
sorely is tempted thereby—
by his own if by nobody else's—
and often undone. I must say
that in view of my former agnostic
indulgence, I think I did well
to resist for as long as I did.
I expected my Maker, for one,
to appreciate how I had tried,
unattractive as chastity seemed.
Though depicted in flattering colours,
or rather in glorious white
by her partisans, Virtue is always
envisaged as up on her toes,
like a basketball player, perhaps—
and I didn't find athletes at all
unattractive, however averse
to athletics myself. As to gender,
philology taught me that *virtus*
was masculine by definition
for all allegorical painters
affect to the contrary. Vice,
on the other hand, garishly painted
in black by short-sighted detractors,
displays all the hues of the rainbow
in fact, though the colours aren't fast
and will wash all too easily out
in the come. In the languorous aftermath
pleasure too often subsides
in reproaches and tears and remorse.
Often said to be rampant, if anything
vice is heraldically couchant.
The charms of the celibate life
were apparent to me somewhat later;
they take getting used to, and never
appeal to the multitude. Habit
and snobbery reconciled me
in the long run to chastity. Yet
at the moment, that virtue at least

seemed disheartening, dull and old-fashioned,
what Freya might call maladjusted,
perverse, antisocial, or worse.

Father Hapgood, however, did not,
as evinced by the grim disapproval
with which he appeared to be hearing
my maiden confession. I needn't,
I told myself later, have made
it to him, with a whole Roman Catholic
city at hand, choc-a-bloc
with confessors who wouldn't have known
me from Adam. The Saturday after
my christening nevertheless
I repaired to the Campion Club
for a different sacrament, filled
with misgivings, like those of a bride
on the wedding night. Penance, I knew,
unlike marriage and baptism, could
be repeated *ad nauseam*: grace
in the form of forgiveness appeared
a renewable resource. Instructed
to take as my guide the Mosaic
commandments, or decalogue, when
I examined my conscience, I found
their archaic prescriptions not only
of anthropological interest
but wickedly relevant. Like
an unnerved hypochondriac reading
a medical handbook, I recognized
symptoms I hadn't suspected,
in my case, of sin. Of the first
and the second commandments, I reckoned
that I had infringed them in numerous
ways: was there nothing I had not
preferred to my maker, at times?
Satisfaction, repose, even virtue
herself I would worship in place
of the simple, ineffable truth.
That the truth could be also an idol—
a protestant one—I should never
have guessed from the Catholic Church,
where its image was rarely if ever
depicted, however its name

was perpetually taken in vain.
In the light of the third I confessed
that on Sunday I'd read an epistle
of Horace instead of St. Paul.
When I came to the fourth I remembered
I still owed my father a letter
explaining my longer than usual
silence. Composing these dutiful
regular, dull and above
all expected epistles required
as much effort as writing in Latin:
we didn't quite speak the same language.
The fact I had something of import
to say, for a change, would not make
the impossible task any easier.
Nervous, with reason, concerning
parental reaction to what
he'd condemn as a reckless flirtation
with Rome, I instinctively shuddered
to think what he'd say when he heard
the flirtation had ended in marriage.
The fifth I felt free to omit
as irrelevant, even while killing
my natural self, as I skipped
to the seventh: some library books
overdue. Yet the sixth, which the Church
all too broadly interpreted (no one,
not even myself, had accused
me as yet of adultery!), loomed
like a sheer insurmountable obstacle.
"Hm," was the only remark
Father Hapgood had muttered so far,
in a tone that reproached me for nothing
more mortal than wasting his time.
Are the sins of the flesh after all
so essential? I wondered naively:
the average lasted no more
than a matter of minutes, an hour
the luxurious limit. My listener's
pregnant, nay, ominous silence
suggested the seriousness
in the eyes—or the ears—of the Church
of such trifling transgressions. Was guilt
not a cause of my recent conversion,

dictating my attitude now
on my knees in the posture of penance?
I hadn't seen fit to inform
my instructor-become-my-confessor
of all the events that preceded
my sudden desire for instruction,
which he had ascribed, I presume,
to prevenient grace. Under seal
of confession, I sketched the irregular
triangle wiped from the slate
of my life by the waters of baptism,
mentioning merely in passing
for sake of comparison, any
regrettably fresh peccadilloes
or laughable venial sins.

If I thought Theodora had taught
me a lesson in reticence, if
nothing else, I was wrong. Indiscretion,
on which the Commandments were silent,
appropriate, so one might think,
to confession, created the same
consternation. We dream we are loved
not in spite of our failings but for
them, and fancy they interest others.
A sermon ensued not unworthy
of Savonarola, indignant
and vehement, doubtless rehearsed,
for my weakness was hardly unique.
He denounced my offence as the grossest
of bestial crimes (in a hierarchy
ranking ambition "the fault
of the angels", and greed quintessentially
human), a lapse all the more
reprehensible for being easy
and outwardly harmless. Such animal
lust, I discovered, excited
more righteous disgust than ingratitude,
cruelty, murder or fraud.
Father Hapgood explained one could sin
against God and one's neighbour, but also
oneself—though one couldn't forgive
oneself, naturally! If a common
and perfectly natural act

which was nobody's business but mine
had offended our heavenly father
as much as it seemed to affront
my confessor, I marvelled that God
was so easily shocked. Had he nothing
to read but the chapter of faults?

Such impertinent, childish objections,
like pebbles awash in the torrent
of clerical eloquence, vanished
unspoken, and with them all trace
of the sceptical bedrock beneath.
Under all of my fluent credulity
lay a deposit of doubt
in abeyance, awaiting a doubt
to reveal itself. Meanwhile I winced
at the ultimate priestly reproach,
that a penitent, having received
the exceptional gift of conversion,
had fallen so soon and on such
an ignoble occasion. If guilt,
universal, irrational, blind,
in proportion no doubt to the urge
it subverted, had driven me into
the Church, it was shame that precluded
my hasty retreat and completed
my sudden and total reform.
I resolved I would never commit
(so I'd never have cause to confess)
this particular outrage again.
As I muttered the Act of Contrition
I'd memorized under my breath
with peculiar fervour, sincerely
I made up my mind to amend.
What is more, I succeeded, in spite
of mundane, diabolical, carnal
temptations, and turned an immaculate
page, which I kept, with some effort
unspotted. My true *metanoia*—
conversion of morals—I date
from that day. Unexpectedly chaste
at the profligate age of eighteen,
I maintained this unnatural posture
for half of that year, like Persephone,

only my winter was summer,
from Easter till practically Advent,
a feat of which I am uncertain
if I should be proud or ashamed,
though I flattered myself at the time
I had driven out nature for good.

Book Two

Lazarus House

Nudum nudus Christum sequi.
FRANCISCAN BYWORD

Iɴꜱᴛᴀɴᴛᴀɴᴇᴏᴜꜱ Spring had attacked
Montreal overnight like a laxative,
loosening snow from the slopes
of the mountain, from rooftops and sidewalks
and streets, where it piled up in barricades
during our annual siege,
till the city began to resemble
a dissolute snowball dissolving,
while under the mud and the mess
deliquescent and delicate music,
a faint, subterranean gurgle
of muttering rivulets sang
a disturbing, subversive refrain.
As it thawed, the whole winter's deposit
was briefly revealed in its various
strata, distinct geological
faults that appeared for an instant
then vanished as quickly. The thaw
illustrated the truth Heraclitus
pronounced πάντα ῥεῖ, and as everything
melted and trickled and ran
all about me, the world, for a fortnight
at least, manifested its permanent
state of continual flux.

While reluctant and gradual elsewhere,
this miracle hit Montreal
with the force of a genitive blizzard,
a freak revolution in nature
as sudden and eager as all
adolescence, a heartbreaking promise
of freedom and joy, so that even
the cheerless approach to the airport
seemed really *La Côte de Liesse.*
In the wake of an outburst so lyrical,
summer, which followed at once,

in a week, without further transition,
appeared histrionic, the trees
that stood nakedly tragic all winter
arrayed in a green crepe de Chine.
There were no intermediate phases,
one morning the stupor of April,
the next the excitement of May,
as the campus, transformed in a week
from a tatty, traditional Xmas-card,
suddenly looked like a battlefield
strewn with the limbs of both sexes,
the scene of a massacre where
indiscriminately the remains
of the quick and the sluggish together
were laid in promiscuous heaps,
here a thigh, there a buttock or breast,
on the lawn by the fountain or under
the shady and overdressed trees.
I averted my gaze from the carnage
of winter's survivors, so lewdly
alive, livid flesh in a tasteless
profusion of beauty and youth,
and their indolent pathos and pride,
underage, underdressed, underdone,
all a curious, carious colour,
the pallor of underground things
or (extending the metaphor) like
a Last Judgement, the great get-together
arranged for the end of all days
when the flesh shall arise in a body
redeemed from the season of sleep.
I exaggerate, yet what a gorgeous
(would I had been free to participate!)
pastoral orgy! Its pretext
ostensibly was the belated
but instant absorption of knowledge:
preparing for finals, the whole
student body pretended to study
their texts while they studied each other
sub rosa, or dreamt to the whine
of a portable radio's mindless
erotic accompaniment.
On their laps or beside them, neglected
lay books, *Introduction to Chemistry,*

Physics, Biology—anything
other than life; but no matter,
for life, as they say at commencement,
needs no introduction. And meantime
the springtime was passing its final
exams with the old flying colours,
obtaining an effortless first
to graduate *summa cum laude.*

"The poet is always at home
in the centre of winter," I wrote
(for I wrote and moreover had published
some poetry then) in my notebook,
alarmed by the world as it burgeoned
around me, the general blooming
of bliss. My adoptive religion,
in spite of the verdure of Easter,
envisaged a monochrome landscape
and hardly this amorous green.
But the world that withstood my analysis,
try as I might to explain
it away metaphysically, showed
no intention of vanishing yet,
as it offered itself for inspection
complete with a wealth of seductive
detail. Until long after midnight
it kept me awake with the echo
of Dixieland from the fraternity
house down the block, Beta Upsilon
Mu. Irritation commingled
with yearning for what I should call
an unbearable nuisance today—
or tonight—but which struck me as vivid
if raucous, back then, reprehensible
maybe, but real. This division
within my existence—or was it
between my existence and me?—
constituted a practical problem.
To paraphrase Wittgenstein: life
is not only the life of the mind
or the body, but life in the world,
and my life in the world was becoming
intolerable, like a marriage
in which one is forced to cohabit

for life, for the sake of appearances.
Blessed are they who have learned
to exist in their element like
salamander or eagle or earthworm
or shark, so sublimely adapted
that no one can tell where environment
ends and adjustment begins!
This ability, verging on natural
camouflage, whether acquired
or innate, I conspicuously
was devoid of. My awkward estrangement,
a form of internal, uncomfortable
exile, expressed as a look
of astonishment at my surroundings,
appeared through the plain and unflattering
glasses I wore at the time,
a transparent but visible bulwark.
I'd speculate later, too late!
at my different fortune and character
if I had worn contact lenses,
but contacts were rare and expensive
in Canada then. As it was
in the midst of exam week I broke
this unique, indispensable pair,
and for several days had to peer,
while awaiting repair or replacement,
at questions I answered and quizzes
I passed for all practical purposes
blind, while my handwriting, all
but illegible, grew even more so,
which may be the reason I garnered,
with no preparations to speak of,
top honours, assuring me plenty
of funds for the following year,
by my modest, ascetical standards
at least, unenthused as I felt
at the prospect of duly returning
to secular studies next fall.
I had chosen, in place of the plastic
mock-tortoiseshell glasses I'd broken,
new frames of some metal like silver
or steel: they were circular, long—
well, a decade—before "granny glasses"
grew fashionable. I suspect

I imagined they gave me an air
of austerity, like reproductions
I'd seen of El Greco's bespectacled
portrait of Cardinal Ximinez.
Yet what a photograph shows
is a curious, faintly bemused
but profoundly ingenuous gawk:
in their glittering prisons the eyes
as if rimless or lidless disclaim
any intimacy with the world.

In the porch of S. Ronan's, the Irish
parochial church I had taken
to haunting instead of the Campion
Club since my shameful confession,
I ran into Freya one morning
inspecting the gothic façade.
When she recognized me I was slightly
put out: one expects an interior
change to produce corresponding
exterior signs, a complete
transformation of body and soul.
What was *she* doing there? I refrained
from demanding, but she telepathically
told me, "I look for druidical
influences in Quebec,
for example, that gargoyle." I blushed
for its antics reminded me weirdly
of Mark, after whom I inquired.
"I have not had a letter," his mother
dismissively answered, and neither
had I. "He was never a great
correspondent." I offered the pain
that I felt at this absence of news
to the sinners in purgatory. "What
about you? Is it true what I hear,
you converted? Of course! I foresaw
this already! Inevitable!
Either this or becoming a Jew,
and the Catholic way is less painful."
Now Freya, at least to my knowledge,
subscribed to no creed, though a sibyl
of sorts. "I approve of your choice,
not of course for its Judaeo-Christian

ingredients but for its pagan
foundations and fabulous folklore.
They got it all backwards to start
with, for man creates God in his image
and woman in hers, not *vice versa*.
This virginal mother of God,"
she declared with a certain authority,
"She is as old as belief:
Aphrodite-Astarte-Athena—
her names in the Mediterranean
region alone are too many
to count, not to mention," she lamely
concluded, "the rest of the world."
Father Hapgood's half-baked mariolatry
wouldn't have borne such comparisons;
personally as a renegade
puritan I was immune
to this cult. As if sensing my coolness
to everything feminine, Freya,
herself an unwomanly woman,
exlaimed, "But you must meet Immanuel
Star!" I remembered the name
or one like it I'd heard on one never-
forgotten occasion of sin.
"An unorthodox Freudian analyst,
Jewish by birth but a Catholic
convert, a very old friend,"
she recited, as if from *Who's Who*,
"He is living in Ottawa now
but will move here next fall." My indifference
as to the movements of this
perfect stranger, ironic in view
of events that I could not foresee,
(although Freya uncannily might)
I concealed, or revealed, with a yawn
which I blamed on my eight o'clock mass.
"I am leaving myself in a week
for Minorca. But what are you doing
this summer?" A sensible question,
but I had no plans for the interval.
Spring had provided a prelude,
allegro con brio to summer's
andante con moto, the long
intermission to which were disbanding

my classmates, to work or to play,
to resorts at the shore or the mountains
as waiters, to day-camps as counsellors,
some for the summer transformed
into lumberjacks, factory hands
and professional roustabouts. Back
in the 'fifties the summer ambition
of students was gainful employment,
and few would be going to Europe
with Freya and Mark. The unfortunate
young unemployed were condemned
to vacation at home, being bored
on verandas and beaches, in parks,
lackadaisically mowing the lawns
of their neighbours and families, caught
in the backwaters, shady and calm,
of some sleepy provincial retreat.
But I couldn't go home any more
since becoming a Catholic. British
Columbia seemed even farther
away than before, ever greater
the distance I'd covered six months
ago now, interstellar the interval
stretched, as if measured in light years
not miles—in light years and dark hours.
"I'm afraid I don't know: what I'm doing,
this summer, I mean." Her concern
though abrupt and erratic, as well
as her wisdom and kindness, were genuine,
more than politeness demanded.
"I wish that the Stars would be here,
but they won't, before Autumn. Let's see:
is there anyone else? I remember
a man in the slums; Alan Waterman,
that was his name." She had opened
her practical purse and extracted
a notebook: "A saint, so they say,
though I don't have much faith in such things,"
and she tore out a page with a name
and address in her vigorous handwriting.
"Take this. Good bye, and good luck."
With a click of her heels and a masculine
handshake she turned at the corner
and took herself out of my life.

I must vacate my room at the Old
Presbyterian College at once,
by the end of the week, and had nowhere
to go. All the others had already
gone, like my godfather Mike,
who had taken a job in the arctic.
What's more, I had nothing to do.
That "the devil finds work" is a proverb
that's proven by many a grandiose
scheme and impossible project—
the pyramids, merely to take
one example, and various dams.
But the converse is equally true,
as the number of madrigals, sonnets,
cathedrals constructed in nutshells
and charity benefits shows.
Should I take out an ad in *The Catholic
Worker*: "Ascetic beginner
desires uncongenial work
in unpleasant surroundings"? I'd told
Father Hapgood my problem, and we
had begun to discuss my prospective
religious—it might be, monastic—
vocation. To give him his due,
while delighted at having recruited
a foot-soldier with sub-lieutenant
potential, a possible candidate
for holy orders, he counselled
delay. When I'd finished my college
degree there'd be plenty of time
to consider my future. Three years!
an eternity, then, at eighteen,
like an endless old-fashioned engagement.
The fact that I'd just been baptized
hardly dampened my ardour. A working
vacation became my vocation,
my novel vocation replaced
the vacation I neither desired
nor deserved. If becoming a Catholic
weren't enough—and it wasn't,
the romance of Rome was beginning
to tarnish already—the glamour
of Poverty, Chastity, even

Obedience offered a headier
thrill in the search for estrangement.

We canvassed the various orders
of regular priests: Father Hapgood
explained the distinction between
these and secular priests like himself
who must live in the world, while the former,
unworldly in principle, followed
the rules of their orders, accordingly
known by their regular habits.
The Jesuits ranked as the Catholic
salvation army, the militant
wing of a church absolutely
triumphant, a disciplined body
of odd-balls, whose uniforms bordered
on camouflage: clerical black.
As polemicists, diplomats, spies,
their deserved reputation of God's
secret agents for intrigue as well
as their arid pneumatical drill,
and the sorry example of Hopkins,
deterred my enlistment. The mendicant
orders, Franciscans, Dominicans,
called themselves friars, or brothers,
and emphasized poverty, much
as the Jesuits peddle obedience.
Nowadays commonly cloistered,
they used to infest mediaeval
society, spreading the plague—
and the faith—with their quite indiscriminate
kissing of lepers and burning
of heretics. So the Dominican
Order of Preachers had fathered
the dread Inquisition, and though
they had mellowed of late into biblical
scholars, their earlier zeal
must disqualify them in my hopelessly
tolerant view, though their habits
were not unattractive. Franciscans,
originally thirteenth-century
hippies, while perfectly harmless,
seemed too simple-minded for my
intellectual taste. Their Duns Scotus,

unread and uncanonized, rivalled,
they claimed, my Dominican namesake
Aquinas. Their costumes were brown.
I admit that this question of get-up
appeared to exert an unconscious
but too disproportionate influence
over my choice of career,
not inspired altogether by vanity
but by a love of disguise—
dressing up—which while culpably childish
befitted my sense that estrangement
required transformation. It seemed
there were few in religion deserving
the title of monk, any more
than the sisters you see in the street
in their picturesque habits are nuns.
The original monks were invisible,
monachus meaning "a hermit."
This promise of solitude, false
as it proved, plus historical snobbery
drew me at once to the oldest,
most (by definition) exclusive
enclosed cenobitical orders—
from *koinos* for "common," and "*bios*"
for "life," the more lively, I learned,
the more common: to whit, Benedictines,
Cistercians, Carthusians. These last
as the strictest if hardly the oldest
contemplative outfit I knew
from *La Chartreuse de Parme* by Stendhal
which I'd read at fifteen, little guessing
that some day I'd follow Fabrizio's
footsteps. Their motto was "Never
reformed because never deformed."
Eremitically really, each lived
in a house by himself (an arrangement
I found most attractive) and rose
in the midst of the night for communal
devotions, dividing the rest
of the day into ten-minute segments
for labour and study and prayer,
which appealed to my punctual nature
and nervous obsession with time.
Underneath their voluminous homespun

they wore, Father Hapgood (who never
infringed on the seal of confession)
informed me, hair shirts, for the purpose
of sensual mortification.
No wonder their numbers had shrunk
to a handful! But seeing they hadn't
established a charterhouse yet
on this continent, I must reluctantly
fail to increase their enrollment.
Cistercians, or Trappists, so often
(unlike the Carthusians) reformed
I had read of in Merton's best-seller.
Their habits were, like the Dominicans',
piebald, their discipline called
for, not solitude, but a gregarious
silence, the last thing I wanted!
This left the primordial order
of monks, Benedictines, the oldest
and biggest—and richest?—extant,
subdivided in various national
houses, as German and French
and American. Scholars and teachers,
they followed the Rule of St. Benedict
mostly in spirit; but some
even followed its letter. Of these
Benedictines of strictest observance
or primitive life, Father Hapgood
had heard of a recent foundation
in northern Vermont just across
the American border. I wrote
to the prior proposing a visit,
or rather, proposing myself
as a postulant. Black as their habits
appeared, I imagined their souls
to be white. There were dozens of other
religious to choose from of course
in the Church—Trinitarians, Passionists,
Maurists—too many to number.

Like tourists examining maps
and brochures as they plan a vacation,
we planned my vocation, consulting
advertisements, hearsay, and guides.
From the moment I entered the Church

(or the moment thereafter, perhaps)
I determined to carry the thing
to excess—an excess, to begin
with, of chastity. If, as I fear,
I have failed to explain my conversion
(it's hard to explain what you don't
understand) I may equally fail
to explain my monastic adventures,
events of a nature almost
to defy explanation.
                          Awaiting
but hardly expecting an early
reply from Sweet Saviour Priory,
what was I going to do
in the meantime? Whatever one does
in the meantime, it takes one a lifetime
to learn, is at least as important
as anything done when the meantime
is over: the meantime is life.
I had kept the address of the "saint,"
Alan Waterman, Freya had mentioned
in passing or given me as
a viaticum. Down by the waterfront
(not a salubrious neighbourhood)
lived, and for all that I know
to the contrary, lives a unique
individual whom I despair
of describing, such radical charity
being notoriously
indescribable since unbelievable,
monstrous, inhuman, unkind
in the etymological sense.
Alan Waterman, therefore, portrayed
as a monster of goodness, seemed worthy
of pilgrimage, through a dispiriting
district of unrelieved squalour
and brick, a Victorian slum
amid warehouses, railways and wharves,
where he worked with the poor undeserving
incurable drunks who frequented
the neighbourhood, always at home
to the homeless, and likewise to me
when I called. I approached through a maze
of malodorous streets with misgivings,

for this was a quarter of old
Montreal I had never explored
in my rambles with Mark in the past,
when we'd tended to cling to the easier
slopes of the mountain in cowardly
contrast, I felt, to my present
heroic descent. For the past
is an underworld even in daylight;
but hell, I reminded myself,
must involve separation from God,
a condition as common in comfortable
homes as in dusty, impoverished
sordid surroundings like these.
Yet the desperate looks that encountered,
or rather avoided, my own
in the street seemed to multiply near
the address I was seeking; a legion
of loitering layabouts, men
for the most part, their gender submerged
in their general misery, dressed
in a motley collection of rags
like some crapulous uniform, shambled
along like an army of sleepwalkers.
Guessing their goal, notwithstanding
their aimless appearance, I followed
the herd. On the sidewalk in front
of a house like its neighbours constructed
of brick, undistinguished and mean,
where the crowd congregated, I noticed
their similar famished expressions;
unshaven, unhappy, unwashed,
whether pale or unwholesomely rosy,
decrepit or viciously vigorous,
varying also in age
and condition on closer inspection
than I was prepared to conduct,
I'm afraid I recoiled from the halt
and the lame and the blind, the unlucky,
the worthless or innocent failures,
the lost, the obscure, that assembled
in silence (though some of their lips
were in motion incessantly) here
on the steps of what must be the place
I was looking for, Lazarus House.

An indignant if indigent straggler
admonished me, "Get to the end
of the line!" As I did there appeared
in the doorway a man whom the derelicts
speechlessly greeted with something
akin to respect—expectation,
the look of a dog for his master,
albeit this figure was far
from imposing, a wraith in his sixties,
as grizzled and shabby and worn
as the worst of them. Smiling a wonderful
smile, he invited them in,
and the zombies obeyed him. With faltering
gait, two by two, and with gazes
abased they ascended the steps
to the entrance, like penitent sinners
ascending the stairway to heaven.
He welcomed them all with a courteous
word, like a clergyman greeting
his flock in the porch of the church;
they responded by bobbing their heads,
which were palsied as often as not,
and by blinking their eyes which were frequently
twitching or rheumy or blank,
or with leers or a hideous rictus
of lips over gums that were either
edentate or sown with the ruins
of teeth. I had followed this ghastly
procession as far as the portal
of Lazarus House, when the man
who must be Alan Waterman bade
me, "Good morning! God bless you! Come in!"
as if I were the last of his guests.
I rejected his charity: granted
that fortune had negative favourites,
I wasn't one of them yet.
As he vanished inside, through a door
partly open, whence issued a scraping
of chairs and of feet and a strangely
delicious aroma of stew,
I elected to wait in the hall
for a chance to present my credentials
and qualifications, whatever

they were, to my host. Father Hapgood
had heard of his work, and agreed
it would do me no harm, for one summer
at least, to apprentice myself
to this radical Christian, a local
disciple of Dorothy Day,
one who honoured the gospel injunction
by feeding the hungry and clothing
the naked and comforting those
in affliction, of whom I supposed
he accounted me one, and no wonder!
My clothes were a mess. I was homeless
in fact, till invited to visit
Sweet Saviour Priory, or
till the Fall when McGill would reopen
for business, whichever came first.

I examined an oleograph
in the hall while I waited: a picture
of Dives and Lazarus during
their disparate early careers,
the occasion when Dives was throwing
a party and Lazarus lay
at the gate with the dogs—an embarrassing
spectacle, still, who remembers
the names of the guests at a function
like this? Yet apparently neither
the host nor the eyesore outside
is aware of the change that will soon
overtake their respective estates
when their true situations will set
in cement for eternity? Dives'
reversal will come as a nasty
surprise, for we read of the millionaire's
righteousness—those contributions
to charity! that philanthropic
foundation! The leper however
proved less than forgiving or generous:
what could a drop of cold water
have cost him in heaven? The moral?
Confronted by this and by similar
proofs of the working of providence,
ought one to blame a mechanical
fortune, inscrutable Tyche,

or worship benevolent Chance?
Or was God a Utopian Leveller
putting the powerful down
from their seats and exalting the humble,
as in the Magnificat? Hungry
as Lazarus during the meal
I could smell but not taste, my reflections
I daresay were just as jejune,
until boredom impelled me to eavesdrop.
The banquet progressed in comparative
silence apart from a clatter
of crockery mixed with a rattle
of cutlery masking more animal
noises like chewing and swallowing;
here there were none of the feeble
facetious attempts at polite
conversation that bloomed in the Old
Presbyterian College's dining-room.
Clear as the bell for communion,
the businesslike tinkle of metal
on glass interrupted the Barmecide
feast, and a saccharine voice
introduced an inaudible grace.
With a mumbled but nonetheless heartfelt
"Amen," the replete, after pushing
their chairs back, began to compete
for the exit as fiercely as ever
they had for the entrance. The dregs
of society hastened away
in pursuit of postprandial port
or cologne, or whatever their tipple;
for Waterman served only water,
the beverage Lazarus couldn't
or wouldn't supply to poor Dives.
I sympathized only much later:
for decades I thought that the richest
repast without wine was a frost.

In the wake of the needy their patron,
whose voice I had heard saying grace,
reappeared. "I'm afraid you're too late
for the dinner today. Is there anything
else I can do for you?" "Thank you,
I'm not really hungry," I lied,

being famished: how else to establish
the gulf that I felt to be fixed
between those he had fed and myself?
I was young, to be sure: so were some
of the bums, even younger than I.
Middle class? But the derelict counted
among them a number of sometime
professionals, doctors and lawyers,
professors and businessmen. What
in our otherwise classless society
marked the degree of my own
education? A year, two semesters,
of mild dissipation at college
redeemed by the sort of omnivorous
reading that warm public libraries
furnish their indigent patrons
in winter along with the shelter
they pay for by autodidactic
exertions like conning the whole
of the encyclopaedia volume
by volume. The fatal distinction,
not only in station but surely
in worth that I snobbishly wanted
to draw between me and the destitute
must, I concluded, be moral.
"I'm here," I informed Alan Waterman
rather toploftily, feeling
unsure of myself, "to contribute
whatever I can to your work."
He regarded me kindly but sceptically,
"Money, you mean?" "In the nature
of service," I hastened to specify.
"What can you do?" I detailed
my irrelevant qualifications—
my only experience really
had been in a library. "Nothing
to offer but willingness," Waterman
smiled, "which is all that's required.
If you're sure you're not hungry or thirsty,
you could, I suppose, do the dishes?"
He showed me the way to a cavernous
scullery. Mountains of china
were stacked in the primitive sink
while the water to wash it in heated

on top of the stove in the kitchen
of Lazarus House, where the tapwater
trickled as chilly as charity.

So it was settled that same
afternoon: while awaiting the call
to contemplative life, I should imitate
Martha, the activist sister
of Mary and that other Lazarus
mentioned in scripture, who rose
from the dead, by performing the corporal
works, as the do-gooders called
them, of mercy. When done washing-up,
Alan Waterman asked me to help
him to sort out the clothing donated
by well-wishers, much of it better
than what we were wearing. We talked
as we worked, and he sketched his adventurous
autobiography, after
eliciting mine (so much shorter
and tamer than his) indirectly:
he made it a practice, he said,
not to pry, but he prided himself
on discernment of character. "Many
are called," he observed of my fancied
monastic vocation, "but only
a handful are chosen." As well
as a carnival roustabout, manual
labourer, lumberjack, dishwasher,
seaman, itinerant fruitpicker,
salesman and cowhand, he'd been
in his youth—which I couldn't imagine:
his face was as finely engraved
as a banknote by age and experience—
also a Capuchin lay-brother,
hence his distrust of untested
vocations. His rackety past
and abandoned religious career
disconcerted my cloistral ambition,
which time would convince me had nothing
to do with religion. Himself
an unquestioning Catholic, born
and brought up in the faith, he had never
forsaken it quite and returned

on the threshold of age to its literal
practice to found an establishment
which he had noted a need
for again and again in his travels.
The Salvation Army and such
evangelical missions were all
very well in their way, though their methods
were not to his taste; but why shouldn't
a wealthy and powerful Church
whose resources are truly infallible
succour the secular failure
today as it says that it did
in the dark middle ages? *The Catholic
Worker*, a movement as well
as a newspaper started by Dorothy
Day in New York had provided
a model; his faith, inspiration.
He welcomed assistance of sorts
in his task as a practical Christian,
when offered: the pay would accord
with my skill and experience, reckoned
as nil. I must live by the rule
Alan Waterman lived by, volitional
poverty, scarcely a hardship
to someone inured to the Spartan
regime of the Old Presbyterian
College; moreover the worst
deprivations are bearable once
they are willingly born. My reward?
Room and board here below, and a similar
set-up hereafter above.

I returned with a brown paper parcel
containing my worldly possessions
that evening, apart from a carton
of books which I stored at the college,
my copies of Virgil and Pound
and the rest of the secular baggage
I longed to be rid of forever.
I brought those necessities which
even voluntary poverty couldn't
dispense with, two changes of underwear,
socks, and a razor, as well
as a crucifix bought in a fit

of aesthetic self-mortification
because it offended my visual
taste with its angular, modern,
unrepresentational pathos:
I nailed it up over my bed
like a primitive fetish, to ward
off temptation and doubt. Alan Waterman
showed me the room I should occupy
during the following weeks
of hot weather: if hardly the cell
of my dreams—for, distempered a dismal
magenta, it lacked that peculiar
air of austerity proper
to cells, in my novice opinion—
at least it was empty, except
for a cot with a thin, scratchy blanket
or comfortless comforter—nothing
superfluous, curtain or picture
or rug on the floor, neither table
nor chair, and not even a view.
When I lifted the blind at the window,
discoloured and torn, Alan Waterman
murmured, "Don't bother. One luxury
Lazarus House can't afford
is a room with a view." Yet I fancied
the breath-taking glimpse of the fire-escape
hinted a last-minute chance
of salvation by means of good works,
a detestable prospect, no doubt,
to all Protestants blandly assured
of salvation by grace, yet I somehow
preferred the idea of working
my way into heaven.
                              "And now,
if you've quite settled in," Alan Waterman
said with (I thought) imperceptible
irony, "you will be ready
for prayers. Every night about now"
(nearly ten, and still daylight outside),
"you will find me reciting the rosary."
Stumped, for I didn't possess
such a thing, as a literate convert,
or know how to use one, in secret
despising as vulgar this popular

aid to devotion as well
as the know-nothing saint who declared
that his beads were his book, I believe
that I shocked Alan Waterman, too,
by my ignorance, which he endeavoured
immediately to correct
with a spare set of beads that he took
from a drawer and presented me with.
He had plenty of piety's second-hand
paraphernalia, whose provenance
I didn't care to inquire,
any more than what blessed material
(plastic and alloy more likely
than silver and wood) constituted
the beads that he taught me to tell
in the parlour that served as the chapel
of Lazarus House, an admixture
like everything there of conspicuous
poverty plus ostentatious
discomfort. I wince to remember
the splintery floor where we knelt
to perform our devotions aloud
in a queer macaronic of Latin
and English, as I in my hopeless
pretentiousness rattled off *Aves*
and *Paters* and *Credos* in place
of "Hail Mary," "Our Father" and Creed.
Alan Waterman humoured me, oddly
enough, though he claimed to prefer
a vernacular service in principle,
back when the dialogue mass
was a gleam in the eyes of the Vatican
fathers. We stuck on our knees
for a further uncomfortable spell
of so-called recollection, a sort
of interior improvisation
or vague, sanctimonious daydream
on topics like Time and Eternity,
Judgement and Mercy; whatever
exceeded the grasp of the rational
mind I considered a suitable
subject for woolgathering
for an hour by the clock before bedtime.
I speak for myself: Alan Waterman's

thoughts were presumably both
better ordered and elsewhere. He certainly
looked (when I peeked) oddly focused,
intent, barely breathing, and yet
wide awake, as if straining to hear
some inaudible music. Howbeit,
while always refusing to teach
me his secret technique, he described
meditation as something infused—
like a tea-bag—reminding me of
the hard-hearted but scriptural motto
of Lazarus House: *Sauve Qui Peut.*
But I found it impossible not
to succumb to distraction, the foe
of contemplative prayer, in the form
of both mental and physical fidgets.
My back inaccessibly started
to itch, like the tip of my nose,
while my ankles and wrists went to sleep
and my knees and my feet seemed to bristle
with needles and pins like a pincushion.
Meanwhile my mind was distraught
by irrelevant images, trivial
worries, and some not so trivial,
dragging me back from such treacherous
ice as Our Lord's Incarnation
and Glorious Body. At last
it was bedtime; before we retired
we partook of a nightcap of cocoa
dissolved in hot water, on festive
occasions in Carnation Milk.

I was going to get pretty sick
in the following weeks of one phrase
Alan Waterman relished, "the Mystical
Body," a flat contradiction
inviting credulity's *Quia
absurdum*, a concept immaculate
as the conception referred
to of meaning, for "mystical" casts
a semantic illusion, a sense
of significance, something hermetic,
not content as such but its absence,
a meaningful vacuum suggestively

vague, as in "mystical marriage"
for instance, or *mariage blanc*,
which is French for no marriage at all,
insubstantial except in the mind
of the mystic or maybe in heaven,
and these after all are the same;
whereas "body" is nothing if not
circumstantial, objective and solid,
too solid at times for my liking.
It occupies space, yet the glorious
body ascending to heaven
transcended (we're told) space and time
and supposedly ended up nowhere,
unless one were modern enough
to imagine it went into orbit?
Jejune speculations like this
all too often would keep me awake
half the night on the comfortless cot
I preferred to a floor as a lot
less luxurious. Nobody spoke
of a body of men or a body
of water as mystical, surely?
A body of doctrine, however,
conceivably might be described
in such terms. I concluded this mystical
body of Christ Alan Waterman
liked to invoke, oxymoron
or not, was no more than a Catholic
catchword defining the Church
as a cosy collective or *corpus
delicti*, the evidence left
here below when the victim absconded.

I rose the next morning and every
morning at Lazarus House
at 5:30 when Waterman tapped
at my door about dawn to remind
me in plenty of time of the 6
o'clock Mass with which weekdays began.
Did you ever awake from a dream
to discover that all that you held
in your arms was a tear-spotted pillow,
the certainty, power and hope
of your vision polluted by day

and the radiance faded wherein
the impersonal truth was announced
as a personal matter-of-fact?
An awakening doubly distressful
to me, since the dream I attempted
to capture again was forbidden
and had to be banished. Reality,
drab as linoleum, took
on the specious allure of a dream
as the glow of temptation gave way
to the commonplace glare of the morning.
Avoiding the view from my window
while raising the blind (a mistake,
like restoring the sight of the dead),
and ignoring the whorehouse décor
of my prison, I hastily dressed
and descended, still groping my way,
to the parlour where Alan (as Waterman
asked me to call him) awaited
me, patiently turning the pages,
as if they were braille, of his missal.

Our choice of which church to hear Mass
in demanded a major decision,
depending on heaven knows what,
for we seldom attended one twice
in the space of a week—which will give
you a notion how richly the slums
of the city were furnished with parishes,
all within reach of the pious
pedestrian. Really what difference
it made which direction we took
was uncertain, the services being
alike at St. Augustine's and
the Cathedral, St. Rose, Holy Cross,
St. Ignatius, Our Lady of Lourdes
or the Sisters of Charity: anywhere
Latin was muttered or sung
the proverbial rule, "When in Rome..."
in liturgical matters prevailed.
In décor variations were minimal
too: tarted up by what must
be the same tasteless hand, all those tawdry
interiors looked like a Christmas tree,

arguably an appropriate
symbol, but rather an eyesore
in June. One significant variant
found in these not very various
places of worship involved
the officiant's speed and agility,
how many minutes each took
for a typical B-minus Mass.
There were some who could get from "the altar
of God" to the terminal Gospel
(beginning, confusingly, "In
the beginning...") in under ten minutes,
the verified track-record standing
at eight, notwithstanding that sacristy
legend, the four-minute Mass;
while the oldest and slowest of celebrants
shuffled away from the altar
in twenty, an average sacrifice
lasted no more than fifteen.
I suspect that in view of the Eastern
position, a priest with his face
to the wall and his back to a small
congregation consisting on weekdays
of Waterman, sundry old women
in black and myself, must have skipped
through the canon inaudibly, dropping
a *Dominus tecum*, omitting
a mumbled *Oremus* or two
undetected amid all the other
obscurely profound hocus-pocus.
There might be a cantor somewhere
in the balcony, clearly a phonograph
record, except when the voice
was too cracked, a soprano or baritone
chanting the musical bits,
out of synch, from the *Kyrie* through
Benedictus qui venit, the signal
for us to nip out of our pews
with a swift genuflection, and scurrying
up to the polished communion-rail
kneel for the first solid meal
of the day. Transubstantial and tasteless,
the papery wafer adhered
to the teeth and the roof of the mouth,

as the Roman communion provided
no wine as an aid to ingestion.
The chalice that holds the New Testament
being reserved for the clergy,
the laity—"people of God"—
are restricted to only one species,
a sordid economy measure
condemned in more bibulous times
as betraying a quite Manichaean
distrust of the innocent fruit
of the vine. My new-fangled devotion,
intense and uncritical, rather
than jibbing at quibbles like these
during Mass, was transfixed by the pantomime
figure in front of the altar
whose gestures and rare and infrequently
audible syllables sometimes
illumined a page of my missal.
One phrase at the start, *Qui laetificat*,
that is to say, "Who rejoices
my youth" (*juventutem*), ironically
rang rather hollow, but after
the *Gloria*, Gospel and *Credo*,
the Preface enjoined us to "Lift
up your hearts," *Sursum corda*. I tried,
as I followed the canon in silence.
My favourite prayer, *Qui naturam
formasti* began *mirabiliter et
mirabilius*—here was the crux—
reformasti: "You formed human nature
in wonderful wise, and more wonderfully
still you reformed it." This cheerful
synopsis, not only of man's
evolution, but also of my
reformation, entailed an emotive
crescendo, *Hosannah* and *Sanctus*
preceding the high point that followed
the formulae, "This is my body,"
and "This is my blood," the miraculous
mute consecration, a private
affair in the hands of the priest.
Elevation succeeded, proclaimed
by a circumspect bell which an acolyte
rang—there was always an acolyte,

not always young, overlooked
in the shuffle. We cringed in our seats
till it tinkled again, when we lifted
our gaze to the altar, in "terror
and trembling," in Chrysostom's phrase,
to behold in a disk of unleavened
farine and a goblet of plonk
the immaculate victim, the godhead
incarnate, albeit invisibly
so. Having taken communion,
I knelt with my head in my hands
as I savoured the state of gratuitous
grace that ensued from the sacrament,
piously picking my teeth
with my tongue, till dismissed with the meaningless
words, *Missa est*. After several
brief uncanonical prayers
to Our Lady (unmentioned almost
in the Canon), the priest made a dignified
exit to breakfast; the candles
and other, electrical lights
were extinguished, compelling the faithful
to find their way out by the rubicund
glow of the lamp that announces
the fact that the Host is at home.

Once outside, temporarily blinded
by sunlight much brighter than faith
which embellished the homely, derivative
sooty façade of the church
and its grubby surroundings, I blinked
at the delicate beauty suffusing
the streets on our route of return
and their hideous hovels of brick
with the fleeting distinction of dawn,
a phenomenon capable even
of gilding the gallows, the gaol,
and the garbage cans blocking the sidewalks.
In transit I fancied the city
beginning to tremble and hum
as if pregnant with squalour and sin,
with the life of the senses, in short,
which I pitied and dreaded and shunned,
fascinated and frightened, deploring

the myth that the poor are at home
in the slums just as I, unaware,
was at home on the campus before
this regrettable nonsense began.

We returned in broad daylight to breakfast
at Lazarus House, not unlike
two fraternity boys on a toot—
to a breakfast of watery cocoa,
again (even tea was esteemed
too expensive, and coffee exorbitant),
yesterday's bread resurrected
as toast, but no butter or margarine
(luxuries foreign to lives
of unselfish compassion for others),
though smeared with—on Sundays and Feast Days—
a smidgin of strawberry jam
which, appropriately in the case
of anonymous donatives, came
in a bucket without any label.
We breakfasted briskly, with little
incentive to dally, and putting
our physical nature behind
us, commenced our quotidian chores.
Alan Waterman set me to scrubbing
the floor—or the floors, there were two—
throughout Lazarus House. Having never
done housework before, I regarded
both bucket and scrub-brush as mystical
means of purgation: was cleanliness
not, as extolled in my Protestant
upbringing, next to divinity?
Slaving away at the ancient
linoleum whose indeterminate
pattern no lashings of sunlight
could ever elucidate, punishing
boards that must rival the wood
of the cross in respect to the number
of splinters they seemed to produce,
as I hummed an Ambrosian hymn—
Lux beata, perhaps—I attacked
the invincible grit of the slums
like a personal enemy, Satan
no less, whom I daily engaged

in indefinite warfare, each skirmish
with dirt representing the endless
guerrilla campaign against sin.

When I finished the floor, or gave up,
there was always the laundry whose quantity,
(never its quality), varied
depending on how many non-paying
guests Alan Waterman harboured
along with myself. Its facilities
limited, Lazarus House
was exclusive as flophouses go,
and as flophouses went, too respectable
really for comfort. A sign
I once saw on a fleabag hotel
in the Bowery, TRANSIENTS WELCOME
HOT BATHS was belied by experience.
Given the turnover, bed-linen
had to be changed pretty often
as most of our derelicts, long
before drugs became prevalent, clung
to the bottle—Australian sherry
or hair-tonic—hardly a habit
conducive to personal daintiness;
some were incontinent too.
I immersed this impossible wash
in a venerable washing machine
with a mangle, or wringer, which worked
when it worked, with a handle, by hand,
and a tub of cold water for rinsing.
Instead of expensive detergents
we used an innocuous mixture
of potash and lye, which is bio-
degradable, had we but known,
but which wrought no lixivial miracles.
Hung up to dry in the basement
in lieu of a yard, amid beetles
and soot, was it any surprise
that the bedclothes were neither immaculate,
nor, for that matter, well-aired,
but in spite of my efforts unhealthily
clammy and tattletale grey.
On the whole the most serious drawback
of Lazarus House I accounted

its smell, a pervasive and nauseous
odour that haunted the place
and which nothing so simple and wholesome
as sunlight and water could exorcise:
urine and vomit, the stench
of unwanted, unwashed, undernourished
and moribund bodies, that scent
of corruption that Lazarus must
have exuded: "He stinketh," it saith
in the Bible, a text that was taken
as gospel by many ascetics,
the Stylite for instance, whose lofty
and lifelong remoteness preserved
his admirers from holding their noses,
the odour of sanctity being
too frequently merely B.O.?
Notwithstanding the heat of that summer,
for all my unwearying if
unavailing assaults on the grime
all around me, I seldom if ever
indulged in a bath, although Lazarus
House had a bathroom, no commonplace
luxury then in the slums;
but I shunned this occasion of carnal
temptation: ironically cleanliness
mandated getting undressed.

When the bells of the neighbouring churches
discordantly chorused the *Angelus
Domini annuntiavit*,
I knew it was noon and high time
to begin preparations for what
I had formerly thought of as lunch
but which here was referred to as dinner,
the principal meal of the day
when we entertained angels not quite
unawares. The whole morning I'd been
in a stew off and on, contemplating
the problem of how we were going
to feed an indefinite number
of hungry unfortunates, given
our meagre resources: a tin
of sardines and a package of Wonderbread,
barring a miracle like

a reprise of the loaves and the fishes.
And yet we succeeded in succouring
multitudes daily, supplied
with that substance on which (it is written)
the righteous subsist in addition
to bread, an endowment by virtue
of which one could walk on the water
of want and remove any mountains
that stand in the way. Alan Waterman
gave the impression of effortless
bounty while making ends meet,
justifiably proud of his shoestring
ragout. I suppose I should turn
up my nose at such simple and tedious
fare nowadays, but sufficiency
simply sufficed that omnivorous
table, for hunger is not
a gourmet; our objective was plenty,
not quality cooking but quantity
cooked. Certain critics (and Lazarus
House had its critics, especially
high in the Catholic hierarchy)
claimed this was better than winos
deserved: the desserts of our neighbours
so often appear to exceed
their deserts! Though we catered to satisfy
everyone's hunger, their thirsts
proved insatiable; water, however,
remained undisturbed in the glasses
I'd filled at each place. Alan Waterman
did all the serious cooking,
an art he had learned in the navy,
or was it the merchant marine?
But he taught me to make a delicious
and nourishing—and economical—
pudding or sweet which we dished
up at dinnertime day after day.
I began by collecting the leftover
crumbs from the table, the fragments
of loaves that some generous baker
donated, as yesterday's crust
doesn't sell. Though the bread of affliction
be stale, it is perfectly edible:
what we discard in the garbage

of Western, which is to say wasteful,
economies, can be redeemed
or recycled by following Waterman's
recipe. See you have plenty
of bread, for it shrinks with inflation;
white bread will be best, but whole wheat
is o.k.; pumpernickel and rye
are unsuitable. Pack some capacious
container, a vat or a dishpan
until overflowing with this.
In addition a handful of nuts
or red currants or raisins as well
as a cupful of sugar, though dear,
will contribute to flavour. Add water
to taste, till the mixture is soggy,
then cover the mess with a dishcloth
and set in a corner to soak
overnight. This you bake in a moderate
oven for hours; when ambrosially
brown it is ready to serve
in minute individual portions
improved out of all recognition
when soaked in Carnation and syrup.
Except for this triumph of Waste-
Not-and-Want-Not cuisine, the invaluable
Lazarus House Hospitality
Cookbook remains to be written.

In setting the table with various
lacklustre cutlery, I
was advised to forget about knives,
for that primitive tableware—older
than tables, by far—could be dangerous,
(Alan regarded his charges
as patients or prisoners, not
without reason), redundant as well,
as the meat, when there was any, had
been apportioned in such tiny pieces
that "bite-sized," provided our clients
had dentures to bite with, could barely
describe them. The spoon, an effete
neolithic invention along
with the pot, must suffice, though we furnished
some newfangled forks to the fussy.

Apart from the pepper and salt-shakers
(peppermills being as rare
as roast duck on the humble Canadian
table), such middle class frills
as a tablecloth, napkins and cruets
were not to be seen on our board.

Preparations completed, I took
up my post in the doorway behind
Alan Waterman, counting, like Noah,
the animals boarding the ark.
But if Lazarus House were a vessel,
for me, of salvation, for them
it was merely a ferry to fetch
them across the unfordable straits
between morning and night. At an average
sitting we entertained twenty
or more at our makeshift, hospitable
board, an erection of plywood
on trestles. My casual census
became a review of the damned,
as I came to consider these permanent
drop-outs, for though I soon greeted
the regular faces by name,
I could never get used to the misery
stamped there, a pain for which time
was no cure, hence remote from my own
adolescent distress. To suppose
for a moment that derelicts pass
beyond shame into freedom accumulates
insult on injury. No,
the romance of the road is a myth
when it means the descent to Avernus,
that highway to modern perdition,
the street. If my pity and horror
appear too naive and subjective,
how *could* I be sure what the destitute
felt in themselves? To concede
to another's experience similar
weight with one's own is impossible:
by definition subjective,
experience must be hermetic.
With nothing to go on but sensible
evidence, all circumstantial

at that, or analogy based
on the faulty assumption that anyone's
inner reality mirrors
our own (for the basic mistake
that we make about others is thinking
of them as ourselves in disguise),
I presumed from the look on their faces,
that terrible look, the indelible
print of despair, that their state
was deserving of pity and possible
succour. Their dress indicated
as much: they resembled some cruel
couturier's summer collection
of scarecrows, in tatters and rags,
overdressed for the season, the colour
and cut of their garments distorted
by dirt and neglect. Their dispirited
gait and their air of dejection,
their downcast demeanours and obvious
want, the occasional words
that escaped them (monotonous oaths
for the most part), as well as their voices,
as ravaged and sad as their faces,
persuaded me that, if in fact
they were human and blessed—or accursed—
with free will, it sufficed to be human
and free to be damned. Alan Waterman
didn't agree that they were,
though conceding that freedom entailed
disagreeable moments, he preached
paradoxically as we prepared
a free lunch for the radically free:
"Who are freer, the rich or the poor?"
Never having been either I couldn't
express an opinion, but wanly
supposed one was never so free
as in giving things up. Both the Communist
Church and the Catholic Party
pretended that freedom consisted
in perfect surrender of will—
"In His will is our peace," a determinist
tag that predicted our modern
alliance of science and force,
Beneath Freedom and Dignity? "Under

their wretched appearance I cling
to their inner inviolabili:y!"
Faith being blinder than love,
which is merely near-sighted, why not?
"Every morning we worship the physical
presence of Christ in a wafer
which sceptics" (I crossed myself nervously),
"scoff at as nothing but bread."
I reflected that similar faith
was required to accept the half-baked
definition of Wonderbread purely
as bread with no chemical additives.
"So we may see," Alan Waterman
talked like a book, or at least
like a paper, *The Catholic Worker*,
"the lineaments, under the least
prepossessing exterior, even,
of Christ who reminded us, 'When
I was hungry, you fed me; when thirsty
you gave me to drink, for whatever
you do for the meanest of these
you are doing for me.'" I could never
accustom myself to these novel
translations of scripture which Catholics
plainly preferred to the grand
if inaccurate authorized version,
the Bible uniquely remaining
a text that exists in translation
without an original. Some
of my efforts to see the divine
in the doubtfully human had proved
too successful, as when I discerned
through a gap in the rags that disfigured
a bum disconcertingly perfect
and shapely and elegant limbs.

We admitted them all to the feast,
undeserving or not, undeniably
needy enough to enjoy
macaroni and cheese or a temperance
boeuf bourguignon (Irish stew),
a hot meal in the heat of the day.
As I waited at table, replenishing
plates with the generous helpings

that Alan dispensed from the kitchen,
admiring as almost monastic
the general silence and haste
which the indigent ate in, distraught
by their frequent, imperious gestures
for seconds, I dreamt that the gutter
might do just as well as the cloister
in terms of ascesis, while beggars
may so far be choosers that under
their beggarly raiment they wear
an invisible scapular.

              After
a hurried vernacular grace
they departed without any further
expression of thanks than a mumbled
Amen. Having taken pot luck
in the kitchen, I tackled a mountain
of dishes barehanded. As morning
and noon had been given to feeding
the hungry (though hardly to quenching
their thirst, save perhaps in the matter
of righteousness), each afternoon
was devoted to partially clothing
the naked, the garments to do so
provided by well-to-do donors,
in Westmount and elsewhere, persuaded
by self-seeking spiritual motives:
generosity earned them a mark,
they believed, in the heavenly ledger
which they, like all Catholics, kept,
where a secondhand jacket was worth,
as a prudent investment, an *Ave*,
a worn pair of pants, on the layaway
plan of salvation, a *Pater*;
but few could afford to contribute
an overcoat longer and fuller
of holes than the *Credo*! Their Bentleys
and Cadillacs crowded the kerb
outside Lazarus House when they dropped
off their glad rags much saddened by wear,
reminiscent indeed of a camel
attempting to squeeze through the eye
of a needle; they haughtily gawked
at the primitive race they had come

to relieve, while the poor for their part,
with a mixture of envy—or pity—
and equal aversion, were gaping
at them. But the rich have been Christians
for centuries, since the half-hearted
conversion of Constantine; stays
of the Church in its palmiest days,
their redemption was never in doubt
once some Council or other determined
the kickback that conscience demanded;
if martyrs with money to burn
were statistically never significant,
bishops are drawn from the affluent
classes, and abbots and cardinals
too, so what Nietzsche despised
as a servile religion emerged
from the ages of faith as elitist
in practice if seldom in theory.
Some, like SS. Francis and Vincent
de Paul and King Wenceslaw, born
to the purple (at least in the pink)
couldn't wait to divest themselves, like
a hair shirt, of the trappings of wealth,
such as comfort, position and privilege
(respectability's often
the first inhibition to go),
and thereafter displayed an inverted
but virulent snobbery, posing
as beggars and thieves to embarrass
their betters: examples abound
in *The Lives of the Saints*. Hagiography
isn't extinct as a genre
today, although saints are in shorter
supply. Alan Waterman may
have been one, though as far as I know
he had given up nothing; and yet
while we laboured and lived side by side
through the dog days of summer, I never
quite got him in focus; his kindness
and piety made him a likable
cypher, who though he had plenty
of character, lacked personality.

Strange and impersonal, too,
were the Avenues, Crescents and Squares
where I went to solicit the castoffs
the charitable were too busy
or lazy to bring us themselves.
After several snubs I remembered
to go round the back; if a butler
or parlourmaid answered the door
I would beg for a word with their mistress.
Demanded my business, I answered,
the rag trade, and Lazarus House.
"I shall see if the missus"—or "Madam,"
depending again on the servant—
"is home." It would be very strange
if they were not already informed
on this point, I reflected: the houses
in Westmount, though big by Canadian
standards, are hardly Versailles
or the Vatican. Yet I'd encountered
this anglophile ruse in Victorian
novels perused in more lighthearted
days, when the fiction I read
for amusement was labelled as fiction,
unlike those dogmatic inventions
I conned nowadays for instruction.
As often as not the domestic
returned empty-handed, regretting
that Madam was out—indisposed—
or too busy to see me—and sometimes
(not often) suggesting that I
might return at a less inconvenient
time. On occasion one might
reappear with a bundle of "suitable"
clothing, a threadbare tuxedo,
a tattered Dior, or a pair
of plus-fours, which they hoped might prove useful
to someone. I piously trusted
they would. At one bogus chateau
I was summoned summarily into
the chatelaine's boudoir; this bountiful
lady reclined on a sofa
half-dressed, with her beads in one hand,
The Ascent of Mount Carmel, uncut,
on her lap, and unblushingly pressed

me to take what I wanted. I made
my excuses and fled from her presence
like Joseph from Potiphar's wife.

Such repulsive temptations aside,
it disturbed me to wander in search
of donations among the evocative
scenes of the winter before
through the shady and somnolent streets
with their Protestant names, like McTavish
and Mountain, surrounding McGill,
and the privileged enclaves adorning
the slops of Mount Royal. Familiar
and foreign at once, like a ghost
I revisited regions of which
I had been, not exactly a native
perhaps, but a freedman: no more!
and I feared to encounter some former
acquaintance to whom I'd become
altogether invisible since.

The collection of clothing concluded
but half of the battle: too often
it had to be cleaned—"filthy rich"
is no idle cliché—and then sorted
according to season and size,
for it profits a man very little
to get a fur coat in the middle
of August, or elegant shoes
that are either too tight or so loose
that they fall off his feet. Like a gentleman's
outfitters, therefore, we featured
our seasonal specialties, always
on sale, and at rock-bottom prices
at that. Distribution began
every day in the late afternoon,
when a queue like the line that had formed
before lunch, and composed of the same
individuals, lengthened in front
of our door. In so far as I found
it at least as repugnant to give
to the poor as to take from the rich,
I embraced, as a mortification,
the duties of corporal mercy.

I learned it was no easy matter
to outfit a man in the grip
of *delirium tremens*, and erred
in assuming the needy were easy
to please and pathetically grateful
for anything given them. Mendicants
sniff at that hand that is feeding
them, drifters exhibit when choosing
a secondhand wardrobe a dandified,
picky, fastidious taste.
"Don't you think it's a little too loud?"
one might ask of a hand-me-down check,
"or too full in the seat? I'd prefer
a more sober, conservative cut.
Have you anything nice in a pin-stripe?"
The intimacy of the fitting-room
merely confirmed the appalled
metaphysical pity produced
by my customers' physical shortcomings:
rickety bodies so wasted
and worn by disease and starvation,
so filthy they gave an impression
of being androgynous, almost.
(Not quite: but it struck me much later
as queer that we never saw women
at Lazarus House?) Alan Waterman,
striving to quell the disgust
that I sought to dissemble transparently,
comforted me with the words
of St. Francis: "All things that thou hatest
in Nature, by Grace thou shalt love;
everything that occasions distaste
in this world shall be turned in the next
to unspeakable comfort and joy."

If the spectacle, and the aroma,
of fleshly decrepitude caused
me a queasy distress, more distressing
by far was the rare and exceptional
vision of carnal perfection
that crossed my laborious path.
In the midst of our sad clientele
of extreme or at least indeterminate
age, an occasional youth

who was down on his luck would appeal
for a handout, a meal, or respectable
duds, or a bed for the night.
And though clothing my needy coevals—
a seaman discharged or a runaway
younger than I—might occasion
temptation, at least of the eyes,
which I primly averted when possible,
sharing my cell with temptation
incarnate entailed an ordeal
such as Gandhi and monks of the Thebaid
often enjoyed. While I slept,
insofar as I slept, on the floor
and recited the Glorious Mysteries
under my breath, as a desperate
apotropaic device
for repulsing unwanted (or so
I insisted) advances that never
materialized, my importunate
roomate's immodest, monotonous
streetwise vocabulary
and the sounds of suggestive, mysterious
movements compelled me, in spite
of my vows, into sneaking a peek:
a perversion that mystics, aspiring
ones anyway, such as myself,
are susceptible to. Visionaries
are all sublimated voyeurs.
The apostle, my namesake, who scrutinized
closely the Glorified Body,
was surely the first peeping Tom.
After weeks going blindfold, I'd almost
forgotten what masculine vigour
and beauty were like, and the contrast
to what I had painfully got
myself used to provoked admiration
as painful. Long after my tempter,
whose friendly and possibly innocent
overtures I had rejected
had fallen asleep on the cot
I insisted he take, I remained
on my guard, not so much against him
as myself. Yet I never felt smug
at the triumph of chastity, proud

of my victory over the flesh,
rather saddened and guilty as if
I'd succumbed, as I had in a sense.
The temptation to virtue, at times
irresistible, poses to passionate
natures the subtlest of snares
in the long run; the conquest of nature
becomes second nature, a habit
that hardens at last into rigid
self-righteousness. Wasn't that just
the result, the reward for resistance
I coveted? Grappling with phantoms
(I felt) of delight had defiled me
like pitch from the pit. Although glad
that such matches were rare, and relieved
that I had not yet fallen, I wondered,
so shaken, how long I could stand?

Such temptations, and others less drastic,
I took to confession in lieu
of more serious sins. After trying
S. Ronan's, whose Irish incumbent's
response to my self-accusations
of gluttony (mumbling a crust
of dry toast before lunch) was a chuckle,
"Ye mean ye got drunk on a Sathurday
night?" and a lenient penance
imposed in an odour of spirits,
I turned to the church round the corner,
Our Lady of Lourdes, where the curate
(confusingly styled *le vicaire*)
was French-speaking, I found after pouring
my guts out in English to silence
I thought sympathetic but which
was a chasm of incomprehension.
Temptations inflated as sinful
he cut down to size in a jolly
accent de joual; he enjoined
me not only, to go, sin no more,
but to go and think less about sin,
as he smiled at the crazy *scrupules
de ce maudit anglais* and my foolish
folie de s'accuser. Moreover,
enlightened concerning the natural

(many would say the unnatural)
thrust of my dreams and desires—
for the gloomy confessional cast
an unmerciful light on the shadowy
corners of even the candidest
soul—he dismissed the whole question
of sex, or of gender indeed,
in a phrase that was kind for those days
and exceedingly kind for a priest,
"*C'est normale.*" When I met him at last
incognito outside the confessional,
Father Le Bel, a supporter
and neighbour of Lazarus House,
whom I knew by his voice, must have recognized
mine, but said nothing to show
that he did. This professional tact
(for the seal of confession in fact
as a rule is preserved as intact
as in fiction), created a tacit
conspiracy, as of a pair
of clandestine conspirators, Masons
or lovers, on meeting in public.
A handsome, if pallid and rather
cadaverous man in his thirties
(which made him, beside Alan Waterman,
nearly my age), he was said
to possess a weak chest; that disease
of the twentieth century, rapid
consumption, ironically threatened
this celibate pauper, naive
and kindhearted, who came from a francophone
backwater of the Saint Lawrence.
In rural Québec the political
temperature in those days
was more moderate than it would be
in a decade, and Father Le Bel,
unperturbed by the social, linguistic
injustices borne by his people,
devoted himself with sublime
disregard for his personal welfare
to "healing the Church from within,"
and "reforming the sickness afflicting
the mystical body." Complacency
reigned in the 'fifties, and nowhere

more stuffily than in the Christian
community. Philippe Le Bel,
imitating *les prêtres ouvriers*
who were busy but outlawed in France,
as a maverick dreamt about joining
the underground church disapproved
by the hierarchy, if he were able
to find it. A decade or two
of upheaval in which an outsider
might think that the church had turned red,
not alone with the blood of the martyrs
("The Providence Nine," "The Los Angeles
Twelve," and the rest of that crew)
once again would subside into clerical
business as usual, nothing
much changed but the language in which
it was done. Revolution was then
in the air, although not in the streets
or the pulpit as yet, but Le Bel,
like a premature Jacobin, had
to make do for the moment with Lazarus
House and his work in the slums
among young proletarians. Given
his radical, sociological
notions of evil, no wonder
he scoffed at my hypochondriacal
conscience! Perhaps (though I didn't
permit myself such speculation)
a secret affinity made him
au fond sympathetic. If so,
he was never to make me an obvious
sign, save the sign of the cross.

Absolution came after repentance
(exotically labeled contrition)
as night after day; and today
was the same as tomorrow and yesterday
too, every day was the same
as the first and the last that I wasted
in service at Lazarus House,
an identical, slavish routine
undisturbed by a shadow of doubt
or a flashback or flicker of carnal
temptation, as part of what Waterman

liked to describe as the "lay"—
as opposed to the "lie,", i.e., priestly?—
apostolate. We were the leaven,
the yeast in the dough of the Church,
an elite, what was more, an elect
in whose charitable estimation
the mass of the faithful were commonly
called but infrequently chosen.
Obedience, always the laical
virtue, has dwindled since Biblical
times to a nervous observance
of trivial rules, such as weekly
attendance at Mass and the annual
Easter communion, abstaining
from meat once a week and mechanical
birth control all of the time,
and the average Catholic either
observes these injunctions or not,
whereupon one was said to have lapsed,
a condition—apostasy—like
an incurable cancer I prayed
to be spared. Alan Waterman taught
that the layman—or woman—should try
to do more, and adopt as their standards
of conduct the Gospel's untried
admonitions to neighbourly love,
paradoxically rising above
the indifferent herd one conceived
it one's humble vocation to serve.

At the end of a dusty and hot
afternoon of good works and (God help
me!) bad thoughts, before making our evening
repast, an extravagant tin
of baked beans, I would stand at the window,
uncurtained as if to declare
we had literally nothing to hide,
staring out at the horrible street
that had seemed to imprison me once
on arrival, and now as I guiltily
dreamt of departure appeared
in a glamorous light as the way
of deliverance. Fortunately
in those days there were no one-way streets

in the slums, an infliction reserved
for downtown and the shadier quarters
surrounding McGill, so the upwardly
mobile could play snakes and ladders,
a game whose religious equivalent
I was already acquainted
with. Even before I had finished
my short introductory course
of instruction in practical charity
I had determined upon
my escape at the earliest decent
excuse, like a guest at a party
who edges politely toward
the front door. I endured for six weeks
a devotion and drudgery hard
to believe, thanking heaven that none
of it suited my proper vocation
in life, for there wasn't a single
alternative discipline, silence,
hair shirt, bread and water, I wouldn't
prefer to a grubby existence
devoted to others, the stink
of this pitiful room with its heaps
of discarded, unsuitable costumes
suggesting some shabby charade,
and the crucifix nailed to the wall
like a horse-shoe, a naked yet sacred
obscenity avid suppressors
of innocent smut have exposed
generations of schoolchildren to,
to instruct them that nature and grace
are identical? During my moments
(and moments they were) of unscheduled
and guilt-ridden leisure—good works
are in principal endless if rarely
in practice—I found, in the words
of some philistine saint, that "The cross
was my book." Otherwise there was nothing
to read in the house. Alan Waterman
couldn't be called a great reader,
for minutes on end when unoccupied
staring ahead in a mystical
stupour induced by the regular
click of his rosary. Heretics

being notorious bookworms,
not even the analphabetical
attitudes struck by a Church
which has indexed and burnt so much classical
literature in its erudite
bibliophobia could
interdict my addiction to print.
Having browsed through my missal at mass,
when I should have been telling my beads,
I had only *The Catholic Worker*,
if Father Le Bel hadn't borrowed
it. Printed on newsprint recycled
so often it looked like the sheets
I had laundered that morning, disfigured
by woodcuts that crossed Eric Gill
with Rouault, this incendiary organ
of what you might call the Church Militant's
urban guerrillas, apparently
edited by a collective
of radical nuns, who have either
gone secular since or been martyred
in central America, offered
remarkably little worth reading
apart from occasional essays
by Dr. Immanuel Star,
("Disbelief as Neurosis," "The Oedipal
Basis of Faith,") and a throwaway
poem or two by the Anglican
poetess Winifred Odin.
The average Catholic worker
today—Lech Walesa for instance—
would scorn such a dissident rag
as *The Catholic Worker*. The Church
has become a conservative enclave
again, with a hard-hat enthroned
in the chair of St. Peter to bless
the reaction. Another and equally
retrograde pontiff was wont
to pontificate then, blessed Pius
the Twelfth, of inveterate memory.
Strangely, his portrait, though commonly
hung in papistical haunts
like the Campion Club, was not held
up to honour at Lazarus House.

If I wasn't ecstatically happy
therein, or indeed in the Catholic
Church, I had no one to blame
but myself. Alan Waterman, Dorothy
Day, even Pius XII
did their best, or at least, in a so
far unminted cliché, did their thing,
but the place and the pace simply didn't
agree with me. Poverty, then
and thereafter, for much of my life,
would remain its unvarying backdrop,
like solitude, leisure and guilt:
a Bohemian poverty, optional
solitude, studious leisure
and Calvinist guilt—as opposed
to the comfortless want, disagreeable
company, strenuous idleness,
guilty attempts (per instructions)
to "offer it up," of a typical
day in the active but would-be
contemplative life of a premature
drop-out. For such I'd become,
just as much as those hippies to come
with their headbands and sandals and beards,
marijuana and macrobiotics
and quaint unforgettable idiom.
I was a flower-child too,
in my way, an ingenuous pansy
disguised as a celibate weed,
having none of the cumbersome goods
of this world: "Status schmattas," I might
have exclaimed as I sorted the secondhand
clothes, had I known any Yiddish.
However, one *sine qua non*
of the 'sixties I lacked: spontaneity
did not come easy, abandon
was out of the question. Apart
from such sexual hang-ups as must
be assumed to depend on the cross,
and political innocence (pacifist
purely in principle, *pace*
The Catholic Worker, I wasn't
aware of a war anywhere

to protest against), also my quite
accidental abstention from drugs
which I must say I'm glad were unknown
in the circles—admittedly square—
which I moved in, I picture myself
as a humble precursor of what
would be labeled The Now Generation,
as if there were any alternatives!
Nevertheless I considered
the weeks that I frittered away
as a slavey at Lazarus house
as a time—like all times!—of transition.
One detail distinguished that Now
Generation from mine: where I buried
my beads in my pocket the hippies
exhibited theirs round their necks.

Book Three

Sweet Saviour Priory

*J'attache le cours de mes ans
pour vivre à jamais au dedans.*
AGRIPPA D'AUBIGNY

*Je m'étais cru dans un cloître, et je
me suis trouvé dans un carrefour.*
SAINTE-BEUVE, *Port Royal*

O MY pen, do you never grow weary,
or dippy, or dizzy, or drunk
in your headlong descent of the page,
with the metre at sixes and sevens,
the matter all anyhow, what
with quodlibets, digressions and jokes?
By the way, any word of the story?
An author may curse inspiration
for petering out like a stream
in the desert, or flourishing like
a luxuriant jungle which strangles
the path of the narrative; still,
inspiration is rather like ink
when you think of it: nobody notices
either until it dries up.
I could call on the Muse or the Spirit
in mock desperation; I might,
being modern, invoke the unconscious,
a prompter forever on tap
from above or below: the connection
too often will yield a wrong number
or static. In short to compose
any poem from epic to epigram
patience and cunning are needed
to winkle some latent significance
out of an anything but
inexhaustible source, *videlicet*
the world, which our callow protagonist
plans to abandon for good,
having barely attained to the age
of dissent, as if judging a book
by its cover.
                    One warm afternoon
I was scrubbing the hallway at Lazarus
House when the miracle I

had been praying for suddenly happened,
and onto the tacky linoleum
fell, with a plop, not *The Catholic
Worker* or some heaven-sent
contribution to Waterman's work
but a letter addressed to myself,
without question the first and the last
I received in my weeks with the Catholic
underground. C/o the Campion
Club, it had been, as I saw
from the postmark ("Eureka Vt.")
redirected, belatedly, (*Festina
lente*) to Lazarus House.
As the envelope bore an American
stamp on one side and, embossed
on the other, a cross in a circle
surmounting the legend, Sweet Saviour
Priory, drying my hands
on my denims, I anxiously opened
it. Anachronistically typewritten,
here is the text of the Prior's
epistle: "Dear Brother in Christ,
You are welcome to visit us here
at Sweet Saviour whenever you wish—
as a guest, to begin with, and not
as a novice or even a postulant
yet. On the Feast of" (illegible),
"Dagobert Fine, O.S.B."

Disappointed and heartened at once
by this somewhat off-hand invitation
subscribed in an elegant, spikey
and quite unAmerican hand,
I had hoped my vocation would either
be recognized instantly or
(what I secretly dreaded) rejected
in so many words. Though this looked
like polite *a priori* rejection
I hadn't yet learned to accept
indecision, nay, lifelong suspense
as a part of the bargain Pascal
underwrote. I considered the day
and the hour of departure, with nothing
to tie me to Lazarus House

save its master's charisma, with something
approaching—or masking—regret.

The objectives of practical charity,
laudable as I assumed
them to be, are apparently doomed
to defeat by the forces of selfishness,
sloth and indifference. Nature,
innate human nature is such
as to render an enterprise like
Alan Waterman's hopeless as trying
to bail out the Flood with a spoon,
the reformer's most obdurate enemy
being the body, or bodies,
he seeks to redeem, for example
the Church, which has broken the heart
and frustrated the efforts of many
a secular meliorist
with its hidebound alternatives, love
it or leave it! I'd brought very little
to Lazarus House and departed
with less. Of the three "theological"
virtues, my charity sagged,
for the moment exhausted, my faith
was, while stout, indefinably compromised,
only my hope, at that age
an essentially physiological
function, persisted erect.

Nonetheless I abandoned with shame
the impossible contest where goodness,
forever outnumbered, contests
single-handed against astrological
odds, and performs those heroical
deeds in the world that unworldliness
purely conceives and can execute
there, unrewarded, unsung
and unsanctioned to date by the body
they ornament, *viz.* that triumphant
and militant flop-house among
whose more permanent residents I
as a transient celibate one
who distinguished himself from the rest
by humility, kindness and truth.

I set out for Sweet Saviour (*sic*:
this American priory seemed
to affect the Canadian spelling,
perhaps at Dom Dagobert's putative
British insistence?), by 'bus
at 6:30 a.m. after 5 o'clock
Mass in the otherwise empty
cathedral next door to the bustling
'Bus Station on Dorchester Street.
Alan Waterman, smiling his careworn
benevolent smile saw me off
with a blessing and breakfast at Nedicks—
a festive occasion—real coffee,
and butter to smear on our toast.
I afforded my fare from the wages
of sin I had earned by translating
a papal encyclical, *Fulgens
corona*, for Father Le Bel
who pretended his Latin was rusty.
A grasshopper aping an ant,
I subsisted all summer on hand-outs:
my luggage, a brown paper parcel,
no larger than on my arrival
except for a paperback book
by St. John of the Cross (in translation:
my Spanish demanded a crib)
which I'd found in a bundle of secondhand
clothes, and intended to read
on my journey. However the Mystical
Doctor embarrassed and mystified
me with his rapturous language,
familiar, except for the genders,
in print. I reminded myself
(and a brief introduction instructed
me too) of the mystic convention
that pictures the soul as essentially
feminine; still, while this helps
to explain why stigmatics, apart
from St. Francis (the first), for the most
part were female hysterics, I wondered,
the godhead of course being masculine,
whether this weren't a means
of insuring the heterosexual

nature of heavenly love?
Even so, not a suitable book
for a 'bus ride, I thought: if the poem
induced an unhealthy degree
of excitement, the gloss was a frost;
for amusement I thus was reduced
to my beads and the transient view
of the flat Eastern Townships of southern
Quebec. I attempted, instead
of reflecting on what I had left
(temperamentally helpless to echo
the hedonist's *Je ne regrette
rien*), to imagine the slowly
approaching (about 55
m.p.h.) and mysterious goal
of my journey, an exercise fraught
with inevitable disenchantment,
unlike the analogous lay-outs
the readers of novels devise
from the hints that the author provides.
Actuality tends to efface
the erections of fantasy; nothing
appears oriented just like
your fantastical orientation
which vanishes once the banal
and particular matter-of-fact
manifests itself, blotted from memory
even, as if Gresham's Law
would apply to the imagination
like anywhere else, so that bad
realistic appearances drive
out the good suppositional image,
as truth is supposed to eject
all fallacious opinion. And yet,
evanescent and precious, these makeshift
projections compose an alternative
universe, filed and forgotten,
accessible only in dreams
and poetical revery later.
My vague yet amazingly plain
preconception would thus overlay
like a shadow transparently all
through my stay the monastic reality,
tempting me sometimes to seize

not the day, not today, an impossible
feat and pernicious advice
to the young, but the daydream tomorrow.

Throughout that unseizable day,
as my few fellow passengers stared
out the window with little conviction
or else straight ahead with impassioned
intensity, napping or smoking
or reading their papers or palms
without speaking, and got off and on
at irregular intervals, none
of them piqued my oblique curiosity
then, or recurs to me now,
any more than I noticed the border
we crossed about noon when I hardly
remarked the extreme informality
of those American Customs
I later would find too familiar;
of course I had nothing, apart
from that popular opiate, faith,
to declare. All the same I observed,
as Canadians do and Americans
don't, a not quite indefinable
contrast between the oldfashioned
and shabby Canadian side
and the prosperous modern American
scene, as the ramshackle village
cafés at the roadside gave way
to exorbitant roadhouses garish
with neon, redundant by day,
to inveigle the transports of summer,
and neat, neoclassical towns
with evocative names—Arethusa,
New Ilium, Carthage and Aelia
Capitolina, nostalgic
with tree-shaded lawns and verandas.
Not long after dark I got off
on the outskirts of what was announced
on a sign at the side of the road
as Eureka, Vermont, Population
350, a place
(I presumed, for I didn't set foot
in it then) of the standard, idyllic

description, which woke in me passing
nostalgia for secular order,
stability, comfort and peace.
On a journey like mine you are fated
no matter how early the start
to arrive in the midst of the night
in the middle of nowhere with no one
to meet you, not even a stranger
to ask for directions, amazed
in a wood that you cannot make out
for the trees that encompass your path.
I was hungry: I'd fasted all day
unintentionally, when I found
the Canadian dollar as welcome
here south of the border as peso,
quetzal or rial, though the streets
of Toronto are papered with greenbacks.
I'd stumbled a number of times
from the 'bus to assuage my insatiable
thirst at a public (hence free)
drinking-fountain and use the less free
although equally public facilities,
sinks of iniquity, were
one to judge by the vivid inscriptions
from which I averted my eyes,
the hard-line Manichaean in me
overriding the old unregenerate
literate Adam.
        Jejune
and benighted, I'd started to panic,
supposing the letter confirming
my time of arrival had not
been delivered, when out of the shadows
emerged a young man in a costume
as shapeless and black as the night
that enveloped us both. With a gesture
between a perfunctory bow
and a glorified nod, without speaking
he ushered me into a little
estate-wagon parked out of sight
at the crossroads, *Sweet Saviour Priory*
faintly emblazoned in crabbed
Carolingian script on its side.
Amid unmediaeval, mechanical

uproar we lurched into darkness
impenetrable as a cassock
except for the moving, selective
unmerciful glare of our headlights
and rare and remote incandescent
celestial beacons, the headlamps
of heaven, where stars represent
a comparative absence of darkness,
like apertures opening onto
a backdrop of light, and in turn
at each turning obscured by the headlong
sublunar effects of our progress.
Apart from this rustical darkness,
unknown in the city, I sensed
from the silence and earthy aroma
that breezed through the passenger window
we were in the fathomless heart
of the country, which comforts and soothes
as the city excites and alarms.
In the literature of the city
from biblical times to the present,
the epithet favoured is "dreadful,"
so Dante's *dolente città*
is an urban inferno, his Paradise
(Persian for "garden") a rural
resort with a ravishing view
and a rose at its centre, the green belt
around, purgatorial suburbs
providing a heavenly anteroom.
Furthermore mankind encountered
its first Waterloo on the playful
and flowery fields of our primary
private academy, Eden.
These drowsy reflections, provoked
by surroundings (unlike the insomniac
city) conducive to sleep,
were reflectively highlighted by
the illustrative beam of our passage
that fixed in its fugitive course
now a branch, now a fern, now the trunk
of a tree for a moment, caressing
and sketching each Düreresque detail,
then letting it go, but suggesting
as if by the act of selection

the presence of myriad similar
details beside and behind,
an invisible, somnolent nightscape
of meadows and ploughlands and woods.
I had spent enough time on a farm
in my childhood to find agricultural
matters, as limned in the *Georgics*,
a bore, indistinguishable
from the boredom of childhood itself,
with its ruthless demands for amusement,
disgusted by rural routine
and the lack of companionship. Now,
having lived in the city for most
of my life, of necessity, I
was imbued with a pastoral fondness
(as sung in the *Eclogues*) for everything
countrified, even ennui.

My chauffeur hadn't spoken so far,
but I thought, looking sideways, he smiled
to himself, as he hummed *sotto voce*
a tune that I knew though the words
were inaudible: "*Oculi capiant
somnum...?*"—a sleepy Ambrosian
hymn that according to Gibbon
had echoed around the basilica
church in Milan while the Arian
roughnecks in trousers laid siege
to the skirts of the Catholic faith.
Half an hour had expired at an accurate
estimate—wearing no watch
in those days, I could usually reckon
the time to the minute—since leaving
Eureka, and still not a word!
If my guide were unwilling to chat,
or unable, (it struck me as highly
unlikely he didn't speak English)
should I, as a guest, having spoken
to no one all day, undertake
to intrude on a silence that played,
as I seemed to recall, a significant
rôle in the rule of his order?
An ultimate twist in the roadway
exposed to my view a miraculous

valley concealed in a cleft
of the mountains or hills we'd been climbing
unconsciously, further secluded
by acres of hemlock and pine,
while the moon, which had risen, illumined
the orchards and pastures and structures
that furnish a farm, with the large
unmistakable shape of a barn
in the midst. The whole scene seemed asleep,
save a building I took for the farmhouse
whose windows exuded a brightness
eclipsing the moon's. I conceived
the conceit that the glowing interior
blazed like a fiery furnace
as if it were framed out of flame,
and I marvelled at all that exuberant
splendour created by prayer
and inhabited by supernatural
beings of light, a community
certain philosophers placed
in the sun. Cabalistically dazzled,
descending the slope of the valley
we came to the light house whose denizens
never apparently slept,
though the landscape about them, ensorcelled,
was sleeping, *le bois* (in the story)
dormant, as Bernardus Silvestris
pretends is the state of all nature,
but kept a perpetual vigil
enflamed with incendiary love.

Overwrought by my journey *à jeun*,
when I turned in confusion to question
my driver, he'd vanished, along
with his van, without saying a word.
At the top of the steps to the house,
in the doorway that suddenly opened
a luminous rectangle, stood
as if beckoning motionlessly,
not an angel of light but a solid,
imposingly corpulent figure
in flowing, enveloping black,
middle-aged rather than mediaeval,
clean-shaven, bespectacled, bald.

"Father Dagobert?" "*Pax!*"
he admonished, or greeted, me, under
his breath, with a sketchy embrace
and a sketchier kiss on both cheeks,
introducing me into a vestibule
empty and bleak but ablaze
with mysterious light emanating,
I saw, from a commonplace fixture,
a luminous globe overhead
in the midst of the ceiling, or *caelum*,
a sphere like the sun or the moon,
artificial, indeed manufactured,
man-made but not hand-made, cheap mass-
produced stuff, which the contrast, no doubt,
to the darkness outdoors and the shadowy
wattage at Lazarus House
must have made me mistake for a mystic
effulgence. And yet at Sweet Saviour
Priory darkness and light
always struck me as darker and lighter
than elsewhere, in part the effect
of the habits against all that whitewash
so dear to monastic décor.
As I opened my mouth, not to hazard
a bright observation, but simply
agape, Father Dagobert checked
the presumptive presumptuous words
on my lips with a gesture towards
an injunction in uncial letters
that hung on the wall like a sampler.
REMEMBER, it said in vernacular
speech, THE GREAT SILENCE. The finger
Dom Dagobert raised to his lips
indicated a tacit command
to obey and be still, as he opened
a door to his right and inducted
me into a room that had patently
served as the diningroom of
the original farmhouse and still
must fulfill the same function, to judge
by the benches and makeshift refectory
tables abutting the walls.

In the centre a circle of men—
perhaps twenty, no more—in voluminous
black, and as bald as the Prior,
though not necessarily naturally
so, were immersed (as it seemed)
in profound meditation, their hands
in their sleeves and their foreheads inclined
to the dust, whose comparative absence,
in fact, as a seasoned domestic,
I blinked at. Atonally someone
intoned, not a hymn or a psalm
or a prayer, but a warning, unlike
most liturgical Latin in being
at once comprehensible. "*Fratres,
sobrii estote*," it started,
and hearing it nightly impressed
it verbatim, or virtually so,
on my memory, "*Et vigilate
quia adversarius vester
diabolus ut leo rugiens
circuit quaerens quem devoret,
cui resistite fortes
in fide.*" Which, being translated,
is, "Brethren, stay sober, watch out
for the devil, your enemy, prowling
around like a ravening lion,
is looking for someone to eat;
but stand up to him, steadfast in faith."
This advice the community sealed
with "Amen," which requires no translation
in Latin or English, though often
in French, and the sign of the cross.
With a rustle, like ravens that rise
in a flock from a wood at the onset
of evening, they turned to the door
and proceeded in mute single file
to process from the room. As they passed
within feet of the spot where I goggled,
how could I resist a clandestine
inspection of all these discrete
and discreet individuals, each
set apart from the others as much
as myself, yet possessed of a private,
collective expression that veiled

their hermetical gaze, which would never
return my inquisitive stare.
I could see that these cenobites came
in all sizes and shapes and descriptions
of mankind, their differences plain
at a cursory glance, from a stripling
with hardly a hint of a beard,
to a wrinkled but vigorous gnome,
and Dom Dagobert's portly aplomb.
Their demeanour was almost as uniform
not to say blank, as their clothes,
but I studied the latter more closely
as offering more of a change
from the world, for their faces, however
unworldly, reminded me somehow
of those I had seen on the 'bus.

Now the habit I longed to adopt
I had never so much as set eyes
on before, in the flesh, so to speak:
it was black, as becoming the black
Benedictines, their primitive order,
and even in summer, of serge.
The conventual cassock was girt
with a thick leather belt, the sartorial
symbol of chastity: over
the shoulder, the scapular, token
of servitude, hung like a yoke
to the hemline before and behind,
with a hood, the *cucculus*, attached,
though what *that* was a simile for
I could never discover: dependent
in back but designed at canonical
seasons to cover the head.
Of their habits this much I perceived
as they filed from the room; what they wore
underneath I refused, or I tried
to refuse to conjecture: hair shirts
were discouraged, I knew, by the mild
Benedictines, however avowedly
primitive. Under their robes,
I remarked, the bare feet of that hardier
time and a Mediterranean
clime, like the sandals of Cluny,

had been superseded by sensible
shoes, polished Oxfords and clodhoppers,
even a couple of sneakers.

I hastened to follow the monks
through the door and the vestibule, empty
apart from the overhead light
and the sign that enjoined the Great Silence.
Outside in the premature darkness
(for once I'd lost track of the time)
I divined their direction, toward
a black hole in the starlight (the moon
having set or been snuffed by a cloud),
the abrupt silhouette of a building
I guessed was the barn, now converted,
like me, to liturgical use.
A rectangular glimmer defined
and made light of the door, which I opened
a crack to enable me, slim
as I was in those days, like a shadow,
to sidle inside. The interior
had, as I feared, been redone
architecturally as a church
which betrayed its not very remote
agricultural origins; thus
in the place of the manger an altar
now stood, and an alley or aisle
now bisected the newfangled nave
longitudinally, with the cattle stalls
facing it turned into choir stalls,
with minimal need for adjustment.
Expecting to find the community
there, I was taken aback
by their evident absence, the place
seeming empty at first, till my eyesight
adjusted. Two flickering candles
that furnished the otherwise bare
but freestanding high altar revealed
in the shadowy stalls indeterminate
figures enveloped in darkness,
their hands folded under their scapulars,
cowled, like cadavers erect
in their caskets, which grisly conceit
was dispelled when they started to chant

in monotonous plainsong these words:
"*Nisi Dominus aedificaverit*
domum, in vanum laborant
qui aedificaverunt eam"
they sighed, for like psychoanalysis
psalms do begin with a psi,
"*nisi Deus custodierit*
civitatem, frustra vigilat
qui custodiet eam." This Calvinist
text I in haste misconstrued:
"If the Lord is your architect, surely
your labour is vain who are building
the house; and if God is protecting
the city your vigilance also
is wasted." "*In vanum est surgere*
vobis," I heard with dismay
"*ante lucem, cum dederit,*" here
was a morsel of comfort, "*dilectis*
somnum." I attributed most
of their metrical irregularities
to their American diction.
"In vain you arise before daybreak;
he gives his beloved repose."

I was falling asleep on my feet
when they changed to a sprightlier strain
which I recognized shortly as one
that my driver had hummed at the wheel
sotto voce. "*Te lucis creator*"
he droned with them now (I assumed)
"*ante terminum rerum,*" "Thou maker
of light, ere the end of creation...."
I'd often been taught to ignore
Latin word-order. "*Procul recedant*
insomnia:" "Banish insomnia?"
Perish the thought! "*et phantasmata*
noctis:" "phantasms of night,"
"*polluantur ne corpora,*" "So
that our flesh may not suffer pollution:"
a clinical, cryptic, fourth-century
phrase, a petition or charm
before bedtime that meant more or less
what I fervently took it to mean.
They concluded by saying the *Salve*

Regina, until *Completorium*—
Compline—the final and only
unvaried canonical hour
was completed in silence, to wit
the Great Silence extending in principle,
sacred, inviolable,
as I learned, until Prime the next morning,
or breakfast, whichever came first.

The majority quickly dispersed
in the darkness, like phantoms, or simply
like men who are ready for bed.
As I followed them out of the barn
I remarked that a few had remained
in their stalls: for the night? or forever?
I mused in a dream of the sort
that insomniac age is inclined
to begrudge to somnambulist youth.
Father Dagobert loomed by the door
and repeated the shibboleth, "Shh!"
Even sign-language being prohibited,
less by the Rule than the rule
of the darkness, I followed his bulk
to the house we had left in a blaze
now extinguished except for a little
electric *veilleuse* on the second-floor
landing, to show me my way.
Like a child who is packed off to bed
with a mute benediction instead
of goodnight, I reluctantly mounted
the stairs. At the top among several
doors, I decided that mine
was the open one. When I had closed
it behind me, the blackness enveloped
me, black as a cowl and apparently
empty. Our senses are tempted,
confronted with nothing, to think
nothing there. But upon the impervious
nothingness presently opened
a glimmering square of perspicuous
gloom, which at first I mistook
for a mirror (and asked myself what
a monastic would want with a mirror?)
but found, on intrepidly crossing

the room, an invisible obstacle-
course with no obstacles, only
a wide-open window. The body
of night was embalmed with the sensuous
scents that the country exhales
after dark in the summer, the smells
of fresh hay and of cattle, the odours
of apples and grass and manure,
so delicious to senses deprived
by the city of wholesomely rank
stimulation. Inebriate, briefly,
of air, as I drew a deep breath
the environment made itself known
to my nose, and at last, bit by bit,
to my eyes, for the frigid and tenuous
starlight illumined as if
incidentally almost enough
for my sleepy immediate needs
of a cell as ascetic but less
unaesthetic than that I had lately
vacated at Lazarus House.

I discovered that I had forgotten
the brown paper-bag that contained
all my worldly possession, besides
The Dark Night of the Soul—on the 'bus?
in the Priory pick-up? However,
my reflex anxiety changed
into joy, even as I undressed,
at the thought of arriving at Sweet
Saviour Priory practically naked.
Of all the excesses of youth
this peculiar passion of mine
for denuding myself psychologically
seems inexplicable now
when maturity wants all the garb
it can get. The material comforts—
to judge by the sheets on my bed—
of monastic existence exceeded
those standards to which I had tried
to adapt. I remember repeating
a verse of the psalm like a lullaby,
"Dederit somnum dilectis,"
"He giveth his favourite rest."

I awoke toward dawn, I supposed,
for the casement, though paler, fell short
of auroral effulgence, on hearing
a bell intermittently tolled,
a lugubrious summons I knew,
without sending to ask, was not tolling
for me, and accordingly went
back to sleep as the physical triumphed
for once over all metaphysical
yearnings to hear the Night Office,
since Matins, and Lauds were restricted
in the fact to the Fully Professed.
Once again when I opened my eyes
(my night office discharged) I could tell
by the angle or angel of sunlight
that fell on the scrubbed wooden floor,
it was late by monastical standards,
say eight or eight-thirty. A radiant
stillness surrounded me, marred
but not broken by distant, subliminal
sound-effects suiting the precious,
precarious cool that prefigures
a hot summer day in the country.

Ashamed to be slugging abed
at that still indeterminate hour,
I got up, but again was detained
by the window which showed me my whereabouts.
Under the brow of the valley,
as background, an orchard extended,
but though I could hardly distinguish
one tree from another, I couldn't
help noticing what a variety
of miscellaneous fruit
could be glimpsed through the branches: ripe apples,
and nectarines, curious peaches,
and pears, though no melons or grapes.
In the foreground the chapel or barn
I had seen the inside of last night
in the matter-of-fact understatement
of morning presented, apart
from the rough wooden cross on its roof,
a disarmingly secular aspect.

I shivered deliciously, feeling
how soon I should sweat; as I stooped
to recover the clothes I had strewn
at the bedside, I spotted a garment
I took for a dressing-gown hung
from a hook on the back of the door:
how considerate! Black and voluminous,
heavy and homespun, I realized,
hefting it, this was no monkish
kimono but rather the coveted
habit itself in a singular
one-piece design that was called,
as I later discovered, the cope.
Though I couldn't begin to, of course,
I was tempted to try the thing on.
And why not? There was nothing to stop
me, except for my conscience, which branded
as sacrilege donning the sacrosanct
raiment before being fully
entitled to do so. But once
I'd adjusted the scapular guiltily
over my shoulders, surprised
at how lightly the yoke seemed to lie
there, compared to the weight of the cloth
when I lifted the robe from the door,
I submitted to wool next the skin
as a penance. My fingers got lost
in the ample, superfluous sleeves,
and the generous folds of material
swathed and impeded my feet
while the world disappeared temporarily
under the hood that enveloped
my head, as if made for a giant,
reminding me wryly of childhood
and how I tried on the familiar
forbidden parental disguises,
enjoying the franchise of grown-ups
to dress and undress as one pleased.
But on looking around for a looking-
glass such as I used to admire
myself in, I imagined that mirrors
except of the soul were taboo
in a cenobite's cell, as if monks
were like vampires in casting no shadow

or mirrored reflection? Encased
in a woolen cocoon like a chrysalis,
raising my arms in the shape
of the cross, which I'd read was adopted
at solemn profession, I mimed
for one make-believe moment the symbol
of reincarnation, the moth
not the bat, which is drawn to the flame
of the candle as I to the life
of the spirit, whose audible stirrings
downstairs, indistinct but inviting,
induced me to doff the ill-fitting
uncomfortable habit and hastily
don my own travel-stained clothes.

I became as I bended to tie
up my laces aware of a feeling
of emptiness somewhere inside
me, yet nothing so grand as catharsis.
The hunger I felt after fasting
for twenty-four hours many millions
endured every day of their lives.
But for history's darlings like me,
deprivation, when not accidental,
is optional; nakedness, hunger
and thirst, the necessitites of
the majority, furnish the fanciest
luxury goods of the few.
My discomfort would surely abate
in a while, if I only knew where
to abate it. Inspecting the room
I had slept in, I noted its simple
but decent décor, which had none
of the raffish, theatrical squalour
of Lazarus House. On the wall
a presumably valuable ikon
depicted a Byzantine Christ
with one finger uplifted in blessing
in front of his lips in a mute
admonition to silence which might
have been less out of place in a library.

Hunger curtailed my inspection.
I opened the door to the hall

and a tempting aroma like coffee,
a smell that excels, like temptation,
its flavour, which tends to be bitter.
I followed my fallible nose
to the foot of the stairs and the door
of the room where I'd seen the community
gathered in chapter, ajar
on a wonderfully different scene
owing much of its cosy, familial
look to the sunlight that carpeted
tables and benches and floor
as it curtained the windows that framed
a matutinal farmyard. Remains
of a frugal but copious breakfast
still littered the tables, a jumble
of breadcrumbs (enough for a pudding)
and numerous mugs with the dregs
of some beverage, coffee or milk.

I appeared to have missed by some minutes—
or hours?—the community breakfast,
a word that assumed in this setting
its etymological sense,
like *déjeuner* in French. I was thinking
of breaking my fast with the leftovers
strewn on the table when checked
by a cough. "*Benedicite?*" There
in the doorway a youth of my age
with an apron on top of his cassock
in place of a scapular, smiled
interrogatively, an ingenuous-
looking American, freckled
and friendly. "Perhaps," I imposed
on his baffled good will, "you could tell
me the way to the bathroom?" I groped
for the apposite term, euphemistic
yet crude, the American idiom;
"lavatory," let alone "loo,"
even "w.c." would no doubt
be affected because out of place.
"Father Abbot believes the flush-toilet,
he calls it a Renaissance toy
and a pagan convenience," as
if reciting by rote he expounded

this lore with a straight if vermilion
face, "undermines fundamental
monastic morale." "Father Abbot?"
I queried, the title (redundant,
as "abbot" means "father") surprised
me. "Dom Willibrord," stated my nameless
informer, as if that concluded
the matter, "I thought that Dom Dagobert
was your superior here?"
"He'll explain all about it, don't worry,"
he begged me, unwilling if able
off-hand to describe the interior
organization of Sweet
Saviour Priory. "Anyway, there
is the outhouse," he pointed, "in back
of the chapel. Perhaps you will catch
them at Terce." This canonical hour,
indicated, I knew from my studies,
the third in the classical day,
about nine or nine-thirty a.m.
Had I slept in so late after rising
at dawn every morning at Lazarus
House? "Do you meant that I've missed...?"
"Our conventual Mass is at eight,
the community always communes
at the priests' individual Masses
at six, before breakfast or Prime."
The first time since I'd entered the Church
that I'd risen too late for my heavenly
breakfast food, *panis angelicus*,
filled me with panic akin
to an addict's or drunkard's withdrawal
on skipping a drink or a fix,
an ironical state of affairs
here, like starving to death in a bakery.

"*Deus*," I heard as I skirted
the barn, *adjutorium meum
intende et me adjuvandum
festina*, the opening words
of the office, and Psalm LXIX,
"To my succour incline yourself, Lord,
and make haste to my instant relief."
I was not so naive as to think

that monastic manure doesn't stink,
but the times I had spent on a farm
as a child had inured me to such
unhygienically earthy arrangements
as those that I faced in the Priory
privy, deserted at present
except for a legion of flies
and the murderous spiders ensconced
in their flimsy but fatally intricate
webs, and the odours that lingered
(this morning abounded in odours)
maliciously, like some unsavoury
character, pointing the moral
of fleshly corruption.
                            Emerged
from this private retreat so conducive
to such meditations as make
Manichaeans of even the heartiest
Catholic, *Deus est caritas*
greeted my ears as I entered
the church, where I stood at the back
near the door to await the conclusion
of Terce. "*Et qui manet,*" they chanted
the final capitulum, "*in*
caritate in Deo remanet
et Deus in eo." The nature
of God being charity, he
who abides in the same is abiding
in God, just as God within him,
I translated, perhaps tautologically.
What I imagined this meant
at the time I am now at a loss
to explain. It depended in part
on the meaning of charity: *agapé,*
Eros baptized and chastised
and emasculate? or human kindness,
good works and forbearance, the virtues
required for community living,
which also incarnate the secular
socialist ethic? Whatever
it was, I determined to keep
it in mind as I crossed myself fervently
backwards or forwards, unable
off-hand to distinguish my left

from my right, in the physical sense
and too often politically too.

As they stepped from their stall with a bow
to the altar and filed from the chapel,
more spritely (I thought) when uncowled,
I observed that their number had shrunk
since last night; but among these I spotted
Dom Dagobert, whom I approached
in the sunlight outside. "*Benedicite!*"
("Bless me!") he caught me off guard
with his Anglican accent in Latin
as well as his lofty yet affable
manner: I found in the former
a comfort of sorts in this foreign
as yet unexplored situation.
"You slept pretty well, I am glad
to infer, as we didn't, I think,
have the pleasure of seeing you either
at breakfast or Mass?" I assured
him that missing communion afflicted
me more than the pangs in the pit
of my stomach. "All tasks are assigned—
after Prime—you remember our motto,
Labora et Ora?" "Of course,
but I thought that the order was different?"
"Different? We would prefer
to describe it," he sniffed, "as unique!
I assume that on this, the first day
of your working and praying vacation
you'd like to be free to explore
on your own. Follow me," he at once
contradicted himself as he waddled
away to the farmhouse I'd slept
in and straight through the hall
to the kitchen in back, a commodious
cave with an old-fashioned wood-burning
stove, a gigantic monstrosity
doing its bit to increase
the already unbearable heat
of the day.
                At the cast-iron sink,
as he flayed a defenceless potato
the youth who had shown me the way

to the outhouse stopped whistling *toute suite*
when Dom Dagobert entered, the melody
"Home on the Range," though appropriate,
sounding a trifle profane.
I remarked that his hair, although short,
was not shorn like the others' on top
in a clerical tonsure. "Ahem!"
(I had never heard anyone actually
utter this quaint interjection,
so much like "Amen," heretofore),
"Frater Thomas, our guest has not broken
his fast. Can you offer him—" here
he consulted his large ostentatiously
functional wristwatch, "Elevenses?"
Visibly stifling a shrug,
my baptismal, obedient namesake
removed an aluminum pot
from the back of the stove and impassively
poured me a mugful of brackish
and black simulacrum of coffee,
a mixture, I later discovered,
of acorns and chicory. Handed
a basket of crusts from the table,
I breakfasted shamefully standing.

While eating in company can
be convivial, eating alone
a peculiar pleasure, to eat
in the presence of others who aren't
partaking is simply embarrassing.
Primitive peoples whose sexual
openness shocked anthropologists
primly regard the ingestion
of food as taboo, a display
as distasteful as public excretion.
A snack such as mine constituted
a solo performance as staged
for the camera: why are there no
pornographic descriptions of eating?
Another man's meat, if not poisonous,
does not provide secondhand
satisfaction. Perversity largely
consists in the real or assumed
nonchaloir of the audience faced

with the symptoms of ravenous hunger.
Discreetly I mumbled my crumb
in a matter of minutes or less.
"Frater Thomas à Kempis," Dom Dagobert
switched from the vocative case
to the nominative, "is a postulant."

Envy, one sin I had seldom
if ever been tempted by, ruined
my appetite, turning the bread
in my mouth into ashes. Just why
had this hobbledehoy with his haircut
befitting a conscript engaged
in K.P. been accepted for such
basic training, and I with my hair
not much longer, rejected, or rather
deferred? *sine die?* Of course
his ill-bred *bona fides* was written
all over the simpleton's face,
like a map of the Vatican. Striving
to feel for my rival, whose galling
success was congenital, something
like charity, smiling I gave
him my cup which he rinsed at the tap
and replaced on the shelf as Dom Dagobert
opened a low, inconspicuous
door in one wall of the kitchen
and ushered me into his cell.

This was snug and austerely luxurious,
furnished in fussy good taste,
with a carpet (the first that I'd seen
in some weeks) on the floor.
Father Dagobert squeezed himself into
an armchair in front of the desk
by the window and told me to sit
where I liked. There was nowhere to sit
but the bed with its cumbersome eiderdown.
Seated, our knees almost touching,
I thought of the intimacy
of two strangers who ride vis-à-vis
on a train, for Dom Dagobert's study
resembled a first-class compartment.

He studied the flies on the ceiling
in silence for several minutes
as if the exiguous chamber
were bugged, as it was, and I couldn't
help thinking he looked like a spider,
in which irresistible simile
I was the fly he'd invited
to enter his parlour, the Priory—
yet I'd invited myself!
"My dear boy," he began with a practiced
urbanity. Neither incensed
nor especially charmed by his puerile
endearment, I blamed our respective
and disparate ages and status,
suspecting the title of Father
had gone to his head, and recalling
the words of Saint Paul, that we all
are the children of God by adoption,
those children the gospels describe
as so praiseworthy. Nietzsche mislabelled
the Christian religion as servile,
whereas it is childish, the Church
an immense kindergarten or nursery
many intelligent people
outgrow.
          "So you wish to essay
the contemplative life, having toyed
with the active?" I bristled, submissively
silent. "The skeleton key
that unlocks such apparently different
vocations is poverty, re—"
he protracted the word as if bleakly
prolonging the act, "-nunciation!"
and added inconsequently,
"And how *is* the dear lady?" "Dame Poverty?"
"None of your childish Franciscan
personifications! I meant
that resplendent if rather too radical
modern example of practical
charity, Dorothy Day.
You belong to her movement, The Catholic
Worker, I think that you said
in your letter?" Dom Dagobert's questions,
though hardly rhetorical, brooked

no reply. "I expect you could write
a whole book about poverty, worldly
and otherwise? Not that you will!"

I ignored the implicit proscription
and tried to explain the in part
geographical distance dividing
the Bowery and Lazarus House.
"Montreal?" he appeared to consult
the address book that served as his memory,
"Then you must know Verecundia
Valentine? Everyone does!"
In his discourse a series of audible
question marks mingled with mute
exclamation points, so it was not
always easy to say which was which.
At the Campion Club as at Lazarus
House I had heard—who had not?—
of this darling of *Commonweal*, pillar
of pious *belles-lettres*, recusant
apologist, bigot, papistical
spokeswoman, whimsical scourge
of heretical notions, who'd authored
or pasted together a paperback
popular guide to the grossly
maligned middle ages, an era
on which, with revisionist tact,
she affected to throw a misleading
but kindlier chiaroscuro:
according to her the crusades
were a picnic, the so-called Black Death
not as black as it's usually painted.
Dom Dagobert, seeing me shaking
my head, was inspired by his stern
theological virtue to drop
an alternative name, "Or Immanuel
Star?" But again, lacking foresight,
I had to acknowledge my ignorance,
"Only by hearsay." "Dear Very!
So philoprogenitive! How
many Valentines over the years
we received at St. Chrysostom's School
when I served as headmaster!" His history
hinted the source of his haughty,

if not hoity-toity, pedantic
yet worldly demeanour. "But not
many Stars—though no doubt a respectable
recusant name!" There are several
species of snob in this world,
and no doubt in the next, but the Prior
appeared to belong to the harmless,
straightforward, exclusively social
variety. "Wistan and Hrothgar
and Grendel and Offa!" The names
(I presumed) of the Valentine offspring
were English enough; for the Catholic,
Calvin and Luther were equally
ultramontane. Like a banished
aristocrat pining for vanished
prerogatives, riches and honours
extinct as the pseudo-dentata,
Dom Dagobert cherished the privileged
past, represented by numerous
silver-framed ikons displayed
on his desk and the walls of his cell,
the illegibly autographed photos
of fashionable, famous or rich
co-religionists, most of whose scions
had passed through his hands at St. Chrysostom's,
none of which noble alumni
I'd heard of, including one clan
with as yet unfulfilled presidential
pretensions. However I recognized,
even before being told,
Verecundia Valentine's faded
flamboyant coiffure. In the 'fifties
most photographs stuck to the circumscribed
hues of monastic couture
and were candidly dim. The predominance
elsewhere, if not in the cloister,
of grey, I was slow to discern,
inasmuch as *grisaille* is a shade
which the young would appear temperamentally
blind to. These monochrome habits
imbue my monastic experience
after the fact with the tones
of an old, black-and-white silent movie
with subtitles dubbed in by memory.

Just at the moment Dom Dagobert
seemed to be bent on producing
a talkie. Ignoring his ponderous
chatter, I failed to ignore
the resemblance between Verecundia
Valentine, suitably framed,
and that same *bien-pensante* odalisque
who had clutched *The Ascent of Mt Carmel*—
or was it *The Grammar* she clasped
of Assent?—on her sagging but generous
lap, in my shocked, insusceptible
presence? If so, I refrained
from informing Dom Dagobert how,
if I had, I had made and declined
her acquaintance. He routed me out
of my revery. "What, may I ask,
do you seek at Sweet Saviour?" Before
he could cite (though I doubted he would)
the old Augustinian bromide,
that one cannot seek what one has
not discovered, impertinently
I considered propounding a similar
poser to him: had the world
or the flesh or the devil incarnate
in boarding-school life as depicted
in Henry de Montherlant's drama
La Ville dont le Prince est Enfant
been his reason for seeking his present
retirement? Instead in a mumble
I fumbled and dropped like a bombshell
the ultimate Name, to Dom Dagobert's
open delight. "Isn't He
in the world?" he inquired. "In and out,"
I replied, "here and there, now and then,
but invariably in disguise."

"Where we look for him least, in the closet
where children are told that the bogeyman
lives? And surprisingly often
in power and wealth and success,
as church-history proves!" But this proof
of the deity's whereabouts failed
to convince me as much as the usual

proofs of His fabled existence.
The myth that the search is the sought
I dismissed as a sophistry, mere
serendipity making the best
of a fruitless and tedious quest,
as I'd never much cottoned to shopping
(that favourite American pastime)
as such, though with time I became
more acquisitive, making the common
mistake of desiring the end
without willing the means. Hide and seek,
I perceived, was the name of the game
in contemplative circles, if not
blind-man's buff. "A monastic vocation,"
Dom Dagobert sighed, "is a process
of losing, you'll find, and not finding
at all." I inclined to agree,
for the more that I saw of the brethren,
the more they appeared like a bunch
of unbeautiful losers. "Our vows
circumscribe the extent of our loss.
So obedience mandates the loss
of free will, in the smallest as well
as the greatest particulars. Reverend
Father—our Abbot, Dom Willibrord—
will, as the pastor that all
must obey at Sweet Saviour, instruct
you therein, health permitting." A mysterious
hint by the postulant Thomas
compelled me to ask, "But I thought
that as Prior, since this is a priory,
you were the Father Superior
here?" "In most practical matters,"
he granted, "I am. You might call
me the manager, but I'm no more
than a glorified guestmaster!" Was
it a come-down, I wondered, from headmaster?
"Why, if this isn't an abbey,"--
I'd done my research!—"do you talk
of an abbot?" "A courtesy title,
awaiting our long overdue
elevation," he rolled up his eyes,
"to abbatial status, befitting
our Abbot Elect. And Dom Willibrord

clings to the title he bore
for so long as the Abt of Einsamkeit."
During, or after the War—
or before? I repressed further personal
questions until I should meet
face to face with this future and preterite
prince of the Church, but agreed
with Dom Dagobert's dictum that "Germans
are frightfully keen on obedience!"

"Coming to chastity," shrewdly
he cast me a glance whose professional
edge had been honed on untold
generations of guilt-stricken schoolboys,
"I don't have to tell you what sacrifice
that must entail! Père Clément
as our Master of Novices speaks
with authority here." I detected
an accent again of regret,
or perhaps resignation, beneath
his impeccably fruity delivery.
"Everyone knows that the French
(for he comes from the ancient and famed
Abbaye de Thélème) are notorious
experts respecting the sins
of the flesh!" Such outright Francophobia
puzzled me, coming from one
who had chosen an old Merovingian
name in religion, although
he was seldom if ever so Frank.

"Leaving poverty plainly to us!"
he concluded elliptically, "Here
we own nothing, you know, of our own,
while enjoying the usufruct, holding
the simplest possessions in common.
This habit, this pen, for example,
are 'ours' and not 'mine.'" He produced
from the folds of his robe a magnificent
fountainpen, lacquer and gold,
of the sort that the Pope, as the *servus
servorum* himself apostolically
pushed in the autographed picture
I saw on his desk. All these small

creature-comforts and luxuries filling
his cell, the mementoes and books,
were they equally "ours?" I exclaimed
at this communist practice, when even
naive, apolitical newspaper-
shunning Canadians such
as myself were aware of the red-baiting
fever that racked the inert
body politic just to our south,
an infection to which we were scarcely
immune, only one in a series
of regular spasms convulsing
that rich but hysterical nation,
to wit, Prohibition, the War
against Organized Crime, and crusades
against drugs and pornography. "Mark's
is our scriptural warrant, not Marx,"
an improbable pinko, the Prior
assured me, "as well as the Rule."

Having fathomed the pitfalls of scripture
enough to appreciate how
inconsistent divine revelation
can be, I accepted with thanks
the well-thumbed little leatherbound volume
he took from the depths of his desk.
I had read of the Rule of St. Benedict
(always referred to as "holy"
by those who observed it) and had
to repress an unworthy temptation
to claim I had read it already,
the kind of untruth that too easily
slipped past my puritan conscience
almost undetected. Dom Dagobert
urged me to "read it religiously,
just as you used, I imagine,
to study your Bible. I know,"
he confided, "for I am a convert
myself from the Episcopalian/
Anglican Schism!" In spite
of this clue, I could never be sure
if the Prior were English (if so
he would never say British!) and not
an affected American anglophile.

Still, I discerned in his manner
of speaking another unspeakable
source of nostalgia. "I see
you're admiring my library! Didn't
you say in your letter that you
were a poet as well as a student
at, was it? McGill?" He implied
he had heard of the place, and the effort
to place me intrigued him as much
as my putative talent. "Perhaps
we can find some congenial task
to employ your creative abilities!
How many languages other
than English—so few of our novices
properly speak even that!—
do you know?" "Only Latin and French,"
I demurred to exaggerate, "plus
an iota of Greek." Incredulity
lifted an eyebrow. "Indeed?
We've been looking for someone to translate
a monograph for us from French
interlarded with Latin quotations,
let's see..." He had barely to turn
in his chair to consult a compendious
bookcase that bulged at his elbow.
"Emmanuel, Evelyn, Graham,
François," the collection appeared
to be shelved in some loose alphabetical
order according to authors'
first names: "Verecundia, Winifred,
David, oh dear! out of place,
well the first shall be last, I suppose!"
(the anathemata in parentheses)
"Here it is! Under Anon.!"

I accepted the gift with misgivings,
a paperbound work—or *corvée*—
of a staggering number of pages,
L'Expérience Bénédictine
by *Un Moine de Thélème*. "We shall lend
you our typewriter, also our Dictionary,
though I am sure you don't need
one!" Dom Dagobert beamed, for the first

time that morning, at me, and extracted
a *Petit Larousse* from the shelf,
though what use this would be for translating
from French into English I hadn't
the faintest cedilla. "Tomorrow,
you may," he cajoled, representing
the chore as a choice opportunity,
"take your first step in obedience.
You will be doing this house
and the order a service, as well
as the Church, while acquainting yourself
with the rule in its many historical
manifestations, perfecting
your French and improving your typing."
In other words, since I was ordered
to translate, my labours would pay
for my keep and afford me a free
education in cenobite life
simultaneously—and why not?

I misread his intention, however,
if not his *ipsissima verba*,
and said, mistranslating his drift,
"Do you mean...?" The illusion of meaning,
so dear to the heart of the literal-
minded, a ghostly, elusive,
intangible something transmitted
or (frequently) lost in translation,
had blinded me to the effect
of his words, which is all a translation
can modestly hope to convey.
"Do you mean the obedience due
from a novice or postulant?" "Heaven
forbid!" His disgruntled expression
implied that it normally did.
"That is something for Reverend Father
of course to decide, but I fear
that in light of your recent conversion....
You cannot expect, when you enter
the house of the Lord, to go straight
to the drawing-room, skipping the vestibule!"

Was I expected to sit
in the monastery waiting-room scanning

back issues of *Life*, I demanded,
indefinitely? "If you have
a vocation, you will persevere.
But take time to consider the worth
of the world that you want to give up
and the riches you wish to renounce,
the innocuous burden of wealth
generations of God-fearing Christians
have borne without murmur." It struck
me incredulously that the Prior
supposed I was rich. I could not
disabuse him at once, since his error
afforded him such satisfaction
and gave my abortive but generous
gesture a weight that it lacked
in reality. "How I have always
admired the impetuous ardor
of youth! Though it was my professional
duty to dampen it, often!
Its essence is freedom from doubt,
an unthinking affirmative attitude
that is so very American!
'Yes' in a nutshell, its answer
to life, whereas 'Maybe' sums up
middle age's evasive response!
And the watchword of age? An implacable
'No!'" I discounted the fortune
he credited to my account,
being callow, as mere faery gold,
disagreeing concerning the certainty
youth, aporetic by nature,
enjoyed in his roseate view.

With surprise I perceived that Dom Dagobert
looked upon no one as poorer
than he. "We were frightfully worldly,
I fear, at St. Chrysostom's: cocktails
on feast days, and lobster in Lent,
not to mention the telly!" I hadn't
yet seen, let alone fallen under
the spell of this new diabolical
instrument, nor did I wish
to. "Ah, well! Our observance was lax,
I'm afraid, but I miss the indulgences

sometimes! Maturity has
such a lot to give up in comparison,
youth is endowed with a blessed
obliviousness to discomfort!"
Moreover its greatest endowment,
the fabulous wealth he attributed
wrongly to me must consist
in sublime disregard for material
want as opposed to imperative
physical wants.
           An innocuous
knock at the door interrupted
these rum ruminations. Dom Dagobert
cooed, "*Benedicite!*," clearly
the all-purpose password and greeting
at Sweet Saviour Priory. Muffled,
an echo replied through the portal
which, opening, framed Frater Thomas
as cupbearer. "Time for your Bovril,
your Reverence!" Like a male nurse
or a steward—but how did I know,
having never embarked on a ship
or a plane, or been hospitalized?—
he deposited, square in the midst
of my letter on top of the desk,
the salubrious beverage, visibly
steaming. "Already?" the Prior
affected surprise at the length
of our interview, glancing askance
at his Rolex (or "ours"), which he covered
along with his bouillon and books
and the furniture, photos and comforts
that cushioned his cell, with a needless
apology, "Little concessions
to age and infirmity! Go!"
he dismissed me off-hand with the sign
of the cross as he reached for his Bovril,
"in peace! Frater Thomas will show
you around before Sext." As I rose
and performed my obeisance, some remnant
of youthful intolerance, one
of those juvenile assets I meant
to renounce in religion but didn't
succeed in suppressing the thought

of as well as the verbal expression,
supplied the definitive text
on the subject of poverty, culled
from a muddled misreading of scripture,
the Protestant's Bible: *To him*
who has something much more shall be given,
from him that has not, even that
which he has shall be taken away.

In the kitchen my rival (I really
must check this competitive view
of the sanctified life as some kind
of exam), my eventual brother
in Christ, Frater Thomas à Kempis,
the postulant detailed to show
me the ropes (a midshipman instructing
a landlubber), smirked like a schoolboy,
obliquely in reference to
his superior's idiosyncrasies.
"What can I show you?" his friendly
obedience changed him again
to a floorwalker eager to interest
me in the latest in heavenly
fashions. "You've seen our provisional
chapel." I caught the quotation-marks
scoring the adjective not
(I presumed) in his everyday, working
vocabulary. "Father Abbot
has plans for a fancy new fabric,"
I wondered anew if the word
were his own, in this context? "Designed
by some world-famous Catholic architect
friend of Sweet Saviour, he says,
but its realization awaits
the success of our building fund." So
well-informed for a parrot, he couldn't,
I hazarded, show me these plans?
"They are safe, as we all are, in Reverend
Father's omniscient keeping,"
he solemnly stated. "We've started
to work on the cloister already."
That must be the source of the distant
and tentative taps punctuating
my chat with Dom Dagobert, like

some tremendous stone typewriter's slow
hunt-and-peck. Frater Thomas regarded
me enviously, I was startled
to note, if askance. Did he covet
my secular flannels and turtle-
necked sweater as I his invidious
cassock? "Who knows? When we're given
our duties tomorrow you may
be assigned to construction?" Dismaying
to me, this idea appeared
to amuse him, in view of my own
rather weedy construction. "The vegetable
garden, more likely. Stoop labour,
but somebody's got to produce
all the heaps of potatotes and onions
and carrots and turnips and parsnips
that I have to peel, not to mention
the lettuce and cabbages, radishes,
beans and tomatoes and peas
I prepare for the pot everyday,
for in Reverend Father's opinion
a postulant's place is the kitchen."

Remembering Lazarus House,
I admired the impeccable order
displayed in his homely domain,
the Gargantuan cauldron that fragrantly
bubbled on top of the stove,
the aroma of baking that rose
from the oven, and guiltily dared
to repudiate all of it, like
Cinderella on fitting her foot
in the slipper of glass. "As a matter
of fact, I have got my assignment,"
I showed him the books that I clumsily
clutched to my chest. The incredulous
awe and contempt of his question,
"How come you know French?" indicated
the proud monolingual American,
prompting my equally chauvinist,
"Everyone does in Quebec!"
"You're Canadian?" Strange to recall
that the terms were coterminous then!
"But not Canadien," the distinction

escaped him but didn't divert
him, apparently. Most of his countrymen's
notions of Canada (when
they had any) derived from the movies:
a snow-covered wilderness peopled
by Mounties and wolves and untrustworthy
French-speaking half-breeds and picturesque
reindeer and Eskimos. "Not
many English Canadians really
know French, though we're taught it in school,
in a manner of speaking," I modestly
boasted, implying that I
was the speaking exception; but neither
my prowess nor Canada's earnest
but quite unsuccessful bilingual
experimentation excited
the postulant much. "Montreal's
in Quebec?" I observed that it was
when I left, and suppressed an unkind
observation: geography played
as much part in his high-school curriculum,
seemingly, as foreign languages.
What did they study, I wondered—
American history, civics,
and driving? A bell intermitted
our colloquy. "Sext!" Frater Thomas
exclaimed in alarm, "and I ought
to be setting the table. So much
for your guided—" or misguided?—"tour!"

My proposed cicerone, God knows,
was no Virgil—but then my poetic
ambitions, obscured by my fancied
monastic vocation, envisaged
my being no Dante, however
exemplary he might be thought
as a Catholic poet, moreover
Sweet Saviour Priory was
no inferno; albeit the heat
of the kitchen suggested a hurried
retreat to my room, or my cell,
as I liked to pretend, to deposit
the texts that Dom Dagobert lent
me, and with them the task he'd imposed.

As I hurried downstairs and outdoors
to the barn, I imagined the scapular
over my shoulders, the swish
of a cassock around my impoverished,
chaste, and obedient limbs.

In the chapel, more barnlike than ever
at midday, a handful of fieldhands
in habits of denim was droning
in unison, "*Vices qui temperas
rerum, et splendore mane
instruis meridiem ignibus.*"
Garbled, this might be translated,
"Thou temperest nature's vicissitudes,
strewing the morning with brightness
and noon with incendiary splendour."
For Sext, the sixth hour of the day
in the ancient monastic horarium
marked a meridian: everything
afterwards tended downhill.
Like so many significant hours
this was sparsely attended, and sparely
observed by a minyan of manual
labourers fresh (or perhaps
not especially fresh) from the fields
and the building-site. *Habitus facit
monachum*: their overalls robbed
them of much, if not all, of their monkish
mystique. Was it merely my hunger
that made the canonical hours
reassuring to me, as to others?
The infant that has not been properly
fed will grow up to become
the neurotic adult who insists
on a regular schedule—or so
it is said! But whatever the cause,
as a creature of habit forbidden
the habit (and others I blushed
to remember) I clung to a rigidly
structured existence, the stricter
the better. Besides, I rejoiced
in the knowledge that Sext was the signal
for lunch, in the country styled dinner,

or *cena*, from which some have fabled
that cenobites borrowed their name.

"With all watchfulness keep in thy heart
because life issues from it. The heart
is a very wild creature and often
it lightly leaps forth. As St. Gregory
saith, 'There is nothing more light
or more like to escape than the heart.'"
At a lectern between the two tables
a youth in a coarse cotton smock
was attempting to read from a volume
entitled *The Ancrene Riwle*
above, not a babble of tongues
but a bubble of silence, apart
from the gnashing of teeth that accompanies
any communal repast,
not to mention the rest of the wholly
unmentionable, irrepressible
din of digestion now raised
to the power of twenty yet quieter
still than the similar racket
at Lazarus House. "Once King David,
God's prophet, lamented his heart
had escaped him, and later rejoiced
it was with him once more. If a person
so holy and wise should endure
such an escapade, others may well
be afraid that their hearts would escape
in a similar manner. And where
was it David confessed he had lost
it? God knows, through that window, his eye,
through a something he saw, through a sight
he beheld, as you presently shall..."

I supposed that the reader was chosen
by lot, for he did not enunciate
nicely, but mumbled, and stumbled
at each unfamiliar locution,
of which there were plenty; and yet
his incompetence scarcely appeared
to perturb his intent but uncritical
audience, whose unremitting
attention embarrassed and dumbfounded

him. "It is monstrous, a crime
against kind, being dead, thus to dote
on the living, and act with them wickedly:
mortificatus in carne
sed vivificatus in spiritu..."

Plainly the effort of reading
aloud which contorted his regular
features discovered no sense
in the text; it was only the letters
that caused him dismay. Underneath
the laborious surface, calm depths
could be guessed, of unquestioning faith
and respect for the word; here was one
to whom scripture was incomprehensibly
sacred—a brutish idolatry.
"Lucifer looked at himself
and beheld his own beauty, and leapt
into pride. Thus he fell, and from being
a beautiful angel became
a most hideous devil. And Eve,
when she gazed on the apple and saw
it was fair though forbidden, began
to delight in the sight of the fruit
and desire it, and presently plucked
it and gave it to Adam...." And so
on and so forth throughout the Old Testament,
culling examples of ancient
voyeurs, he progressed in the steps
of our erudite author to citing
the fathers-in-law of the church's
patristic statistics. "St. Augustine—"
(hitherto speechless Dom Dagobert
humphed, "St. Augustine!") "—declares
that the eye is the messenger of
a concupiscent heart. What the mouth
cannot utter for shame, the light eye
will convey in a moment. The eyes
are the weapons of Cupid, and glances,
the arrows of lust." This Petrarchan
conceit one and all disregarded,
the reader's concupiscence fixed
on his page, while the rest of us listeners
lusted inscrutably, eyes

on our plates, like St. Lucy the patronal
saint of myopia. "Blind
is the heart, and most easily vanquished
by sin, as St. Bernard observes.
For as death did first enter the world
through the portals of sin, through these windows
the eyes, thereby death is accustomed
to enter the soul"
                          "*Miserere!*"
the reader broke off with emphatic
relief at Dom Dagobert's groan,
"*mei Deus secundum—.*" The monks
who had sat with their hands in their scapulars
rose to their feet as they crossed
themselves. "—*misericordiam tuam...
et dele,*" they begged as they quit
the refectory, "*iniquitatem...
in iniquitatibus ecce
conceptus sum, et in peccatis
concepit me mater....*" The meal
which was sandwiched between two canonical
hours, thus concluded in penitence:
"Mercy, my God, in Thy mercy,"
the psalmist is nothing if not
pleonastic, "and take my iniquity
from me. Behold in iniquities
was I conceived, and my mother
conceived me in sins." As if washing
their hands after eating, "*Asperges,
me, Deus, hyssopo,*" they prayed,
"*et mundabor, lavabis me et
super nivem,*" they swore, "*dealbabor*":
which means, "Thou shalt purge me with hyssop,"
—whatever a hyssop is!—"I
shall be cleansed, Thou shalt wash me and I
shall be whiter than snow." But this optative
sentiment melted away
on the way from the house to the chapel
for Nones, in the somnolent afternoon
atmosphere, *tenax vigor*
in the words of the hymnodist, *rerum
immotus in te permanens,*
"pertinacious the strength of creation
abiding in Thee without change."

I emerged after Nones—if it seemed
that I popped in and out of the chapel
all day, it was surely no more
that the Rule of St. Benedict mandated?—
blinking, to find my quotidian
schedule suspended. The doldrums
with which afternoons are too prone
to begin, in the cloister admitted,
I knew, no siesta, effeminate
secret of Mediterranean
civilization, taboo
as it is in the workaday world,
though Dom Dagobert's age and infirmity
might be indulged in a lie-down,
referred to as "prayer horizontal."
The rest, I assumed, had returned
to the sole Benedictine alternative,
work. I had nothing to do
till tomorrow, and furthermore, nowhere
to do it. Tomorrow comprises
a movable feast, and I loitered
in front of the church, till a voice
at my elbow inquired, "You are free?"

Looking down I discovered the gnome
I had noted the previous night
as the oldest inhabitant. Older
by daylight, his vigour eclipsed
the effete middle age of the Prior,
for I was not one of the young
who confound every age over thirty.
As wrinkled and gnarled as a root,
he appeared to have sprung from that primal
material wood of which everything's
made, the enchanted primordial
forest, the setting and source
of all fairytales, dreams, superstitions,
and much *art nouveau*, where it's wise
to be wary of going awry
and digressing as I do, misled
by an anagram. Laying his claw
on my sleeve, he repeated his statement
or question—pronounced in his chipper

batrachian accent, it might
have been either. "I hope so," I lied.
At nineteen, who is ready for freedom?
At thirty, or fifty, or ever?
No sooner escaped from parental
preventive detention than drafted
(though Canada had no conscription),
we worm our way into some prison
or other—society offers
a choice: education, career,
unemployment and marriage, or other
more subtle illusions of freedom.
At least I had chosen, so far
as one can, an unfashionable form
of imprisonment nowadays, here
in the cloister, which earlier centuries
took as a grand penitentiary.
Nobody likes to be free
when they are, never mind what they want.
All too often our precious free will
is no more than the right of refusal;
since God gave the Virgin the veto
the option of wrong is our own,
and though helpless to make a decision
for good, uncreative and passive
in all that concerns our salvation,
one negative virtue prevails:
it is never too late to say no.

"Do you wish for a small promenade?"
Although lexically fluent enough
and grammatically almost correct,
he produced the effect of a deft
simultaneous oral translation,
a trick that dissemblers employ
when they think in one language and speak
in another designed to deceive.
I responded in French, not so much
for the sake of politeness, much less
showing off, but attempting to talk
the same language, forgetting that then
I'd be thinking in, therefore translating
from English. "*Mais oui, un petit
promenade serait trés agréable.*"

He grinned, "You speak French?" His polite
interrogative, nearly incredulous
tone I explained by the French
disbelief, reinforced by the foreigner's
weakness for syllable stress
and confusion of genders, that no
one speaks French but a Frenchman—or -woman.
The opposite holds in American
English, whose standards or borders
are permeable to a fault;
so I presently noticed the novices
treated the Abbé Clément
(whom they called Father Clement) as one
of themselves.
      We directed, or rather
the priest who would be my director
of conscience at Sweet Saviour Priory,
turning his back on the chapel,
directed our steps to an overgrown
thicket not far from the cloistral
foundations, which oddly resembled
an archaeological site,
with its wide excavations, and nothing
much standing above ankle height.
Half a dozen monastics in work-habits
puttered about lackadaisically,
faintly astonished at what
they'd discovered, although, as with most
pre-Columbian ruins, they'd built
these themselves, and remembered that Rome,
like Tikul, wasn't built in a day.
"Very well, it begins," Abbé Clément
with a nod and a wink of ironic
approval sat down on a log,
an immense fallen idol like those
which an axe-wielding crank of his Order,
St. Boniface, butchered in droves
in the groves of the heathen. It lay
where it fell to remind any twentieth
century druids, in part,
of the folly of tree-worship. "Seat
yourself," Abbé Clément with a quaintly
hospitable gesture invited
me, much as Dom Dagobert proffered

the foot of his bed. "When I read
as a child of the great North American
forests in Chateaubriand
I have never imagined they were
so untidy. The forests of France
are like splendid reception rooms such
as one sees at Versailles, very lofty
and grand, but with nowhere to sit."
Nor had I ever been to Versailles,
I confessed in the same conversational
tone, which would suit a salon
of the sort he described. "Neither I
any more. I'm already a monk
from my seventeenth year, and our Order
is cloistered, so all that I know
of the world is from hearsay and memory."

Did he learn English by hearsay,
I wanted to ask, though he spoke
it by rote; but determined to make
a linguistic impression, I pointed
to where the monastic foundations
extended explicit at some
little distance, and quoted in French
a remark from Sainte-Beuve's *Port Royal*,
where the author, supposing himself
in a cloister, discovers he stands
at a cross-roads. "St Beuve? But who is
it that she is? At last! there are so
many saints in the calendar!" Puckish
good humour so masked his disdain
for my accent and subject, I couldn't
be sure when the Abbé Clément
wasn't teasing. "Oh, yes, I remember
myself, the free-thinker—no saint
after all. But I hope—" I would not,
if I could, reproduce his inaspirate
accents phonetically, scorning
to sprinkle the page with apostrophes
like some Victorian novelist's
dialect scenes, "—you are not
of the Jansenist side, like so many
Americans?" Tired of explaining
a trifling distinction which none

but my countrymen seemed to appreciate,
I was inclined to let slide
this inaccuracy. "Well, I've read
Les Pensées de Pascal," I admitted,
as if I'd been sneaking a peek
at de Sade. "There is not any evil,"
he stunned me by murmuring this
metaphysical secret, until
I retranslated, "No, they were good
and sincere, but so gloomy!" He seemed
to rejoice, like a child, in those English
expressions that had no exact
French equivalent: "gloomy," "untidy,"
but French also lacks any loan-words
for "cosy" and "home." "Like all heretics.
You for example, you have
altogether the Protestant air."
His indifferent ignorance touching
my national status (the French,
having lost Lower Canada might
be excused for forgetting its further
existence) fell short of excluding
my shady sectarian past,
which inspired him, like everything, seemingly,
under the sun, with a fit
of the giggles. His merriment then
and in retrospect set him apart
from the others I met in the Priory—
nay, in the Church. Notwithstanding
the fake Chestertonian jollity
favoured by Wordy and Twee,
Verecundia Valentine's publishers,
most of the faithful exhibited
visible symptoms of strain:
Alan Waterman, Father Le Bel,
Father Hapgood, Dom Dagobert, even
the postulant Thomas à Kempis
could none of them really be envied
as carefree; the world they inhabited
seemed, no hilarious Belloc's
but grim Graham Greene's. Among Catholics
only this French Benedictine
appeared unaffectedly happy,
not merely serene but amused,

as if dying to share an ineffable
joke. "I am calling myself
Father Clement," he told me redundantly.
"Since I am Master of Novices
here, it is good that I say
you a word on the subject of chastity."
Dreading a fatherly pep-talk
like those I was glad to be spared
by my reticent parent at puberty,
did not the practice, I reasoned,
suffice, without prosing about
it? Of all the religious imperatives,
this was by far the most private,
assuming of course we were talking
about the same practice. "The most
part of novices find it more hard
to begin," he allowed. I should find,
to my puzzled relief, that the sexual
temperature dropped in exclusively
masculine, that is officially
sexless society. Social
constraint was the key, for temptation
insisted on solitude, something
as rare in the cloister as company.
Strange to relate, how this casual
carnal refusal became
almost effortless, simple as giving
up cigarettes, which I had done
incidentally when I extinguished
the smouldering butt of desire.
My return to the world at the end
of the summer, symbolically marked
by my first cigarette in some months,
would result in my leaving the Church
and resuming the natural vices
befitting my age. In both cases,
the taste, though familiar, seemed acrid
and flat, disappointingly tasteless
and almost disgusting: if that
was the best that forbidden sensations
could offer, they hardly seemed worth
denying. I'm getting ahead
of my story, but not very far;
nonetheless, at the time an inviolate

ironed lace curtain divided
the ignorant present from what
would have seemed an unthinkable future.
My ghostly adviser agreed,
as if reading my mind without straining
his eyes on the footnotes' fine print,
"It is nothing, this boring affair
of the flesh, a distracting illusion,
a shadow compared to the sun
of the heavenly love where desire
is consumed like a match in a furnace."
I piously hoped so; and yet
as I shrank from the shriveling heat
of the sun that invaded the grove
we were partially shaded by, sweating
like blazes, I envied the Frenchman's
composed Anglo-Saxon *sang-froid*
in remaining as dry, notwithstanding
his thick, woolen habit, as parchment.

"In place of a selfish denial,
the chastity truly entrains
an abandon of self in a union
superior. Do you not know
that ambiguous painting of Titian,
'The Sacred and—' what you may call
'The Profane'?" I had seen few original
paintings, apart from the brash
post-impressionist brush-work that passed
for Canadian Art, and my visual
memory, falling far short
of my verbal, was drawing a blank
when the subject entitled itself.
"In," I blushed at the rather too relevant
term, "reproduction." A miniscule
monochrome plate in some reference
work I'd consulted had stuck
in eidetic remembrance. "And which
of those ladies, you think, is the sacred,
and which the profane?" He was hugging
himself like the dwarf in the story
who posed an insoluble riddle,
in that case his name. "Well, the clothed
one, I guess, would be sacred?" Experience

taught me that nudity went
with profanity, only one reason
for shunning the locker room scene
after gym. Rumpelstiltskin was not
more triumphant than Abbé Clément,
"You have wrong! For the sacred is naked
like truth, which not only has nothing
to hide but possesses such beauty
no person that sees may resist."
"Like the Doukhobors!" I interjected,
forgetting to ask how a monk
of Thélème was acquainted with Titian's
profane allegorical picture,
in awe of the general culture
of Europe, which had, I was sad
to discover, its limits. "And what
is it they are?" he wondered. "A sect,"
I informed him, "of Russian religious
enthusiasts—'wrestlers in spirit'—
who settled in some of the Western
Canadian provinces. During
my childhood in British Columbia
Doukhobors used to parade
down the main street of town in the nude
on occasion—though what the occasion
and why, I could never find out."
"Antinomian, semi-Pelagian,
antelapsarian heretics!"
Abbé Clément theologically
chortled, "But see! it is love
of the spirit is putting them naked,
however they take it too much
at the foot of the letter." I said
I had heard they were sponsored by Tolstoy.
"Tolstoy!" he exclaimed, "that explains
itself! One of the very small number
of modern romancers that Reverend
Father approves." "Abbot Willibrord?"
"That which he seeks is the primitive
tone of the true Benedictine."
Surprised to be told that the novel,
forbidden (I'd gathered from one)
to the proper Victorian Miss
before lunch, was allowed in the cloister,

I said so. "Tolstoy he permits
as a preacher, an almost sixth century
spirit. In principle, though
Father Abbot insists that no matter
what fell from the time of some Council
of Constantinople is decadent,
compromise often is needed
not least in the reading. Imagine
yourself what a meager selection
of texts the Dark Ages provides."
"But the Fathers—St. Augustine, Origen,
Gregory, Basil, Tertullian,
Clement—" I faltered, recalling
that two of his namesakes, the Vth
and the VIIIth, neither sainted, had steered
into schism the barque of Saint Peter.
But he, whose patrology vastly
surpassed my derivative smattering,
smiled. "During Lent in refectory
somebody read from the *Dialogues*
said of St. Gregory surnamed
the Big, where we heard of a nun
who in ignorance swallowed the devil
concealed in a lettuce, and after
became diabolically pregnant.
See there! the Dark Ages are crazy
for fictions as much as our own."
What a bad dietary example
for novices leery of greens!
But I had to admit that, however
seductive the notion of earlier
centuries literature
is our time machine for exploration
of, one great advantage of ours
is the size of our libraries public
and private. "But yes!" telepathic
Dom Clément agreed, "the collection
of Charles d'Orléans in the fifteenth,
the core of our National Library,
numbered no more than a hundred
of volumes, the most part religious.
The Rule of St. Benedict tells
us to labour and pray, not to read."
"Isn't study both labour and prayer?"

I submitted. "I see it is also
a pleasure for you." "Is a labour
of love less laborious then?
Isn't that what is meant by vocation?"

His silence perturbed me much less
than his answer. "Vocation is more
than your clean inclination. If study
sufficed there would be no occasion
of grace." I retreated appalled
from the edge of this precipice, "What
of Dom Dagobert's library?" prompted
impertinence, seeing the shelves
full of colourful wrappers and even
occasional paperbacks, "not
mediaeval, so far as you'd notice?"
"Dom Dagobert follows the rule—
of St. Valentine," Abbé Clément
understated straight-faced, "as I follow
the rule of Thélème even here."
What this was I refrained from inquiring
half-heartedly, certain I'd read
of it somewhere, though "Do as You Will"
as a motto seemed far from monastic.
Retreating headlong from the subject
of rules—or The Rule—to the safer
yet relevant topic of libraries,
"Wouldn't a reader in, say
the sixth century, have all the classical
authors," I wondered, "and more
of them surely, than we, at his fingertips?"
"If he could read them!" he tartly
retorted, "You can?" I enlarged
on my modest proficiency. "What
is the use, without grace?" he seraphically
asked; it was plain he regarded
the grandeur of Rome and the glory
of Greece as in fact the Dark Ages
and pictured the years Before Christ
as a countdown, the tale running backwards
to zero, which afterthought called
The Year One.
                    We were sitting, I said,
side by side in a filagree patchwork

of shade on the edge of an overgrown
heterogeneous grove.
As one raised in the city, or near
it, I could not identify much
vegetation except for coniferous
or, in the winter, deciduous
trees. The insidious seminal
scent of a neighboring shrub
therefore doubly disturbed me because
I was helpless to name it or say
what the odour reminded me of,
which though grossly familiar resisted
identification. I turned
to the language of Proust for a clue
in the hopes that his countryman (peasant,
I thought from his rustic
demeanour, as well as compatriot)
might be inspired to enlighten
my native botanical ignorance.
"*Qu'est-ce que c'est...?*" I began.
"*La nature,*" he replied, and for once
in his own native language, "*elle-même.*
She is not at all chaste, as you feel."
I reminded myself that, in French
physiology, feeling and smelling
were one. "Are you saying that chastity
is—" surreptitiously, also
I fear, superstitiously crossing
my fingers instead of myself,
I put forward, "—unnatural?" Wasn't,
for me, the alternative equally
so? I debated, contrasting
the shame of my maiden confession
to Father Le Bel's understanding
indulgence, if now was the time
to be frank? When I was I should find
Father Clement not shocked but incredulous,
locked in the pre-scientific
conceit that there were no unnatural
beings but only unnatural
acts, of which chastity couldn't
be called an example. "But no!
The correct subjugation of nature
depends on her collaboration."

His metaphor doubtless derived
from the late (and subjectively long)
occupation of France in the Second
World War, which I scarcely remembered
although it was only a decade
ago, but which Abbé Clément
must remember as if it were yesterday:
how the routine of Thélème
as of Monte Cassino itself
was disrupted by certain upheavals,
like harbouring refugees, Jews,
or the children of Jews, whom the monks
in addition to granting them timely
asylum, brought up in the Christian
religion as camouflage. "What
did you do in the war?" was the question
I couldn't quite put to this father;
however, I trusted the ghostly
Gestapo would rout my own carnal
Resistance. As though overlooking
my mutinous, muted misgivings,
he varied his simile, "So
in a typical garden of France
not a grain is permitted to grow
like it wishes for fear it will spoil
the allover effect." "Overall,"
I corrected unthinkingly. "Isn't
it something to wear—overalls?"
indicating the denim-clad monks
who were laying the cinder-block cloister
nearby, he persisted, "That smells
of the tyranny. Chastity ought
to resemble a *jardin anglais*
as we call it, a formal arrangement
that seems to be rather informal
where each panorama and alley
is planned to achieve the impression
of chance." "Or of nature?" I wondered
if nature and chance were the same?
"They are not," he was adamant, "Nature
has reasons, but not always ours,
as Le Nôtre conceived. Whereas Chance
like some mathematicians, Pascal
by example, explain, has not any."

"And what if there weren't any chance?"
"Then there needn't be reason," he reasoned,
more French for the moment than Catholic,
granted the two are distinct.
"But you other Americans all
are the same!" (I protested in vain.)
"You have only the wilderness, natural
anarchy every-which-way,
or the pavement, the sidewalk, the parking,
the asphalt where nothing will grow."
"You're forgetting the suburbs, the green belt,"
I argued, remembering Westmount.
"American gardens are nothing
but yawns," I misheard him to say,
"endless yawns without flowers or weeds,
like a carpet or *parterre* of green."
Disapproval infused his bemused
horticultural scorn, as he spoke
like a stumped Capability Brown.
"And 'the desert,'" I quoted, "'of love?'"
It had struck me as strange that the landscapes
of Greece and of Israel, equally
lunar, respectively nurtured
the cult of the body and worship
of bodiless spirit. "You read
of this thing?" Dom Clément was unsmiling,
"I pray that you never encounter
it. Deserts are not for the novice
or visitor." Typed as a tourist,
I felt a touristic malaise,
an uneasy estrangement arising
as much from the alien accents
and dress of the natives, as from
the peculiar ways of contemplative
life. "You permit me to say,
you are not a long time a believer?"
Apparently Protestants couldn't
lay claim to belief! But of course
he was right. I'd been hardly a practicing
Protestant save in the radical
negative sense, and my atrophied
make-believe muscles were sore
from unwonted exertion, bestraddling
my new metaphysical bicycle,

standing on credulous tiptoe.
"Not long," I conceded. "What made
you to enter the Church? As a Catholic
born, of a Catholic country,
I ask myself what irresistible
magnet attracts the unfaithful?"
I temporized solemnly, "God
only knows! The mysterious promptings
of grace? or of guilt? Curiosity?"
Abbé Clément, who had shown
himself somewhat inquisitive also
rebuked me for this: "Curiosity
took the first bite of the fruit
of the knowledge of evil and good.
Curiosity opened that box
where Pandora discovered the ills
of mankind. Curiosity questions
and cheapens each gift. Intellectual
pride—intellectual greed—
intellectual lust: curiosity
spoils its environment, tortures
and kills many millions of animals,
victims of science, at last
curiosity sullies the stars
in the sky!" And to think that this same
reprehensible impulse that led
into error so many had brought
me to truth! I supposed that my Catholic
guru detected no irony,
none was intended. Accordingly,
incuriosity, ignorance,
indolence, wholesale neglect
of the faculties must be accounted
the positive manifestations
of chastity. "This is much more,"
he affirmed, "than mere abstinence, for
it contains all the other religious
avowals, of poverty as
of obedience."
            None of these noble
injunctions, the vows I was dying
to take, like an eager fiancé
who hates an old-fashioned protracted
engagement, oppressed me as much

as the scent of the nameless excrescence
that filled the undisciplined grove
and inert afternoon with a genital
fragrance I'd rather forget.
"Will you hear my confession?" Uncertain,
now, how to conclude our meandering
colloquy, which like a stream
in the badlands had petered digressively
out in the sands of irrelevant
backchat, forgetting conclusions
pertained to the other's prerogative,
furthermore fearing that such
invitations to intimacy
constituted a kind of indecent
proposal, I blurted this out.
"If you wish." He evinced no surprise
at my sudden request or its somewhat
incongruous natural setting,
which seemed to be all that a pantheist
might have desired, but withdrew
an exiguous violet stole
from the depth of his habit and kissed
it, arranging it over his shoulders.
I slipped to my knees in the leafmeal
and wanwood surrounding the log
and prepared to examine my conscience,
while Abbé Clément, all attention,
examined the marvellous clouds
as they passed overhead. I recited
the quaint hyperbolical formulae,
begging his blessing because
I had sinned; it had been, I declared,
three whole days since my latest confession.
I fancied he stifled a smile,
as Dom Dagobert murdered a yawn,
in its cradle. The Prior might prove
almost too sympathetic, compared
to the heterosexual Frenchman
who viewed my Platonic desires
as peripheral, transient, nebulous,
shifty as clouds in the blue;
but to me they appeared as substantial
and central, if not as the sun
and the varying moon, as the fixed,

though remote, and significant stars.
Having nothing specific just then
of a sensual nature in fact
to confess (for I'd learned in my weeks
in the Church that the sins of the flesh
had a special prestige), I accused
myself idly of sloth: sleeping in,
and thus missing Conventual Mass.
My director of conscience, however,
excused me for being fatigued
from my journey; the perils of jet
lag had not been defined, or he might
have alleged the transition from time
zone to time zone, one morning the twentieth
century, followed the next
by the sixth. At a loss for a real,
individual fault to unbosom
myself of distinct from the general
swamp of subjective unworthiness,
conscious of wasting my confessor's
time, as so often, I drew
from my pocket a crumpled and creased
but still legible letter received
on the eve of departure from Lazarus
House, and forgotten till now
in the flurry of novel impressions,
the latest but far from the last
in a string of increasingly cross
and indignantly Protestant fatherly
diatribes crossing the continent
often enough to upset
my unbalanced monastic complacency.
First he impugned my conversion—
perversion, he called it—to popery:
what would my Scotch Presbyterian
ancestors think? His suspicions
of Lazarus House (my infrequent
polemical answers disclosing
my whereabouts) paled at the mention
of Sweet Saviour Priory. One
of his favourite lines, which he drew
in rebutting the filial charge
of naivety, was, that he wasn't
brought up in a convent. Submitting

this writing in evidence, muttering
something about the commandment
(I couldn't remember its number)
to honour one's parents, I bided
my time while the abbé adjusted
his spectacles, slowly deciphered
my father's exemplary penmanship
(formed by a lifetime of writing
on blackboards), and handing the document
back to me, murmured, "I see
you are not truly free after all.
For your penance I wish you to say
Pater Noster." "*Qui es in Vancouver?*"
Is blasphemy ever in any
but dubious taste? When he took
me again, as he said, at the foot
of the letter, the letter in question
was T. "If you think that your heavenly
father is merely the earthly
enlarged, you are fooling yourself.
He contains all the wisdom that lack
the most dutiful fathers as yours."
As a child I had fostered the commonplace
childish pretense that my parents
were not my "real" parents, until
I discovered this fancy was fact.
If I therefore thereafter appealed
to those shadowy lovers my actual
absent progenitors, as
to a higher tribunal, no wonder
I sometimes imagined our heavenly
father withdrawn from a world
he acknowledged paternity of
but had not the remotest intention
of nurturing—save, as the sign
of the cross my confessor absolved
me with claimed, for one personal visit,
incalculable in effect.

I arose from my knees in the bracken
unfairly dissatisfied, like
a hard-core hypochondriac leaving
the doctor's who tells him he's perfectly
fine. In dismissing me, Abbé

Clément had omitted the ritual
wheeze about sinning no more
and moreover had aired no opinion
and offered no airy advice.
Temporarily fed up with fathers,
I greeted the straggling approach
of a band of work-habited brethren
with wonder. "They are in this moment
accustomed to bathing themselves,
with permission of Reverend Father,"
the Master of Novices smiled
his discreet disapproval, "a pastime
with precedents evidently
Romanesque!"
                  Having, some of them, laid
down their tools on the footling foundations,
and others, forsaken the vegetable
patch where impartially they
had uprooted the radical radish
along with the alien cornflower,
leaving a desolate area
strewn with innocuous weeds
like a scene in the Thirty Years' War,
they were tracing a path through the woods
a trite track within yards of my sylvan
confessional, looking (I thought)
like the pilgrims in *Tannhäuser*, each
of them toting a towel, in token
perhaps of their cleanly intentions.
In view of the heat, which was virtually
visible, tempted to join
them, I looked for permission to Abbé
Clément, who conveyed his consent
with a wink, as he rose to withdraw
in another direction. I watched
him until he had quite disappeared
in the wood I suspected he sprung
from, then ran to catch up with the sportive
novitiate, lest they themselves
disappear. If they saw me they didn't
say boo to the goose that I was
in those days, to invite or forbid
me to merge with their woodland ballet,
an impromptu rehearsal, perhaps,

of *Swan Lake*: but what wouldn't I give
to take part in the full-dress performance!
The deeper they entered the forest
the more they spread out; the illusory
bunch was dispersed into stray
individual atoms that blundered,
unseen but not silent, about
in the underbrush, making a crackle
of twigs underfoot and continual
crashes and bangs amid ladylike
oaths—nothing stronger than "Ouch!"
for at Sweet Saviour Priory "damn"
was anathema. Blindly I chased
these crepuscular cries though the shadowy
thickets where twilight persisted
in spite of the skylight that broke
through the network of branches and twigs
intertwined overhead like a foliate
baldachin. Vesper appeared,
in the coppice at least, to anticipate
Vespers. However, the woods
hereabouts, although dense, were not deep,
and I knew we were nearing the eaves
of the copse when the daylight regilded
the colourless trunks of the trees
and the foliage grew as translucent
as Tiffany glass. Had we walked
in a circle? I blinked, half-expecting
to see the same layout we left
a few minutes ago, agricultural
buildings converted to clerical
use, thus reversing the normal
historical order, apart
from one famous basilica built
on the site of a stable. Instead,
in a smaller but similar valley,
as green as the mythical vale
of Cunghanedd, asleep in the sunlight
a little, imperfectly circular
pond like a mirror reflected
the burnished Tiepolo dome
of the sky; and surrounding the luminous
water an overgrown meadow
extended, the pasture of shadows,

neglected though recently cleared
and as rough as a soul lately shriven
in which the inveterate bushes
and seedlings of sin are beginning
to sprout once again. By such fanciful
standards, it looked many years
since the landscape's purgation by axe,
and as if in response to this laicized
not to say lapsed or apostasized
atmosphere, painfully pagan
compared to the ordered religious
domain in the other more thoroughly
Romanized valley, the fun-loving
novices (some of them postulants,
some of them newly professed,
but my envy ignored such invidious
quibbles), burst out of the fence
of the forest, descended the treacherous
slope in a rout, as they scampered
disrobing, with laughter and shouts
that were hardly Gregorian. Following
hard on their heels, though the ground
was uneven and soft, to the verge
of the beckoning pool, I demurely
began to undress uninvited,
determined as always to join
them. Ironically, seeing the coveted
habit discarded, I reasoned,
divesting myself of my worldlier
garments, perhaps in the natural
state all distinctions of cleric
and lay would be blurred and forgotten?
Instead of by formal investiture,
("taking the habit" monastic
initiates called it, or final
profession) I might be received
in the fold prematurely, perforce
temporarily, wearing the barely
respectable habit of Adam,
which all the scholastics were sporting
like classical statues, erect
on the rim of the pool, at a glance
indistinguishable were it not
for the clerical tonsure; as cropped

as a conscript's, much shorter than even
my 'fiftyish haircut, it rendered
the hairiest regular Roman
religious as bald as a Calvinist.
Naturally had I asked
myself what to expect underneath
the monastical uniform, I
should have hazarded, simple humanity.
Yet I had been long enough
in the Church to imbibe a profound
superstitious regard for the clergy
as creatures of habit, distinct,
quintessentially other, a caste
set apart from our own, with peculiar
prerogatives, duties, and magical
powers. The taboo in respect
to depicting them naked suggested,
unlike sacred love in the painting
referred to above, they had something
to hide, not a tail or a hoof,
or perchance rudimentary wings,
like those shamans and witchdoctors credited
with superhuman or subhuman
characteristics, but simply
our common humanity, evident
now as they poised on the brink
of the drink, in their commonplace manhood.

My shocked observations (for I
was still callow enough to be shocked
by the obvious) took much less time
in the flesh than they do in the letter.
A series of splashes, split seconds
apart, as the naked novitiate
gaily regained a degree
of comparative decency, shattered
the aqueous mirror and fractured
the peace of the valley. Facetious,
provocative voices rebounded
along the irregular shore
and reminded me, dumb as I was,
of the myth of Narcissus and Echo.
The active contemplatives' members
erupted repeatedly free

of the surface, emerging one moment
submerging the next in the vitreous
element, thrashing about
indiscriminately like a school
(not for nothing were most of them labelled
scholastics) of glistening dolphins
distrained from their fathomless deeps
and confined in a teacup the size
of the tank at Marine World. I marvelled,
unable to float, at the various
strokes of the swimmers: the breaststroke,
the backstroke, the sidestroke (yclept
the Australian crawl) not to mention
the desperate dog paddle; some
of them floated face down as if dead
or face up on their backs. As I stalled
on the bank, with their habits cast off
at my feet like cocoons, an unwilling
voyeur on the verge of exposure,
unnoticed, I fancied, excluded
and shy, I attempted to count
them, the first opportunity since
I had seen them approaching the log
where the Abbé Clément and myself
were concluding our pastoral dialogue.

Masculine dryads they'd seemed
in the wood, as uncountable as
the deciduous trees that had screened
them, and now in the pond, unmistakably
male notwithstanding their fleeting
resemblance, at least in behaviour,
to naiads, more numerable:
it was merely a question of counting
their close-shaven heads as they bobbed
up and down in the water: a dozen,
perhaps, altogether; and had
I been able (as I was so eager)
to add to their number, my total
immersion (believe in it? I'd
seen it done!) would have made it thirteen.
Having so far ignored me (however
I couldn't complain it was I
who had been overlooked) an egregious

cygnet white-breasted, bronze-necked,
Frater Thomas à Kempis besought
me, "Come in!" and demanding for heaven's
sake, eschatologically, what
I was waiting for, called me a chiliast
coward. But I couldn't swim,
and the swimming-hole, small though it was
in diameter, looked to be bottomless:
none of the bathers was wading,
they floated and paddled and swam
with an ease that I envied as keenly
as if they could fly. When I made
my predicament patent by pantomime,
feeling not only ridiculous
starkly conspicuous stuck
on the bank, but immodest as well,
Frater Thomas produced out of nowhere
an innertube, fully inflated
and tossed it, contemptuously
at my feet on the grass. I stepped into
it gracefully, hoisting it over
my loins as a seemly and suitably
black undergarment of rubber,
and took a deep breath in the form
of a prayer (though unable to cross
myself), jumped, as I had a few months
ago out of my depth in the fountain
of faith, and without any improvised
lifesaver too, to a clap
of applause that was drowned in the splash
I made. Undisturbed, unmolested,
but not unperturbed by the bathers
about me, completely at home
in this watery world, and what's more,
self-supporting, I floated secure
in the hole of the doughnut (as pessimists
picture creation) sustained
as it were—as I was—by an inner,
pneumatic elation at finding
myself in the swim with a host
of the heavenly infantry, breathlessly
taking a dip in the god-given
sunlight, my nether extremities
dangling unseen in the bone-chilling

depths, as outsider and newcomer
spared the exuberant horseplay,
the duckings and playful aspersions
indulged in by most of the others,
relieved that I wasn't expected
to share the misfortune of Hylas,
the minion of Heracles, drowned
by the water nymphs smitten with love
for the beautiful boy.
                           As the sun,
that all-seeing voyeur, in his headlong
descent from the heady empyrean,
veiled his inquisitive face
in a cumulus cloud, a perceptible
chill supervened on the frolicsome
scene, and a shadow engulfed
our surrounding, creating a ghostly
and monochrome sketch of a landscape
with etiolated, subfusc
vegetation, a tenebrous pasturage
tufted with bushes and shrubs
paradoxically stripped of their shade
by the general mimic eclipse;
and as in an eclipse, in the train
of the chill and the darkness, a solid
wet blanket of silence descended
to stifle our shrill pandemonium
instantly. Odd, is it not,
that while God in the anthropomorphic
convention appears as a face
at the end of the universe, hell
is envisaged as bodies contorted
in torment? As if at a signal
the monkish apprentices scrambled
pell-mell from the water and into
their habits, and I followed suit.
You would think that a party of ladies,
as in E.M. Forster's immoralist
Room with a View, had surprised
us, or else (the monastic enclosure
presumed as to female intrusion
inviolate) one of our Reverend
Fathers in God, disapproving
of such anabaptist or pagan

gymnastics. So, chastened and damp,
they retraced, as I brought up the rear,
the identical path through the woods,
but how trampled and tame it appeared
to me now! As the sun reemerged
from its nebulous closet to play
peek-a-boo through the ramifications
around and above us, I pined
for the mortal ennui of the pastoral
lie, the acedia bred
in Arcadia: *Et in Arcadia
ego*, not death (an abstraction
at twenty) but rather the daily,
desirable death of the ego.

Magnificat anima mea,
"My spirit enlarges my saviour,"
they chanted in chapel at Vespers,
their voices, so recently rowdy,
subdued in lugubrious plainsong;
anonymous now in their habits,
yet equally so, for the matter
of that, in the flesh, for there wasn't
a novice, except Frater Thomas,
I knew by his name in religion,
and not even he had addressed
me by mine, an American custom
too often encountered inside
the monastic community where
utter strangers would hail one another
as Frater. Debarred from pseudonymous
fraternization, what alias
should I adopt in the Priory?
Thomas and Gregory there
were as common as William, the pomp
of religion forbidding familiar
curtailment, and Daryl, *tout court*
although mere Anglo-Saxon, was never
a saint's name, and therefore uncouth
in the cloister, albeit the Prior's
"Dear boy" was a perfect translation
thereof. To the Abbé Clément
I assumed I was Thou, his refusal
to speak his own language disguising

the small, all-important distinction
of number, alas! obsolescent
in mine. Now my spirit which magnified
everything afterwards anyway,
during the droning of Vespers
enlarged the events of the day
as one blows up a negative, seeking
the miniscule, tell-tale detail.
Recollection enjoys in religion
a blameless perennial vogue
in a sense rather other than that
which it held for the great nineteenth-century
poets who were (as Dom Clément
divined), my undoubted confessors
and doctors and martyrs, my secular
saints. If I had any faults,
(and of course I believed as an item
of faith I had many) the worst
was not one I considered as such,
for it did not appear in the Catholic
catalogue. Who can assess
his most serious failing objectively?
Envy accuses herself
of ambition, and vanity prattles
of pride. My besetting shortcoming,
not yet diagnosed, was—and is—
a refusal, or failure, to dwell
in the present instead of the past
and the future. Both recent impressions
and archaeological memories
promised to furnish me matter
for many a future confession
as well as for future confessional
poems. Regret, an ambivalent
feeling at worst, was resigned
to dividing my soul on a time-sharing
basis with equally dubious
anticipation. "*Ne mens,*"
in the words of the vesperal hymn
I was listening to semiconsciously
"*gravata crimine vitae*
sit exsul:" "Nor suffer the mind
overburdened with vice to be exiled
from life," "*dum perenne nil cogitat,*"

"while it eternally thinks
about nothing," "*seseque in culpis
ligat*" "as it ties itself up
in its sins." For the future, of course
I aspired to a place in the heavenly
choir, but before that, to taking
my place in the choir at Sweet Saviour
where all of the brethren were choirmonks,
the feudal but (Reverend Father
maintained) insufficiently ancient,
though quite out of date institution
of lay brother, latinless Morlocks
who did all the labour while leaving
the prayers to their literate betters,
a thing of the past, and not only
because in the twentieth century
none of the postulants knew
any Latin at all. By the end
of the summer I should be permitted
to stand at the back of the choir
but forbidden to open my mouth.
I could sing like an angel, but rarely
in key.
          After Vespers I waited
outside for the Abbé Clément,
having gleaned a few scruples to add
to my pardoner's tale in the course
of my dim meditation inside
the extemporized chapel, which smelled
more and more like a barn notwithstanding
the bogus aroma of incense,
like eau de cologne unsuccessfully
masking the masculine odour
of sweat. But the Master of Novices,
scurrying past like the rabbit
in Alice in Wonderland, told
me, "Not now! It must wait for the Chapter
of Faults." I attempted to quash
the ridiculous image of Sweet
Saviour Priory seen through the looking-glass.
Reverend Father might be
the unseen Cheshire Cat whose mysterious
influence proved so persistent.
Dom Dagobert could be the Duchess

or else Humpty Dumpty, but if
Frater Thomas à Kempis could play
the Frog Footman, the others remained
Tweedledum or perhaps Tweedledee,
in their uniform habits and faces
composed in expressions of uniform
piety, donned with their scapulars,
pawns in the chess game whose aim
was becoming a fully-fledged monk.

In the quiet refectory nobody
read from *The Ancrene Riwle*
and the frugal collation of yogurt
and blackberries (plucked in the woods
to provide an excuse for the outing
in which I had joined) was enjoyed
in comparative peace, till Dom Dagobert
pushed back his chair from the head
of one table (the only such article
there, as the humbler monastics
were seated on benches), intoning
the psalm, "*Dixit Dominus Domino
meo.*" The rest of us rose
and abandoned the fruits of the earth
to respond, "*donec ponam inimicos
tuos scabellum:*" "The Lord
said to *my* Lord, 'I'll prostrate your foes
like a footstool....'" Antiphonally
they continued some while in this bellicose
strain, as I thought of the oceans
of ink with which wise men had whitewashed
these primitive texts for the sake
of our edification. "*Confitebor
tibi justorum in toto...
consilio....*" Carried along
like a phonograph needle that skips
from one band to the next, they swept on
to the following psalm, "I shall make
my full-hearted confession to Thee
in the upright assembly." Dom Dagobert,
straightening up from the solemn
salaam of the "*Gloria patri,*"
announced that in view of the strictly
unscheduled vacation that same

afternoon, recreation tonight
would be cancelled, and we would proceed
straightaway to the Chapter of Faults.
Recreation I found on the following
nights of my stay a sedate,
indeed sedentary bore, a much milder
occasion of harmless amusement
and innocent mirth than the Chapter
convoked with such ominous awe.

"Frater Patrick?" Dom Dagobert recognized
one of the monks, who'd stepped forth
like a member of parliament catching
the eye of the Speaker, no easy
achievement, I thought, on the part
of the pink insignificant shrimp
with invisible eyebrows, who whined
in a wet, sanctimonious whimper,
"In charity, father, I have
to accuse Brother Thomas à Kempis
of blasphemy." "Jesus!" the Prior
was moved to exclaim, automatically
adding, "have mercy!" I looked
round the room for the nearest approach
to a friend I had found in Sweet Saviour,
and spotted him next to the exit,
repressively biting his tongue
while his fluent accuser retailed
the particulars, licking his lips.
"I was passing the kitchen some time
after Terce when I happened to hear
the accused—" "Frater Patrick, you seem
to forget this is not a judicial
proceeding," the acting superior
acted extremely superior,
"Try to continue less like
a whodunit." "But he *did*!" Already
high-pitched, he became in his wrath
a castrato. "I heard something break,
like a plate, then I heard Frater Thomas
à Kempis say—" "What?" "I don't like
to repeat it." "The name of Deity?"
"No." Frater Patrick, embarrassed,
turned pinker than ever. "Our Saviour's?

His mother's? or one of the saints'?
Were you able to judge his intention?
An infinitesimal chasm
may separate prayer from profanity."
"Excrement!" gasped Frater Patrick,
"or words to that vulgar effect."
It appeared that the rules of the Chapter
of Faults—in the nature of rules
presupposing a game—would permit
no defense. The defendant awaited,
with outward composure, the verdict
pronounced by the Prior who acted
as judge and as public defender
as well. "There is nothing," Dom Dagobert
sniffed, "by its nature profane—
at least blasphemous—even obscene—
in such utterance. Nor is there anything
pious, befitting a son
of Saint Benedict. Frater, your penance..."
Obeying the impulse of faith
to anticipate punishment, Frater
à Kempis (I hate the American
use of first names on the least
provocation) first knelt, then extended
himself at full length and face down
on the floor. "*De profundis clamavi
ad te,*" he began indistinctly,
like one who calls out from the depths.

"That will do for the moment," Dom Dagobert
said as he finished the psalm,
and the penitent got to his feet
to rejoin his inscrutable brethren
whose faces were veiled by their cowls
which they'd raised till they covered their foreheads.
A sinister circle they made,
like a coven of monks in some gothick
romance. "As for you, Frater Patrick,"
the Prior resumed, "May one speculate
why you were eavesdropping here
in the house, when at Prime I assigned
you to weeding the garden?" "I thought—
that is I—" *Qui s'excuse*, as the Abbé
Clément might have phrased it, *s'accuse,*

though the converse obtained in the Chapter
where self-accusation induced
exculpation. "I mean, I forgot—
something—" plainly unable to think
of a plausible object, the tattle-tale
mumbled. "Harumph!" Father Dagobert,
called "the big cheese" in my hearing
by certain irreverent novices
that afternoon, who included
this sneaky albino, observed,
"You'd forgotten yourself, and your vow
of Obedience." Keeping in mind
that the cell where the Prior had interviewed
me on the morning in question—
this morning—abutted the kitchen,
I might be expected to share
his sublime indignation. However,
apart from the dubious interest
of anything said on that recent,
already historic occasion,
I felt I myself had done nothing
but eavesdrop all day, like a spy
in the camp of the stars, *astra castra*:
what else was I doing tonight?
In his turn Frater Patrick prostrated
himself like the other, and grizzled
(the rest of the psalm was inaudible)
"*Humiliatus sum nimis*"—
"Exceedingly humbled am I."
Frater Thomas à Kempis, I lip-read
inaudibly mouthing the following
verse: "*Omnis homo*," I thought
that I saw him articulate, "*mendax*,"
"All men are untruthful," unfazed
by the logical paradox that
undermined his untrue understatement.

His penance or humiliation
complete, Frater Patrick returned
to the ranks of the penitent faceless
from which his sucessor stepped forward
dramatically doffing his cowl
to expose an emaciate face
of granitic austerity marred

by a singular frivolous feature,
luxuriant eyebrows turned up
at the ends in a quizzical, quite
diabolical manner. His stoop,
though it couldn't disguise his unnatural
height, reinforced the effect
of comparative age which his visage,
more lined than the juvenile novices',
gave. "I accuse Frater Bernard
of sloth. He was napping at Matins
again." Father Dagobert censored
a yawn, "Frater Anselm, your vigilance
during the vigil—which doubtless
extended through Lauds—would be praiseworthy
were it not strangely misplaced.
Your attention at that solemn hour
should be given to things of the spirit,
or failing that gift, to the letter
of things, to the literal meaning
of what we are chanting, and not
to the faults of the brethren, no matter
how venial." Doctrines like that
if obeyed, would, I wager, put paid
to the Chapter of Faults in short order.
Perhaps the directive applied,
insofar as the way of perfection
applies to existence at all
as distinct from the Prior's sublime
a priori pronouncements, exclusively
to the canonical hours
of the night, which I wasn't allowed
to attend, and thus thought of with awe
as the heart of the cenobite mystery,
like Eleusinian rites
which initiates only could witness.
I'd heard that in Egypt, the cradle
as well as the grave of the purest
monastical practice, where anchorites
often dropped anchor (a popular
primitive Christian device)
in the desolate tombs of the Pharaohs,
the office was purely nocturnal,
the monks in the heat of the day
lying dormant and solitary—not

altogether unwisely, in view
of the linen so publicly washed
in the Chapter of Faults, not to mention
those scandals the brethren saw fit
not to mention: sufficient, it seemed,
to the day was the evil thereof.
But I asked myself why, though excluded
from Matins and Lauds, I was suffered
to spy, like a fly on the wall—
and of these there were plenty, inglorious
witnesses bred of the life-giving
filth of the farmyard—on this
intramural embarrassing episode?

Meanwhile the Dormouse in question,
a creature from Wonderland, taxed
with inordinate somnolence, stepped
from the circle, or into its centre,
in silent apology, offering
none but a mumbled, percussive
but meek *"mea maxima culpa"*—
a mumble I recognized instantly
now as the reader's at lunch,
whose appearance, bucolic, compact,
not so much immature as unspoiled
by the world, wasn't otherwise noteworthy.
Hoping perhaps to forestall
any further time-wasting prostrations,
Dom Dagobert hastened to hand
out their penances. "Following Lauds
Frater Bernard, you will"—I remarked
what superior force and authority
vastly surpassing the simple
imperative, lurked in the future
indicative—"stay in your stall
and recite, *Mirabilia sunt
testimonia tua.* While you,
Frater Anselm, will kindly consider
the text, *Quis custodiet ipsos
custodes"*—a verse which I looked
for in vain in the psalter. "Beware,"
Father Dagobert gaped, "of the pitfalls
of sloth, which the worldly mistake
for good nature. Our regular life

and canonical hours guarantee
an infallible cure for acedia:
languor, indifference, indolence,
spiritual laziness, wilful
forgetfulness...." Here a hiatus
suggested that he had forgotten
the drift of his homily. Wasn't
the cure of acedia also
its cause, and ascesis accordingly
homeopathic?
                The night
was still young, or at least adolescent.
Incipient twilight reminded
me how many miles to the south
of the forty-ninth parallel Sweet
Saviour Priory lay. In the room
where, forgotten, the frugal remains
of our supper remained on the tables,
the darkness congealed in the solid,
crepuscular shapes of the hooded
fraternity. Out of this shadowy
gathering tripped an unlikely
accuser of sin, a cherubic—
if cherubs are bald, like a doll
with its wig missing—youth, whom I'd chastely
averted my eyes from when bathing
because of his blatant, exceptional
physical beauty. "Aha!
Frater Boniface!" cooed the susceptible
Prior, "Perhaps, as the hour
is advanced," and he peered at his wristwatch,
the only such timepiece I saw
in the Priory, "surely your conscience
would keep, if you'd care to consult
me *in petto*....?" "Both duty and charity
urge me, implacably, Father."
Whereas Frater Patrick's reproach
had been sly, Frater Anselm's severely
straightforward, I thought Frater Boniface's
preamble coy and seductive.
"I wish to accuse Frater Bede
of concupiscence—carnal concupiscence."
Was there, I wondered, another
variety? psychic, perhaps,

like the sly psychological urge
I had struggled to master at Lazarus
House, and was glad, but a mite
disconcerted, to find so innocuous
here. This would prove the unique
unforgettable mention of physical
lust in this celibate spot,
where desire, theoretically rampant
in masculine enclaves, maintained
a low profile in fact. Such discretion
recalled the No Smoking advertisements
posted in gas-works and -stations
and fireworks emporia, signs
that are nowadays nearly ubiquitous,
not that such notices really
were needed at Sweet Saviour Priory,
where a conspicuous absence
of smoke, one assumed hypocritically,
signalled a minimal danger
of fire. Even so a subliminal
tremor convulsed the attentive
assembly, recalling the sudden
revulsion that fell on the pond
when like Adam and Eve the unfrocked
had acknowledged their nakedness. "Brother,"
Dom Dagobert fished for the telling,
perhaps inadmissibly juicy
detail, "I must ask you to be
more specific—a serious charge
such as yours may be magnified out
of proportion by tactful discretion,
and so, though I might have preferred
to discuss such a delicate matter
in private, if not under seal
of confession, you must, having raised
it in Chapter, explain it in chapter
and verse." Frater Boniface batted
his eyelashes, like Frater Anselm's
inquisitive eyebrows, a salient
feature, and flushed, "In the midst
of the night, towards Matins, I woke
from a dream. I would rather go into
the dream," he appealed to Dom Dagobert,
"later, alone, if your Reverence

pleases?" "Of course, my dear—brother!"
(But "boyther" was how he pronounced
it: a boyishly bothersome brother?)
"The Chapter is hardly the forum
for dreams, which belong, if they have
any place in religion at all,
to the realm of auricular guidance."
Whatever their role in religion,
and dreams, as George Eliot noted
in passing, are less influential
in everyday life than in fiction,
the Prior appeared an improbable
Hermes, as psychopomp, guide
of the dead, and conductor of dream;
but his office hermeticized him.
Frater Boniface blithely continued,
"I thought I was dreaming at first;
it was dark in the dormitory, save
for the candle before St. Veronica's
ikon. The rest of the brethren
were sleeping the sleep of the just-
about-due-to-awaken." Their cenobite
sleeping arrangements excluded
pestiferous guests like myself,
but the quarantine couldn't prevent
an occasional outbreak of dormitory
fever. "And yet I was sure
that I felt something cool and uncannily
comforting stroking my brow
like the wing of an angel, I thought,
or the fingers, perhaps, of our Lady."
Dom Dagobert rumbled, "Now, Brother,
you know such Cistercian, hysterical
fancies are frowned upon here."
"But it wasn't a phantom," the novice
demurred, "of delight. When I opened
my eyes I could see Brother Bede
bending over my bed and caressing,"
he shuddered, "the stubble that covers
my skull, as if stroking my hair."
"You should therefore," the Prior improved
the occasion by prosing, "reflect
on the power of the tonsure, that masculine
veil, to deflect the unwanted

desires of the angels, if we
may believe the Old Testament, which,
anagogically speaking, we must.
Had Delilah been bald, it is certain
that Samson would not have been shorn
of his prowess. Remember that hair
is a snare,"—and, I thought, in this case
a delusion—"and rather than mourning
the locks that you left on the altar,
rejoice insofar as your sacrifice,
making of you a less tempting
albeit unwitting occasion
of sin, will exchange for your cropped
crowning glory a glorious crown."
It had little or nothing to do
with the matter in hand, but I wondered
if that might explain my unnatural
lack of reaction when faced
with this afternoon's naked exuberance.
Baldness—and some of the heads
were as glabrous as vellum, while others
supported the shortest of crew-cuts—
disfigures the young so much more
than the old like Dom Dagobert, whom
it became like a headdress, bestowing
authority, wisdom and sometimes
a spurious nimbus of sanctity.
Skulls, notwithstanding their vogue
as Romantic accessories, lack
all romantic allurement, and hence
their appeal in the looking-glass realm
of religion, where what in the eyes
of the world seems repulsive, becomes
in proportion attractive. The postulant
plaintiff complacently rested
his case, as a willowy, middle-aged
monk with a silvery tonsure
and gentle obsequious face
like a waiter or floorwalker, crept
from the ranks and prostrated himself.
"Frater Bede, I must ask you for some
explanation, but keep it in mind
that the best explanation is not
an excuse!" "I was merely," the prostrated

penitent moaned from the parquetry,
"trying to comfort the lad,
who was having a nightmare, to judge
by the way he was thrashing about
and the terrible things he was muttering."
"What," Father Dagobert pressed,
"for example? I doubt Frater Boniface
really remembers himself?"
I was ready to bet Brother Boniface
hadn't forgotten himself
for a second, awake or asleep,
in his life. "Oh, I couldn't repeat,"
Frater Bede undertook to repeat
the familiar refrain that suggested
enormities worse than the rudest
ipsissima verba, "I couldn't
in fact understand or interpret
the language, that is the bad language
of dreams. The poor soul was unconscious,
delirious maybe." "Quite so.
Frater Bede, we believe your intentions
were blameless, however your actions
might be misinterpreted. Never
forget who forbade our offending
the least of his children, and say
for your penance the *Laudate pueri.*
Yes, you may rise. Frater Boniface,
come to our cell after Compline."
It seemed that the Prior could grant
dispensation to anyone from
The Great Silence, including himself.

The community, purged by their mutual
audit, in which there were items
more decently uttered in silence,
(though chastity proved less deficient
than charity), silently bided
Dom Dagobert's blessing concluding
The Chapter of Faults and announcing
the office of Compline officially.
"*Noctem quietem et finem*
perfectum concedat omnipotens:"
"May the Almighty concede
us a night that is quiet and final

perfection." They crossed themselves, turned
and right-marched from the Chapterhouse, which
their departure restored to its everyday
role as the common refectory;
lives which had seemed open books
only lately, were brusquely withdrawn
still unread when the Chapter concluded.

As, hesitant whether to tread
on their heels as they trouped into chapel,
I dithered, I saw Frater Thomas
à Kempis collecting the dishes
and clearing the tables. When offered
a hand, he rejected my help
in dumb crambo, which meant the Great Silence
had started already. But sign language
proving inadequate as
semiotics for further instruction,
he fished out the stub of a pencil
and scratched on the back of an envelope,
"Reverend Father will see
you tonight after Compline. I'll take
you there." When he had swiftly if sloppily
finished his duties, in which
as I did not belong to his union
I had been forbidden to meddle,
he led me outdoors. There, precocious
because of the latitude, summertime
darkness enveloped our faintly
familiar monastic surroundings,
except for the blaze, less mysterious
now, of the glow in the hallway
behind us, outshining, though empty
the flickering glow from the chapel.
"*Ut pupilla oculi*" wafted
the words from the barn, notwithstanding
a sensible lack of afflatus,
"*sub umbra alarum tuarum*:"
that is, "Like the apple, O Lord
of thine eye, in the shadow, O Lord,
of thy wings...." Imperceptibly cooler
but stagnant, the air constituted
a habit of sorts, an habitual
mortification, to which

by degrees I was growing accustomed
along with the dark. Frater Thomas
à Kempis conducted me out
of the dust of the barnyard and into
the whispering grass of the orchard,
our footsteps bedevilled by windfalls,
apostates from overhead branches
whose fruit-laden ramifications
were outlined in starlight. No moon
having risen (nor was I sufficiently
learned or rustic or moonstruck
to know when one would), Frater Thomas
produced from a pocket concealed
in his cassock, a substitute moon
in the form of a lantern or flashlight,
so "feet followed kindly our ransom
and rescue." He looked a more likely
Destroyer of Argus, which thousand-
eyed monster embodies the star-spangled
vault, than the Prior; his wandering
beacon, effacing the firmament's
faint incandescence increasingly
dimmed by a cloud as a tremor
of wind agitated the foliage,
focused the bio-degradable
bric-a-brac lining the path
in its beam, as the orchard gave way
to the wood. But if that were the same—
and why wouldn't it be?—I was sure
we were taking a different path:
in the word of my paperback guide
and half-read *vade mecum*, St. John
of the Cross, "To arrive at a place
which you know nothing of, you must go
by a way which you know nothing of."
In the thick of the darkness ahead
of us flickered a light intercepted
by trees: it outshone as it drew
ever nearer and grew more distinct
Frater Thomas's torch. We emerged
at the edge of a clearing defined
by an absence of growth intervening
between this amorphous effulgence
and us, and the glimmer resolved

itself into a window, a square,
or a rectangle rather, uncurtained
apparently, set in a tumbledown
cottage like that of the witch
in a fairytale. Hearing a grumble
of thunder, and feeling a drop
on my shoulder, I turned to my erstwhile
companion, to find he had vanished,
all but the mercurial track
of his flashlight retreating apace
through the wood. As the heavenly mumbles
became more disgruntled and rain
had begun to descend with a vengeance,
I dashed for the door which the glow
of the window had led me to guess
could not be far away, but the distance
at night was deceptive. I felt
like the arrow in Zeno's insoluble
paradox, halving the distance,
and halving the remnant, etcetera,
till, when I thought I should never
arrive at my goal, I was there.
Dripping wet, and afraid lest the storm,
as abrupt as a stage-effect, render
my knock ineffective, I knocked
nonetheless. "*Benedicite*! Enter!"

Uncertain I'd heard what I thought,
and half dreaming the thunder had spoken,
I opened the door on the cave
of Aladdin, or rather a roughly
translated *Arabian Nights*'
European equivalent, lighted,
appropriately, by a guttering
oil lamp, the source of the tremulous
brightness that oozed from the window.
Within, a farrago of heterogeneous objects of varying
period, style, and description
affronted my puritan, also
provincial, aesthetic assumptions.
A cuckoo-clock perched on the lid
of a fortepiano or harpsichord
here, while a statue of Dante

in plaster of Paris surveyed
with dyspeptic approval a model
of Jeremy Bentham's panopticon
there. Here lay mountains of books,
no-man-fathomed, not paperback modern
editions like those that adorned
the well-packed alphabetical shelves
of Dom Dagobert, rather unread
and unreadable volumes in vellum
and leather, untitled apart
from the gilt Roman numerals stamped
on their spines, not so much individual
books as the type of The Book.
In one corner—for under the rubbish
of centuries, mainly the teens
of this era, one saw that the shack
was rectangular—stood a complete
set of armour, and next to it brooded
a bust of Napoleon, bearing
the motto, *Aut Caesar aut Nihil*—
(*viz.* Moscow or Bust?). Even bustier
still, stood a dressmaker's dummy
which elbowed the Venus de Milo,
its prototype, torso confronting
inbrachiate torso, as Sacred
outfaces Profane, with a clock
in her stomach. An album of gramophone
records, the 78's
of my childhood, was poised on the nethermost
step of a stepladder under
an astrolabe. Costumes of every
historical period, pattern
and sex—a kimono, a farthingale,
boots, pantaloons and a cod-piece,
were strewn on the period furniture
ranging in style from Victorian
Gothic to Roman provincial,
along with a brittle collection
of bibelots, virtuous objects
in ormolu, ivory, tortoiseshell,
silver and sandalwood, goblets
and reliquaries, teapots and chessmen.
In short (though this catalogue isn't)
I'd stumbled upon a museum

of culture-historical artifacts
jumbled together all anyhow,
like the impressive but meaningless
contents of what one might truly
describe as a catholic mind.

I was looking about for the rich
sensibility that had assembled
such eons of junk as belonged
to the Abbot of Omnium Gatherum
when, from behind an elaborate
tapestry screen in a corner,
a voice neither still nor especially
miniscule rasped, "*Benedictus
qui venit in nomine?*" Blessing
or question, the formula also
expressed a command, which I answered
with reflex Teutonic alacrity,
"*Servus!*" I'd noticed already
how Latin, the language the Roman
communion continued to call
universal—like music, according
to some—though about to be banned
from the altar, preserved in the mouths
of its acolytes accents that varied
according to national origin,
such, I imagine, as flourished
in Europe before the emergence
of local vernaculars, during
the twilight of Rome. I shall not
reproduce Abbot Willibrord's personal
idiosyncrasies—if
I was right to assume they were his—
of delivery, whether in Latin
or English. My accurate pen,
though it were a Mont Blanc, could not hope
to transcribe the Germanic perversions
of W, V, and the rest—
not to mention TH, which apart
from the *theta* of classical Greek
has no place on the sibilant palates
of Europe, and little enough
in America, peopled by refugees
from the inaspirate argots

of lands whose phonetic divisions
are otherwise rather pronounced.
With pronounced trepidation I threaded
my way through an obstacle course
of irrelevant impedimenta,
the cultural baggage of Europe,
towards what I hoped was the source
of the oracle. Screened by a folding
contraption embroidered with scenes
from the life—and the death, in exhaustive
detail—of St. Boniface, lay
on a cast-iron camp-bed or cot
an emaciate figure in black
Benedictine pontificals—but
for the mitre, an effigy sculptured
in flesh of an abbot, as stiff
and immobile as stone. From the yoke
of his robe there extruded a skull
like a head on a platter in vivid
relief, or a medium's fraudulent
manifestation, which spoke.
"You will kindly forgive me for failing
to rise to receive you: my Body
was scathed in the War." Was his spirit
unscathed? Unsolicited, his
information surprised me much less
than his frank, conversational tone,
notwithstanding his audible habit
of capitalizing all nouns.
So disarming an opening gambit,
intended to put me at ease,
condescension befitting a prince
of the church, paradoxically kept
me instead at a distance. "Which war?"
As I struggle to frame the impertinent
question, his answer anticipates
it, "In the Second World War,
as they call it, forgetting our War
with the World is eternal, I worked
with the Christian Resistance in Germany."
Dare I confess my impression
that Catholics, beginning with Pius
the XII, had put up but half-hearted
resistance to Hitler, inured

as they were to authority? "Ach!"
he uncannily ambushed the train
of my thought, "If Authority be
illegitimate...." Stunned by the wholly
correct but unidiomatic
subjunctive that marked the fastidious
English Dom Willibrord spoke
like a book, I misheard his apodosis.
"Man must obey. So as Abbot
of Einsamkeit Abbey deriving
legitimate, *nein*, apostolic
Authority ultimately
from the Absolute, what in the World
can I do but oppose the preposterous
Claims of the State? There was many
a circumcised Monk in the Choir
in my Time." He fell silent in revery.
"How they found out is a Mystery,
one of the sorrowful Mysteries."
Was this gratuitous history
only a further display
of that preoccupation with self
on the part of my pastors and masters
I found disconcerting in those
who supposedly had extirpated
all selfish desires and concerns,
an obsession extremely annoying,
convinced as I was that the subject
that ought to be under discussion
was I? Unawares, I had hit
on the flaw in the frequent confessional
system of private direction—
its crass, egotistic pretensions.
The greater the guilt, whether real
or imagined, the more histrionic
the role of the soul, the perennial
star of its own psychodrama.
Moreover the guiltless confessor
now painting himself as a martyr
who also incarnated some
of the grandeur and power of Rome,
that insidious power and shabbily
compromised grandeur, seemed bent
on extolling his painful experience

like an example or text,
disregarding my claims to be questioned.
"I often examine my Conscience
concerning Our Lord's Admonition
to render to Caesar the Things
that are Caesar's." A duty, I mused,
that the Church hadn't always discharged
with alacrity, tending to confiscate,
rather, the goods of this world,
as the clutter surrounding him showed,
though some churchmen, for instance Dom Dagobert,
rendered to Caesar a homage
as abject as incense. "I ask
myself, what may be said to be Caesar's?
The Coin? But the Copper or Silver
or Gold is not his. As your Protestant
Poet observes, 'In his deep
and unfathomable Mines,'" he misquoted,
"'He treasures His brilliant Designs.'
The Inscription—the Image—the Likeness
are Caesar's, or nothing." He paused
in the midst of his homily; given,
I wondered, how often before,
it required interlocutors less
than the tirades of Socrates. Tortured,
I took him to mean, by the world
at its worst, he could spurn it with extra
ascetic integrity, sparing
the various objects collected
about him, as Caesar's hard-bought
souvenirs. "I revered the historical
Process," he said as if reading
my mind like a visitor's book
he had looked at before in a cheaper
edition. "My little Collection
enshrines, metaphorically speaking,
all History, Everyman's sacred
Possession, the Past—the sole worldly
Endowment we cannot give up
or be stripped of, except by Derangement
or Death, both of which I was spared
by a Hair's-Breadth because of the Goodness
of Him whom I serve—and the Badness
of him whom my Questioners served.

They were brutal but not so refined
as our own Inquisition. You'll find
in that archaeological Midden
a rusty, intact Iron Maiden,
a Thumbscrew or Rack which the secular
Arm used to brandish before
it was tied by the squeamish Enlightenment."

How could I reconcile what
he had suffered himself, and his courage,
if I could believe his account
as of course I implicitly did,
with his sanguine if faintly ironic
defence of the Catholic Church's
disgraceful expedients? Damned
if I could! "Only God," he explained
"has the Right to give Pain." "And a power,"
I added, "to do so exceeding
the cruellest human malevolence."
"What," he addressed me *ad hominem*
now, or *ad juvenem* rather,
in testy reproof, "do you know
of the Matter?" "I've never been tortured,"
I had to admit, "only teased
in the playground and bullied a bit
on the way home from school, as a child.
But I've suffered...." I censored, suppressing
a stronger desire to confide
(as opposed to confess) to this still,
hieratically supine superior
than to the friendly but fidgety
Frenchman, my tale of emotional
torment, "unspeakable anguish
from toothache." Because I meant, heartache,
brought up as I was with a stoic
disdain for complaint and respect
for the truth, I reflexively blushed;
while of course my discomfort fell short
of the pains of the damned, the description
partook of hyperbole: nothing,
I felt, was unspeakable. "Tush!"
or some German equivalent augured
a curt fellow-sufferer's sympathy.

But as I winced at this morbid
competitive spirit evinced
by the sick in regard to their symptoms
(for, say what you will about pain,
it is personal, your very own,
a possession no order, no vow
can distrain), he surprised me by changing
the subject, at last, to myself.
"So you wish to become one of us?"
My assent was redundant. "I see.
And you have been a Student at what
Institution?" "McGill University."
For the first time in my life
and the last I was tempted to call
someone Sir, but I didn't; however
such personal interrogation
evoked an uneasy response
as of guilt, though my conscience was spotless,
at least in regard to the past.
"Montreal?" Abbot Willibrord made
the approximate association
that everyone seemed to in literate
Catholic circles. "Immanuel
Star I recall on the Rim
of the Circle of Stefan George
in Heidelberg, where I imbibed
the religious indeed mediaeval
Ideals that led me to Einsamkeit
later." I drew in my breath;
I had sniffed in George a flavour
of *Knabe und Wein und Gesang*,
but no doubt this was figurative,
like the psalms. "A Professor, I hear,
in the Medical School at McGill?"
I assumed this referred to Immanuel
Star, but refrained from explaining
I thought his appointment began
in September. "A Catholic Convert:
perhaps you have read his bestseller,
The Pillar of Salt?" As a matter
of fact, in the wake of repeated
and various recommendations,
I had: by the prevalent standards
of hagio-autobiography,

most of which took *Astra castra*
to mean *Newman lumen*, an arid
and tedious Dead Sea erection
indeed, as the title suggested.
I shrank from expressing this negative
verdict not simply because
I distrusted my judgement and taste,
which in fact I did not, even under
the promise or threat of aesthetic
obedience; rather, because
I was loath to disparage one Hun
to another; for Star, though he wrote
the same painfully error-free stuff
that the Abbot, Dom Willibrord, spouted,
stylistically clung, like the monk,
to that vigorous tongue, uncorrupted
by Humanist cant, unlike English
and French, so beloved of Winifred
Odin, the Stefan George
of lower Manhattan. As well,
repetition had wearied my ears
with the name of Immanuel Star,
though I'd somehow forgotten his son's.
"But I trust you will seek his Acquaintance,"
Dom Willibrord grimaced in pain,
"at McGill." There it was, the decision
I'd dreaded, already. "You mean,"
I determined to spell out the worst,
"I am doomed to return to the world?"
"In the Harvest, what you call, The Fall,
to resume your scholastic Career."
That career, I regarded, aghast
as a Fall in the biblical sense.
"But I want to renounce—" "Academic
Pursuits, undergraduate Studies,
in time a Degree, although worldly
perhaps, are I fear indispensable
Qualifications, in *your* Case
for any monastic Vocation.
Your Faith is brand new," he exploited
this false etymology slyly,
"the Product still carries the label
proclaiming its Maker: it has
to be tested, and possibly shrunk

in the World before worn in the Cloister.
Also," with this oddly accented
Teutonic perversion of "also,"
the Abbot was candid enough
to exhibit that practical streak
that, surprisingly, runs down the back
of the most otherwordly ascetic,
"you may be of much greater Use
to the Priory with a B.A.
from a real University." Did
he intend to disparage those bastions
of Catholic learning that dotted
the landscape, including those run
by his order? "Perhaps we shall send
you to Europe—to Rome—to prepare
for the Priesthood. We haven't, you see,
very good sacerdotal Material
in our Novitiate: pious
undoubtedly, raised to believe
and obey from the cradle, Good Boys,"—
if that wasn't a stark oxymoron:
he hadn't beheld them in mercury,
shouting and splashing, like me—
"for the most Part exemplary Christians
but not Intellectuals such
as are needed as never before
by the Order." His offer, if that's
what it was, introduced the first hint
that I had an advantage of sorts
incunabular Catholics lacked.
If untried, my belief represented
a plausibly conscious, informed
intellectual choice, and my turning
my back on the godless and secular
joys which alumni of Catholic
homes and parochial schools
never knew, could be seen as a positive
recommendation. That same
intellectual honesty forced
me to ask, was McGill what he meant
by a "real university?" Didn't
his notions of student high-mindedness
date from his Heidelberg youth?
His conception of me I saw through

as generic; he hadn't the time
or the interest to plumb my unique
haecceitas. "You may visit us here
in the Summer, of course," he conceded
as further inducement—and live
at McGill, like a monk, by the Rule
of Saint Benedict? "Under a Vow,
if you like, a provisional Vow
of Obedience, certainly. "But—"
I had always disliked making plans
as opposed to embroidering fantasies,
daydreaming, building alternative
lives. When composing an essay,
or *a fortiori* a poem,
I liked to dispense with an outline
for fear of its cramping my style.
Even more I detested fulfilling
the plans made for me, for my good
as they said and believed, by my elders
and betters. My father's distress
and disgust at my poping arose
from the wreck of his unrealistic
but doctrinaire hopes for my future
success in the Protestant work-ethic.
Freya had other but similar
plans for her son, but I couldn't
have said at the moment if Mark
had rebelled or obeyed. In Victorian
novels, I knew, the paternal
prerogative picked the career
of the son, as it does in the mystery
play at the heart of the Christian
mythology. Hopeless, the scheme,
and not my cup of tea, which I prayed
would pass from me, yet nevertheless
I rejected the filial role
of rebellion. "Obedience," Reverend
Father declared, "is the Secret
of Faith which subsumes all the cardinal
Virtues, though not so completely
as Luther pretends. Without Faith
what is Hope but an animal Reflex,
our temporal Nature's Defence
against daily Despair, the pathetic

but radical Wish of the Flesh
that Tomorrow will be, if not better,
no worse." I had thought this phenomenon,
which I instinctively recognized,
something peculiar to youth;
now I wondered, since it was instinctive,
why hope wasn't more fundamental
than faith? "Without Faith, what is Charity?"
argued the Abbot, "—but charity?
secular Tolerance, worldly
Benevolence—Sentimentality!
Likewise, aside from Obedience,
Chastity seems little but
a Perversion, and Poverty signifies
Want. Have you thought what your Life
would be like without Faith?" I recoiled
from the very idea, a sign
that my faith was already transparent,
a notional option. "Unthinkable!"
stoutly I lied; but as midnight
advanced I foresaw my complete
disenchantment: the habit I'd prayed
for in rags, and the virtues and vows
I was ready to live by reduced
to good manners and self-deprivation,
like horses transformed into rats,
as the vitreous coach of the Church
was restored to its primitive form
as a Hallowe'en pumpkin. "Obedience,"
Reverend Father repeated,
"alone guarantees Perseverance
in Faith." "But the Germans, I mean,"
I retracted my error in horror,
"the Nazis excelled in obedience,
too." Abbot Willibrord snorted
in scorn at this sophistry. "*Ja,*
but the Nazis were Heretics." Memory,
though it is said we're unable
in fact to remember a painful—
or pleasant—sensation, inert
recollection descended like sleep
on his sculptural features, discoloured
as fossilized ivory. Closing
his eyes, he dismissed me in silence.

I bowed, and withdrew—into what?
The deposit of faith, or of memory,
solid and polished as furniture,
objects of dubious virtue
and priceless but hideous junk,
were impeding my steps, and to further
detain me the thought of the forest's
obscure and impervious labyrinth
waiting outside was enough.
I would never get back to Sweet Saviour
tonight. If I wondered, once there
how I'd ever escape the monastic
museum, or find my way out
of the dark sacred wood of the Church,
I dismissed the idea, apostasy
being anathema still.
Cinderella became Sleeping Beauty,
but where could I sleep? There were several
suitable surfaces, some
more or less horizontal. A davenport,
sofa or chesterfield cumbered
with books, was the nearest, which weariness
plumped for. I thought of the luminous
scene at the end of the Gospel
according to John, when the risen
Redeemer, about to ascend
into heaven, addresses his followers,
charging the fisherman Peter
with feeding his flock. But when Peter
demands of the author, St. John,
the beloved disciple who leaned
on the breast of the Saviour at dinner,
"My Lord, what is this man to do?"
He replied, "And what is it to thee
if he tarry until I return?"
I must tarry at least until dawn
unavoidably, with or without
the implicit permission of Reverend
Father concealed by his screen
and so wrapt in remote meditation
or sleep that I felt as if I
were alone in the hermitage. Scorning
to make myself comfortable, stretched

on the moutains of Migne, I extracted
one volume that happened to dig
itself into my kidneys, and opened
the *sortes Augustinianae.*
"*Si sileat carnis tumultus...*
phantasiae terrae, aquarum
et aeris et poli:" "If flesh
and its uproar were silent, as well
as all earthly, acquatic, and aerial,
also celestial phenomena"—
"*anima ipsa si sileat,*
taceant imaginariae—
somnia:" "and if the soul
would be silent, and dreams and imaginings..."
"*et omnis lingua,*" "and every
tongue," "*omne signum,*" "and every
symbol," "*et quicquid fit nunc*"
"*transeundo, si tacerant,*" "everything
fashioned to vanish were still,"
"*audiamus sicut verbum ejus,*"
"we'd hear in a manner of speaking
His Word," "*non per linguam carnalem*
nec angeli vocem nec auditum
nubis, sed ipsum in his
audiamus:" "but not in the language
of flesh, or the speech of an angel,
nor yet from a voice through a cloud,
but Himself Whom we love in such things
we shall hear with no help from the same."
The Great Silence imposed itself finally.
Sleepless, I listened for nothing
and heard not a breath, not a syllable.
Dozing in spite of myself,
I awoke for a moment to find
that the paraffin lamp which I'd read
by had flickered like faith and gone out.

Book Four

Astra Castra

’Αστὴρ πρὶν μὲν ἔλαμπεσ ἐνὶ ζωὄισιν Ἑῷοσ
νῦν δὲ θανὼν λάμπεισ Ἕσπεροσ ἐν φθιμένοισ.

PLATO

(A star, you glittered like the morning when
You shed your radiance on living men,
And now, extinct, among the shades you are
Equally brilliant as the Evening Star.)

THE beginning of Autumn, or Fall,
     which recurs in the secular whirl
at the equinox, dates in liturgical
circles from early September,
and thence it was merely a matter
of days till my scheduled departure.
The total of badly typed pages
in English already outnumbered
the pages in French of *L'Expérience
Bénédictine*. Father Dagobert
urged me to hurry and finish,
while I like Penelope dawdled,
deploying the arts of revision
in hopes of postponing the end
of my task, and the term of my stay.
The canonical hours seemed to shrink
with the shortening days, until Prime
really signalled first light—*prima lux*—
whereas Vespers became almost vesperal.
Labour Day, summertime's terminal
fling, like the Fourth of July
an American popular holiday,
passed unobserved in the cloister
where everyday counted as Labour
and Pray Day. The day of my dreaded
return to the world, calculated
in time for the first day of class
at McGill, like all odious, red-letter
days soon arrived, all too soon;
but a summons again to the presence
of Reverend Father in God
Abbot Willibrord didn't. Dom Dagobert
hoped they would see me again
at the Priory when I'd completed
my secular service, and charged
me with messages for Verecundia

Valentine, Winifred Odin,
Immanuel Star and the rest
of his stellar acquaintance, in case
I should ever be lucky enough
to make theirs. The remaining community,
not having taken official
account of my presence and status—
not even a postulant's—found
no occasion to bid me farewell.
But the Abbé Clément with more generous
tact and affection inflicted
a Frenchman's farewell on my cheeks,
with the tacit embrace of the *Pax*
at the 'bus stop the morning I left
after Terce. In retracing my route
through complacent American townships
with classical names, and reversing
the course of my earlier pilgrimage,
what disappointment I tasted
at moving away from my goal
like a hostage constrained by the Rule
of St. Benedict, hijacked by holy
obedience! North to the border
I sped in a palindrome, faster
by far than I'd fled in the other
direction: reluctance accelerates
just as impatience retards.

If I didn't revert to the shelter
of Lazarus House, my excuse
was its distance from campus, not merely
as measured in miles. Alan Waterman,
when I dropped by on a visit,
insisted on giving me soup
and a hand-me-down sweater, and though
I repeated my name, he persisted
in seeing in me a mere stand-in
for Christ, as he did in the various
vagabonds, derelicts, drunks
and delinquents he saw every day.
I had often been puzzled by pity's
proverbial blindness, because
in my tiny experience, love
was all eyes, until visualized

in its aspect of agapé rather
than Eros. If lust be distinctly
observant and even inquisitive,
Charity can't see a thing.

The McGill I returned to was far
from incarnating Newman's ideal
university, parodied there
at the Campion Club by parochial
Poles and illiberal Irish.
It also fell short of its own
reputation, aggrandized, like most
institutions', by ignorant distance.
A stern, all too legible line
from my father in far-away British
Columbia spelled out his righteous
relief at my quitting the cloister
for normal, by which he meant Protestant,
varsity life, and applauded
what he prejudicially called
my return to my senses—approval
he ought to have saved for my Reverend
Father in God, Abbot Willibrord.

Now, after all my far-fetched
but instructive adventures in wonderland,
here I was, back in the very
same room I vacated last May
at the Old Presbyterian College.
The Campion Club, where I fancied
I might have been happier,
anyway subject to fewer
temptations, afforded no vacancies.
But in resuming my courses
in Classics, I swore I should never
resume the irregular courses
of youth, and the rackety life
I had led as a freshman before
my conversion. A sophomore, saddled
with folly and wisdom in grossly
unequal proportions, but poorly
equipped at the time to distinguish
the one from the other, amid
my habitual prospects I pined

for the habit I'd never officially
donned, and the clerical cloth
that eluded my grasp. Though I sported
a primitive tonsure on campus
this passed unremarked in that crew-cut
decade. Coming back in September
I found that the leaves I had left
on the trees in mid-May a luxuriant
green were becoming senescent
and sepia-tinted and fewer
each week. On the other hand, most
undergraduates, waxen and pallid
in Taurus, were brazen and bronzed
under Scorpio. I, having frittered
the summer away in translating
L'Expérience Bénédictine,
notwithstanding brief stints in the vegetable
garden, and briefer communal
outdoor recreations—the pond,
of which Reverend Father got wind,
being placed out of bounds—now stood out
for unnatural pallour if for
nothing else. Montreal in October
made up for its summery mugginess,
suddenly crisp as the apples
I kept on my windowsill: Gravensteins,
Golden Delicious or Winesaps,
and some Northern Spies, as they scented
the celibate hot-house I lived
in, a fragrant *memento* (or so
I assured myself) *mori.* The portals
of memory swing on such sensual
hinges, our cardinal clues
to the past are a matter of taste,
and of texture and smell, not the dominant
senses of hearing and sight
which, as stereotypical, fiddle
the evidence, serving a tyrannous
mental dictatorship. Atmosphere,
odour and flavour are harder
to fake and, at times, to identify
too, but the echoes they wake
are authentic as well as elusive.
The odour of overripe apples

nostalgically tinged with decay,
and the vigorous chill of the air
that intrudes in the form of a draught
through the window left open an inch
at the bottom to counter the fierce
central heating, to which as a native
of temperate climes I was little
accustomed, evoke even now,
reincarnate in essence a season,
a day at the end of October
1955, a peculiar
person, a ghost who may rise
at a word accidentally spoken,
refusing to answer a summons
sub poena, or visit my heartbroken
séance when formally called.
When the moment is ripe the immediate
scenery suddenly shifts
and the tedious present and all
its particulars vanish or fade
as the past like a backdrop, transparent
as gauze, and as flimsy, descends,
and I hear that extinct, unforgettable
voice, "Hi! I'm Hyacinth Star!"

Introductions are seldom one-sided,
like swords. If I had not yet drawn
on Dom Dagobert's recommendation,
and Freya's and Reverend Father's,
and looked up the Catholic analyst
Dr. Immanuel Star,
my reluctance was less a result
of habitual shyness than pride
unacknowledged, since knowing his name
would be useless unless he knew mine.
As a matter of fact I was not—
though the fact was not one which I cared
to make public—a fan of the *Pillar*
of Salt, with its petrified stance
and unsalty opinions. Moreover
I did not believe I required
psychiatric advice at the time,
an infallible symptom, or so
the profession would say, that I did.

While I tried to adjust to familiar
surroundings in vain, and put off
introducing myself to the father,
the son introduced himself out
of the blue, like a meteorite
or some similar heavenly body,
to me. I had fixed up my room
at the Old Presbyterian College
to look like an anchorite's cell,
to the spare institutional furniture
adding a crucifix, beads,
and a dressing-gown which I imagined
resembled a habit, though plaid,
the capuche of the Cameron order
perhaps? Up and down the linoleumed
hall, behind doors whether open
or shut, other rooms, in an obvious
pun on a currently popular
novel, concealed other vices,
all equally secretive. As
I was reading—my favourite solitary
vice at the time—on the morning
in question, the clock of the library
opposite tolling a secular
Angelus, told it was noon,
when a knock at my door, unexpected
if not without precedent, gently
repeated, announced a mysterious
stranger who entered before
I could say "*Benedicite!*", mouthing
the brief salutation recorded
above. As the door of my cell
was unlocked, it appears my ascetic
seclusion and studious pose,
if not truly a sham, were as vain
as my earlier quest for enlightenment.

Why is it hard to describe,
or recall first impressions of those
who are destined to play a significant
role in our lives? and so easy
to sketch an indifferent stranger?
The chap in the doorway would strike

me today as a boy, in his open-necked
shirt, scruffy flannels and old
mossy jacket—conventional garb
for a middle-class youth of that time
and that place, not unlike what I sported
myself. Although slender and taller
than I, who was five foot eleven
and scrawny enough in those days,
he affected a negligent slouch,
with his hands in his pockets when not,
as one was at the moment, extended
in greeting. The face that is soon
to become the beloved's resists
retrospective depiction: no photograph
captures his bistre complexion,
pale brown, like his hair and his eyes,
and his pleasant, irregular, delicate
features, too witty for beauty.
His salient characteristics
at first didn't seem to be his,
in the sense that his aquiline nose,
narrow forehead, full lips and recessive
but definite chin were: his tortoiseshell
spectacles, which in the 'fifties
just might have been genuine, clumsily
mended with tape, and his name
which he uttered defensively. Tempted
to ask if his friends called him Hy
and his enemies Cynthia, I
was reminded that mine, although shorter
(too short to be shortened to furnish
a nickname in scorn or endearment)
was quite as peculiar but lacked
his high-toned mythological resonance.
Doubtless his father had christened
him this when he entered the church
and translated their surname? Less queer
in provincial Québec than it seemed
at McGill, where he hid it behind
an initial—H. Star (an anthologized
anagram), Hyacinth—or
Hyacinthe—was the name of a German
twelfth-century saint, the apostle,
so-called, of the North, and a church

on the outskirts of Paris, of numerous
Gallican bishops, a notable
portraitist, several pages
of Sade that so far had by me
been unsullied, as well as Apollo's
devoted beloved or boyfriend
or catamite—choose the appropriate
term of abuse or approval
ad libitum. Only this final
allusion occurred to me now,
to be briskly dismissed, with the popular
name of the flower which is said
to have borne on its petals in Greek
the inscription AI which repeated
betokens lament: I must add
that the hyacinth nowadays has
neither petals nor letters: its bells
although fragrant, are mute. If he envied
the bearers of names rather common
than proper, like Roger and Peter
and Dick which they shared with so many
synonymous others, whatever
the drawbacks of Hyacinth socially
speaking—at school, for example—
by hearty Canadian standards,
it signified nobody else,
and soon unaffectedly fell
from my lips, its rococo frivolity
almost forgotten in view
of its personal reference. Hyacinth
didn't present himself first
as the son of Immanuel Star
but as Mark's naughty childhood accomplice
and chum, whose predicted appearance
provoked an absurd, inexplicable
blush, by recalling the night
when I first heard his name—a reaction
he slyly ignored and obliquely
appraised as he picked up the book
on my desk and inquired with a semblance
of interest, what I was studying?
Vowed though I was to humility,
still I had standards, and one
was that I never studied like those

who hung out in the library reading room:
rather, I read, and reread
on occasion but seldom took notes
in the margin. "*The Eclogues*." "Which one?"
He could see for himself but I mumbled
ironically, "*Paulo maiora
canamus*." "*Sicelides musae?*"
he laughed, and extracting a pen
from his jacket, proceeded to sketch
the Sicilian Muses, complete
with moustaches and motherly bosoms
in ink on the virginal fly-leaf
of Virgil—my Virgil, at least,
not a library copy. He drew
rather well, and remarkably quickly,
unasked and untaught, as I learned.
When I'd finished politely admiring
his handwork, Hyacinth flipped
through the text which his Jesuit schooling
had made him familiar enough
with to foster contempt. "Here's the one
that we never translated in class,
though a number of fellows construed
it in private: the second, beginning
Formosum—you know it?" Uneasily
blushing, I quoted from memory,
"*Corydon pastor ardebat
Alexim, delicias domini*,"
not of a mind to translate
this straightforward enormity. Hyacinth
like the psychiatrist's son
that he was and the analyst that
he aspired to become, penetrated
my pious façade at a glance
but said nothing, except to observe
that the textbooks identified blushing
with sexual ardour. Before
psychological jargon grew commonplace,
snap diagnoses like this
disconcertingly showed his vocation
as well as his background. But shutting
the book with a shrug he allowed,
"*Sua quemque trahit voluptas*."
I protested his accent or accents

pedantically: hadn't he—not
that it mattered that much—got it backwards?
and wasn't it *voluntas*, "will,"
that directed each one of us rather
than *voluptas* ("pleasure")? He shot
me a pitying, near-sighted look
which I wasn't far-sighted enough
to interpret. "That's Nietzsche, not Freud!"
I pretended I hadn't read either,
in this no more honest than ignorant
worldlings who claim they've read both.

Introducing himself to my history
Hyacinth showed little will
to withdraw, but no positive pleasure
in staying; he lounged in the window
embrasure, examined my books
(why do personal libraries count
as exempt from the social taboo
against snooping? The nature of print,
which is public while writing is private?),
uncrossing and crossing his negligent
legs and self-consciously brushing
his hand through his hair, which could only
be called hyacinthine, whatever
its colour. He brought out a battered
and half-empty pack of cork-tipped
Craven A.s which he proferred politely.
"No thanks. I don't smoke any more,
since I quit in the monastery." Hyacinth
seldom took no for an answer,
"Go on, I won't tell your superiors!
We've seen them all—Benedictine,
Cistercian, Carthusian—the lot."
"On retreat?" I was edified. Laymen,
I knew, like Immanuel Star,
over Christmas and Easter would frequently
stage a retreat to some comfortable
house of religion, to rally
their forces strategically. "No,
in my father's consulting-room." Crudely
he sketched a contemptuous gesture
by twirling his finger in air
by his ear and then tapping his forehead.

"He's cornered the market in clerical
crises of faith and devout
nervous breakdowns." I took his derisory
tone in the spirit in which
I accepted his cigarette (quickly
stubbed out in the waste basket after
one nauseous puff: did the apple
taste bitter to Adam? one bite
was enough). He enjoyed the prerogative
granted to born or at least
kindergarten R.C.s, of bad-mouthing
the Church, so distressing to converts.
He rose, "I was told to invite
you to lunch," he announced with one hand
on the doorknob. "I never eat lunch!"
I perversely refused without asking,
invited by whom? "Something else
you gave up in that monastery?" Hyacinth
smiled. As a matter of fact
it was not, but a novel austerity
practised in order to conquer
the flesh by omitting the midday
repast at the Old Presbyterian
College, although institutional
food was enough by itself
to determine my fast. "It's too early
for Advent. Come on!" I could hardly
reproach him with being a calendar
Catholic when part of the Church's
ineffable wisdom appeared
in appointing a season for feasting
as well as a season for fasting.
I wavered, as even the silliest
virgin must do when the bridegroom
approaches, the prospect of innocent
pleasure occluding my will,
and we left the Bucolics of Virgil
unread for that day on the windowsill.

Later that year and the next,
as the Autumn surrendered, too quickly,
to Winter, and Winter reluctantly
yielded to Spring, we had frequent
and regular lunches together,

since Hyacinth's Chemistry Lab.
and my Sophocles seminar ended,
on Tuesdays and Thursdays, at noon.
A premedical student, just setting
his feet on the seemingly endless,
laborious ladder toward
the M.D., and beyond, through internship
and specialization, he trod
in his father's professional footsteps,
a course whose apparent advantages
covered its Oedipal pitfalls,
which Hyacinth blindly ignored
notwithstanding his Freudian bias.
When hurried we patronized one
of a number of crowded since cheap
student restaurants close to McGill—
a Hungarian hang-out, a Greek
greasy spoon, and although I persistently
vetoed the tea room on Mountain
of infamous memory, even
the Old Presbyterian College's
dour cafeteria. Often,
our schedules permitting, he bore
me away in his Volkswagen beetle,
as now, to the kitchen in Westmount
where under a seventeenth-century
polychrome crucifix decked
with the dessicate fronds of Palm Sunday
his mother discharged without zeal
the traditional chores that the Church
and that eminent convert her husband
ironically, given the Nazi's
notorious slogan, imposed.
Kinder, *Kirche und Küche*: of these,
only Hyacinth, single survivor
of multiple sad misconceptions
and infant mortalities, thrived,
but both kitchen and church were the scene
of her vigorous daily routine.

Out of thoroughly modern Charlotte
von Dittersdorf slowly Immanuel
Star had confected a fetish
called Mutti, a martyr to marriage

and motherhood, bony and dry
as a fetish, yet handsome and even
distinguished, as fetishes go,
in a style Isak Dinesen's photograph
popularized. A descendant
of Ditters von Dittersdorf, skilled
as the women as well as the men
of that musical family were,
she performed at their small *Musikalische
Abende* skillfully whether
on 'cello, viola or oboe,
or passing around the delicious
refreshments she made in the kitchen.
She welcomed me, too, without question
not only as Hyacinth's friend
(for the friendships of youth are more instant
than Nescafé, needing not even
hot water) but as a prospective
recruit in the war, undeclared,
to the death, with her husband. I sensed
in this capable woman miscast
as *das ewige Weibliche*, qualities
not merely feminine: irony,
fortitude, warmth and tenacity.
Mutti before the conclusion
of lunch had requested I call
her Charlotte, three syllables, rather
than Mutti. The soup, as at Lazarus
House, was substantial and filling,
far from the thin gruel of Old
Presbyterian College and that
which my stepmother dished up from tins,
but much tastier, rich and exotic,
its leftover origins lost
in a medley of seasonings, like
those Canadian stews which unlike
the American melting-pot never
quite came to the boil. I detected
among the outlandish ingredients
garlic and lentils and bits
of Bavarian sausage; each mouthful
presented a hearty and new
gastronomic experience. Never
before had I tasted such—soup

was a wholly inadequate term!
In addition the table was laden
with black bread and butter, a basket
of cold hard-boiled eggs and a segment
of rubbery cheese of a kind
I'd not tasted before and was curious
therefore to try. It was there
I beheld—indeed held—my first peppermill,
pepper in Canada coming
already fine-ground in a shaker
like salt. Drinking beer with the meal
and not milk, which the goyim imbibed
at the Old Presbyterian College,
or water at Lazarus House
and Sweet Saviour Priory, struck
me as pleasant but strange, for while beer-parlours
played an (exclusively masculine)
part in our national life,
no one dreamt of enjoying a brew
with his food. When Charlotte, or Mutti,
began to extoll Alan Waterman,
spooked by that weird paranoia
that Catholic circles induced
with their more than Masonic coherence,
I weakly agreed that the work
he was doing was wonderful; but
when she broached her idea of teaching
the derelict practical crafts
such as weaving and bookbinding, Hyacinth
caught my incredulous eye
and suppressed an unfilial giggle.
Complicity, heady to one
who was starved for coeval companionship,
made irresistible Hyacinth's
jokes, innuendoes, irreverent
sallies and quips, which his mother
disparaged, but tolerantly,
in an accent attractively gruff
and Teutonic, like Freya's, another
acquaintance in common, her friend
of three decades, her juvenile
sidekick, as Mark in his turn
had been Hyacinth's. Now that I looked,
I could see the resemblance: an angular

grace and neurotic distinction
like that of the worm-eaten, wooden
Madonna that stood on a stand
in the dining-room, unsentimental,
severe, thirteenth-century—everything
bore at the Stars' an invisible
label, like those in museums,
proclaiming its age, in reaction
perhaps to the modern new world
which they found themselves in but not of.
Of our mutual friend in Minorca
I asked if they'd had any word
since I hadn't heard anything since
her departure last Spring. "She has quarreled
with Grief, to begin, over some
silly anthropological nonsense
or other." The poet and popular
novelist Reginald Grief
had resided so long on the island,
composing his archaeological
fiction, his residence seemed
prehistoric; he therefore regarded
all visitors, tourists or not,
as intruders or pilgrims, the latter
on minimal notice and less
provocation too prone to revert
to the former. Now Freya, I knew,
was acquainted with Grief, and had likely
offended the master by some
neolithic opinion. "And Mark?"
I inquired, unaware or unconscious—
the states are not always the same—
I was begging the sun that was rising
for news of the sun that had set.
"He was never a great correspondent,"
said Hyacinth, "Somewhere upstairs
in my room there's a postcard from Paris."
"I spent there one week in the 'thirties,
before you were born, and before
I was married, of course. I was running
away at the time from the fatherland,"
reminisced Mutti, but Hyacinth
having presumably listened
to this and to similar fugitive

anecdotes often enough
for one lifetime, respectfully lighted
a cigarette. "One of my grandmothers
only was Jewish, but that
was enough for the Nuremberg Laws.
Although Jews were forbidden to take
any cash out of Germany then,
at the border they never discovered
the thousand-mark note I had folded
again and again, very fine,
like a flower, and pinned to my hat."

After lunch in the kitchen Charlotte
suggested that Hyacinth show
me the house, on our way to his room,
an objective unmentioned and therefore
unquestioned. The typical Westmount
exterior, squarely constructed
of brickwork, contained an amazing
amount of substantial and elegant
stuff for a refugee family,
wardrobes and sideboards and bureaus
and tables and chairs, Biedermeier
and Buhl, an immense Bösendorfer
piano as big as my room,
and incongruous pictures by German
Expressionist masters and mistresses,
Kollwitz, Kokoschka, Kandinsky
and Klee. In his father's consulting-room
near the front door, so his patients
could make an anonymous getaway,
Hyacinth dared me to try
the analysands' couch, which was more
like a daybed, adapted to daydreams,
despite its luxurious cushions
as hard as the bed of Procrustes:
"To snooze is the analyst's privilege,"
Hyacinth claimed. At the windows
three layers of curtains excluded
not only all light but all sound,
like the threadbare but rare Turkish rugs
which were scattered more sparsely throughout
the ground floor of the house over acres
of burnished parquet that presented

a treacherous surface of ambery
ice. On one wall, underneath
a large, eye-catching ivory crucifix,
hung a framed postcard from—Hyacinth
certified—Freud, like a small
unofficial diploma. The Doctor
was absent, of course, at his clinic;
we tip-toed away, even so,
half abashed at invading the medical
fatherly sanctum sanctorum.
The Stars' was the first private home
I had seen with two staircases. I
as a guest was conducted upstairs
on my tour of inspection by way
of the polished front stairs that, uncarpeted,
rose like a shimmering, broad
frozen waterfall out of the well
of the hall. Further intimacy
introduced me in time to the narrow
back stairs where the sun never shone.
At the top of the stairs in a sun-filled
but otherwise empty front room
at the end of the corridor Hyacinth
showed me the loom at which Mutti
was weaving the warp and the woof
of her life, like Penelope biding
her husband's return toward nightfall,
a daily event apprehended
with patience. Bypassing some other
closed doors, with a flourish he ushered
me into his bedroom, a space
that like most adolescents he liked
to regard as his castle, besieged
as it was by parental demands.
Though untidy enough, it was less
metaphorically cluttered than Reverend
Father's retreat. Inquilinous,
at home in an instant, he threw
himself down on the badly-made bed,
recommending the only unoccupied
chair to my notice, where, after
removing an intimate garment,
I perched. On the walls, neither pennant
nor poster, whose heyday would dawn

in the following decade, but Dürer's
engraving, *Knight, Death and the Devil*,
and stacked by the bedside a ramshackle
tower of books which were bristling
with improvised bookmarks like matchsticks
and toothpicks and cinema tickets.
The desk top discovered a similar
muddle of papers and pencils
and paperclips scattered about
like a glacial morraine; and the floor
was adrift with discarded apparel,
worn underwear, socks, bedroom slippers
and handkerchiefs, moultings to feather
the juvenile nest, which resembled,
I couldn't help thinking, the ashtray
that sat on his desk overflowing
with cigarette ashes and butts,
half-burnt matches and orange peels. Yet
though offensive the odour was not
disagreeable. Under the scent
of tobacco and oranges lurked
the more personal smell of a healthy
young masculine body, astringent,
well-scrubbed, *sui generis*. Smell,
in most insects and beasts the supreme
aphrodisiac faculty, holds—
insofar as it does in this age
of deodorants—sway in the bedroom
alone. Only lovers perceive
those olfactory idiosyncrasies
friends are oblivious to:
so I ought to have known that I trod
on thin ice, or had set my infatuate
feet on the slippery slopes
of an active volcano the moment
I animadverted on Hyacinth's
physical odour. Unconscious,
as everyone is, of my own,
which he told me on further acquaintance
was equally fruity, I joked
that comparing our smells was, to borrow
a future cliché, like comparing
the fragrance of apples and oranges.

Dialogue, hard to remember,
is easy enough to invent,
but I hardly recall the agenda
of ours, though I've never forgotten
its fluent facility. Talk
tumbled out in exuberant question
and answer, abrupt, interrupting
each other, our flighty garrulity
loosed and excused by unusual
sympathy. Instant, spontaneous
gush is a strong indication
of burgeoning friendship. When Hyacinth
branded me "verbal," a term
psychoanalysts use, I discovered,
pejoratively, I was flattered
but also amused at the coffeepot's
teasing the teakettle's heady
ebullience. Not even love,
which succeeded so quickly to friendship,
could render us tongue-tied. One topic,
apart from our common acquaintance,
already exhausted, we shared
was religion, where Hyacinth's attitude
struck me as frivolous, not
to say wicked, while he was amazed
and amused at my recent conversion,
the reasons for which I could hardly
explain inasmuch as I didn't
myself understand them; I therefore
took refuge in mystical claptrap,
which Hyacinth challenged with equally
vague and jejune psychological
jargon. On learning my mother
was dead, he declared that explained
my recourse to the cult of the Virgin,
to whom my devotion had ever
been tepid. My passage with Mark,
and indeed Theodora's existence,
unmentioned, I prosed of prevenient
grace to one versed in neurotic
projection. But Hyacinth breathed
not a word of those boyhood adventures
which Mark had referred to obliquely
until we had crossed the unthinkable

Rubicon. Yet while we argued
at best disingenuously
and from different premises, he
on the bank, undermined by the current
unknown to himself, whereas I
out of depth in a flood I refused
to acknowledge, was clutching at frail
theological flotsam and jetsam,
we reached I suppose an unspoken
concurrence of sorts. How unspeakably
shocked we'd have been at the course
of our future relations, could we
have foreseen what was mercifully hidden
from view round the bend which the swift
irresistible river of time
was relentlessly rushing us headlong
towards! Conversation, before
it evolved into intercourse, eddied
and flowed round indifferent topics
submerged in a stream of impatient
palaver unruffled by any
impetuous, turbulent undertow.
Lulled by a spurious sense
of security here in this Catholic
home, in the company of
this obedient son of the Church—
there was even a cast-iron crucifix
next to the door—I relaxed
for the very first time since I entered
the trap, and examined the books
on his desk surreptitiously. Hyacinth's
indolent attitude sprawled
his permission. I opened—why not?
after all he had handled, defaced
or embellished my Virgil—a notebook
of drawings, or rather cartoons,
pen-and-ink over pencil. Satiric,
suggestive, adept, they depicted
a gamut of po-faced grotesques,
of which some were at once recognizable:
Mark with a cast on his leg,
upside-down but still strapped to his skis,
Theodora in Byzantine get-up,
("No, I never met her, but Freya

described her to Mutti."), his father,
presumably, bald and bespectacled
wearing a stethoscope over
a clerical collar, to illustrate
medicine's sacrosanct niche
in the twentieth century; after
the white-coated priesthood, a series
of clerics in black, whose scholastic
equipment identified them
as the Jesuits whom he had recently
quit. There were others, whom I
neither recognized nor can remember,
including one naked, anonymous
couple embracing: the fabulous
Beast with two Backs. With a shudder
I shut the irreverent sketchbook,
which Hyacinth asked me to pass,
with a pencil, to him. "Do you mind
if I draw you? I get so few chances
to work from a model." I froze
just as I was beginning to thaw.
There was something indecent in posing
like that, a life study, although
fully clothed, like submitting to some
life-and-death operation without
anaesthetics, but Hyacinth's pencil
was deft as a scalpel. He drew
as a matter of fact like a doctor
and not like an artist, the final
effect diagnostic and barely
aesthetic at all. "Just a minute!
I'm practically finished. Don't squirm!"
He inspected me with a direct
and perspicuous gaze that, unflattering
as its intent, must occasion
resentment in other conditions.
While stared at unable to meet
his contemplative eye, I pretended
to study the weird, allegorical
etching (if that's what it was)
over Hyacinth's bed, where he lounged
in the grip of painstaking depiction.
The devil, I noticed, looked grimmer
than Death. I had started to tingle

all over, when Hyacinth lowered
his sketchbook and pencil and stretched.
"You can look if you like." Was there ever
a subject, however immune
to the promptings of vanity, who
could refuse? He had captured my likeness
quite well, though my features were masked
by my spectacles, always a godsend
to caricature. Facing pages
displayed a satirical diptych:
on one I was draped in the cowl
of a monk, on the other, though equally
owlish, quite nude; anatomical
guesswork had filled in the blanks
meretriciously. "Sacred?" inquired
the inscription in Hyacinth's legible
hand underneath, "or Profane?"
As I gaped at him, speechless for once,
he proposed that we go to confession
together. I felt no immediate
need for express absolution,
whatever the moral bad taste
of his joke, having taken communion
that morning as usual. Yet,
unaware of a subsequent slipping
from grace, nonetheless I agreed,
if he liked, in the hope,
psychologically sound but heretical,
penance beforehand would act
like a kind of vaccine against future
occasions of sin; but at Hyacinth's
motives I wouldn't for worlds
have attempted a guess. With a wave
to his mother, who plying her shuttle
was deaf to our verbal farewells,
we departed the way we had come
in the family Volkswagen, actually
hers, since Immanuel Star
didn't drive but was driven—like me,
as a matter of fact: metaphorically
driven by what, I should presently
speculate. Hyacinth seldom
referred to his father by name,
like a plagiarist naturally careless

to footnote the author from whom
he derives his ideas, indeed
his whole being.

 We circled the Mountain
(retracing our route) where I'd dawdled
and dallied with Mark, and I almost
suggested a stroll; but the urgent
expression on Hyacinth's face,
like the look on the face of the Knight
in the picture, deterred me, as well
as the drab afternoon, neither lachrymose
Autumn nor furious Winter,
the trees for the most part denuded,
their colourful foliage splattered
all over the place, underneath
a cold sky of dull pewter which promised
the earliest flakes of the season.
We skirted the campus where lights
twinkled on in the various windows,
as nightfall began to anticipate
snowfall. As Hyacinth wanted,
he wouldn't say why, to confess
incognito, the Campion Club
wouldn't do, any more than his neighbourhood
church, so we drove to the draughty
cathedral across from the CNR
station, an equally top-heavy
pile in a similar style
of unwieldy baroque in the heart
of the city, at least of the Anglophone
part. Montreal had two hearts
and as many cathedrals as terminals
then: that their passenger traffic
is sadly reduced nowadays
may be seen in those vacant Victorian
temples of travel and faith.
Montreal, up-to-date, more and more
monolingual, despoiled of her drab
nineteenth-century charm, with the Old
Presbyterian College bisected
to make a new thruway, no longer
possesses two hearts, and the question
remains if it has even one,

notwithstanding the functional transplant
that serves as its pacemaker now.

There was nobody else in the church
at that hour; the cathedral at dusk
seemed deserted aside from its statues,
the vigilant, flickering tapers,
and hanging before the high altar
the lamp that betokened the presence
of God in His Sacrament. Briefly
we both genuflected, perceiving
our host was at home to receive
us, then looked all about for a deputy
ready to hear and remit
our transgressions. Halfway down the nave
in the lee of a pillar we spotted
a booth that, to judge by the toe
of a boot that protruded therefrom
and a sterterous snore, must be open
for business. "You first." "After you,
I insist!" Our politeness before
the confessional flowed from identical
sources: embarrassment, modesty,
shame, a reluctance to take
uninvidious precedence, like
(to anticipate) stripping in front
of each other, to find we were made
in a similar image, apart
from the scar of the covenant. Hyacinth,
seeing our spirits were weak
while our flesh was if anything almost
too willing, suggested we toss
for the dubious honour, and, "Heads?"
he extracted a coin from his pocket,
"Or tails?" I remembered Dom Willibrord's
homily. "Heads," my unconscious
replied without thinking, as that
which was Caesar's described its metallic
trajectory high in the air
of the temple of Mammon, to tumble
unerringly back into Hyacinth's
palm, which he opened triumphantly.
"Tails!" With a wink he retreated
toward the confessional booth

unimpressed by the seriousness
of his mortal predicament, whistling
a popular tune which I thought
that I recognized, "Pennies from heaven...."

While Hyacinth crouched on one side
of the listening post and embarked
in a murmur upon his confessional
voyage, I strove at an altar
nearby not to eavesdrop, preparing
my soul for a similar trip,
and determined, in case that untrustworthy
vessel should founder, to swim
for it. Prayer, the subjective sensation
of floating, immersed in pneumatic
oblivion, failed to sustain
me. The ocean St. Augustine tried
to imagine, when growing up far
from the sea, in a beaker of water
had shrunk to a drop in the bucket
containing the water of life.
*"Mon Seigneur, donnez-moi le courage
à regarder mon corps et mon âme
sans dégoût"*: to reiterate Baudelaire's
prayer in *Mon Coeur Mis à Nu*
was no doubt hypocritical, seeing
the body and soul at my back
were so far from the back of my mind
and the focus of far from disgusted
if so far Platonic regard.
The cathedral, a whispering gallery,
broadcast occasional syllables
clearly not meant for my ears.
The confessor's responses, aloud
in a bored, interrogative tone
as if nothing a penitent said
could surprise him, were "*Naturellement.
En effet. Oui, je sais.*" Why should Hyacinth
make his confession, I wondered,
in French? Anonymity is
one advantage an alien language
affords the discreetly repentant—
no wonder so many of Dr.
Immanuel Star's European

and few French-Canadian patients
preferred to be treated in English
where he was himself an articulate
stranger. "*Souvent?*" It was like
overhearing one half of a 'phone
call, collect and long distance: I could
reconstruct the inaudible poppycock
wasted on ears less attentive
than mine. In a twinkling the prodigal,
pardoned, returned to my side
at the rail of a garish side chapel
in front of a statue of bleeding
Sebastian, a muscular youth
in his underpants, bristling with arrows
and writhing in agonized ecstasy.
Hyacinth nudged me, "Your turn!"
As I rose from my knees in the silence
that filled the cathedral like twilight,
an islet submerged in the fluvial
traffic outside, I rejected
the echoing footsteps I heard
and the sigh of a sacristy door
as irrelevant sound effects. Drowned
and disoriented by this dark
afternoon of the soul, at a loss
for the proper or functional booth
to begin with, I trusted the organ
of smell. Amid various odours
of sanctity, beeswax and incense,
the perfume of prayer and the stench
of humanity's stale aspirations,
the fragrance of Hyacinth's presence
embalmed one confessional much
as it haunted his room. If the lingering
scent of his sins were familiar
already, I couldn't have guessed
just how soon they would also be mine.
The disgrace of my maiden confession
had not been repeated, as yet:
I had kept myself pure, in the Priory
effortlessly, at the Old
Presbyterian College with effort,
at least while awake. In my dreams
the unnatural promptings of nature

assumed a nocturnal exuberance
sorely regretted next morning
but hard to forget. Any sin,
my indulgent director of conscience
assured me, attached to a habit of morbid
perverse introspection. My conduct
was blameless, but still I felt guilty.
With little or nothing to tell
the invisible ear, should I make
a clean breast of unconscious intentions
and imminent acts? But the past
not the future is conscience's bailiwick:
what we will do we are innocent
of till we do it, tomorrow.
Condemned to a menu of leftovers,
tasteless and stale, I presented
those venial scraps that had always
gone down like a treat at the Priory.
Sloth I invoked to describe
the relaxed afternoon I had spent,
for a change, with a chosen companion
who wasn't a book. As for gluttony,
lunch had evoked a conception
of food that was not institutional.
Envy I labelled the feelings
that Hyacinth's presence provoked.
When I finished this rigamarole,
having made my confession linguistically
naked, in English, the priest
remained stubbornly mum, so remembering
Hyacinth's ruse, I repeated
a *précis* in French; but the clerical
oracle seemed to have taken
a vow of perpetual silence.
The longer it lasted the harsher
my probable penance. I couldn't
believe that my sins were so mortal
as quite to defy absolution,
determined to die in a hail
of Hail Maries. Unable to bear
the suspense and concomitant sense
of extreme disapproval, I peeked
through the grille: there was nobody there.
I had poured out my soul *in extremis*

and for the last time (though I wasn't
aware of it yet) *in absentia.*
Crossly I got to my feet
feeling cheated and foolish and snubbed.
St. Sebastian in polychrome orgasm
winked in his niche as the candlelight
fluttered and flared in a draught
from the back of beyond. I omitted
my penance, perforce—but perhaps
I am only performing it now?
With a nod to the sacrament, seeing
that Hyacinth wasn't in sight,
I walked out of the Church. In the narthex
I found him perusing a pamphlet
on birth control avidly. "*Quem,*"
he inquired in the words of the angel
in front of the tomb, from the sequence
at Eastertide, "*quaeritis?*" ("Whom
do you seek?") "*Non est hic,*" I responded,
"*surrexit.*" ("He isn't at home,
he has risen.") Outside on the steps
where amid phantom pigeons and actual
snowflakes we winced at a wind
that blew straight from the Hyperboreans
down Dorchester Street, it was night
though the hands on the clock of the opposite
station said, quarter past five.
"Do you know the Tzigane?" Did I not?
It was there I first met Theodora
and there I last met up with Mark.
"I could do with a Viennese coffee,"
cried Hyacinth gaily, "let's waltz!"
As he sprinted ahead down the steps,
I supposed what he meant, was, let's walk
the few blocks from our Volkswagen parked
on Dominion Square to the verge
of McGill. On the pavement the crowds
after nightfall were scurrying every-
which-way at the onset of winter,
like leaves, ill-prepared for this sudden
event as exciting as Spring.
If I say it was snowing like blazes,
the flakes seemed to burn as they melted
on touching the skin, frozen flames

that descended like judgement upon
Montreal, called the city of saints
for the number of streets that are saintly
in name, but whatever its sins,
not a city, to judge by the average
passerby's looks, of the plain.

In the steamy Hungarian tea-room
where business was humming but service
was not, we were lucky enough
to find places at once at a table
vacated the moment before.
If I recognized few of the patrons,
I hadn't set foot in this den
of *Gemütlichkeit* since last semester,
B.C.; or before my conversion.
In Canada afternoon tea
is a British tradition, "high tea"
a substantial plebeian repast,
not the snobbish occasion Americans
think, like High Mass. As a cultural
maverick—wasn't my act
of conformity really a show
of defiance?—I ordered *espresso*,
but Hyacinth, born if not bred
continental, preferred *cappuccino*.
"I feel," he confessed as he shrugged
off his duffle-coat, hooded, like mine,
with a pseudo-capuche, "I've come back
from the laundry all spotless and starched."
I refrained from explaining the cleaners
were closed when I got there. "I see
it as more like a bank, where you open
a savings account at your baptism.
First you deposit your sins—
your life-savings—and then you withdraw
absolution." "It's not always easy
to balance the books," he complained,
"and it seems so mechanical sometimes.
One moment you're broke, in the red,
and the next you're not only just solvent
again, in the black, but a millionaire.
Usury, that's what it is!"
The refrain from *The Cantos*, a work

I permitted myself to peruse
as not harmful to morals, impelled
me to play *advocatus diaboli*,
taking the Church as my client.
"Transferable credit, unearned
by the chief beneficiary, that
is a brief definition of grace."
"So you take out a loan on exorbitant
terms every time that you make
a confession...." "The system is foolproof:
an act of contrition, that's all
you are asked to put down, with forever
to pay." "I believed I was damned
half-an-hour ago, now I am saved
I'll be damned if I feel any different!"
However he felt, he was looking
unlike himself, having abandoned
his spectacles, fogged by the warmth
of the restaurant; mine, in the heat
of the argument mistily hampered
my view. "But I know that tomorrow,
next week or next month, I'll be bankrupt
again." Repetition, a constant
motif in the life of the Church
as in life (if there be one) outside
it, revolts the idealist. Gravely
alarmed at the mutinous state
of his faith, I prepared to defend
the old firm which I'd recently joined
to this long-term investor, while secretly
itching to cut all my losses
and run. "It coheres," I half-heartedly
pled, "as a system." But what
did I know about systems of faith
or coherence? "A marvellous fabric!"
he threw up his hands, "When you pull
out one stitch, it unravels." That fantasy
structures, while splendid to visit,
are hell to inhabit occurred
to us both. There is this to be said
for reality: seamless and sordid,
it seems to be solid as well
as insoluble. "What of your father?"
I risked an impertinence. "Hidebound,

an orthodox Freudian, orthodox
Jew in his youth, ultra-orthodox
Catholic now, living proof
of the great Judeo-Christian tradition."
"Whose tenets are Hope," I improved
on his error, "and Faith, and Karate."
He sneezed, "And the greatest of these
is karate!" If falling in love
were like catching a cold, one might harbour
infection for weeks, incubating
the virus, before one began
to exhibit the symptoms. My throat
was beginning to tickle, my eyes
were beginning to tear, but I stifled
that hypochondriacal habit
of taking my spiritual temperature.
"Hot in here, isn't it?" Hyacinth
sniffled, "I think that I'm getting,"
he muffled the rest of the phrase
in an almost immaculate handkerchief,
"something contagious." "*Gesundheit!*"
the dumpling-shaped waitress exclaimed
as she tardily brought us our orders.
Awaited so long, the exiguous
pleasure proved brief, but it took,
as predicted, forever to pay
at the busy cash-register where
I insisted on footing the bill,
though I couldn't afford to, and thanking
him lavishly. "Where are you going?
Quo vadis?" His passion for commonplace
Latin quotation, instilled
by the Jesuits, rivalled my own.
I explained I had paid in advance
for my meals at the Old Presbyterian
College's bleak cafeteria,
"Supper is over by six."
"You're too late," he consulted his watch,
which had stopped as he seldom remembered
to wind it. "Tonight you're invited
to dinner with us." Lest I think
that his family dined at a fashionable
hour, "It depends," he declared,
"when my father gets home from the clinic."

The household revolved round the hard-
working doctor like clockwork, as if
one so normally waited upon
could as naturally not be kept waiting.
I had to admit that my plans
for the evening were subject, for once,
to last-minute revision: tonight
The Interior Castle could wait.

The implacable snow was descending
much harder and faster outside,
Montreal had mysteriously
disappeared in the blizzard; we might
have been lost in the midst of a featureless
plain, an occasional headlight
or random pedestrian all
that remained to be seen of our urban
environment. Somehow, by instinct
or luck, we located the car,
as reluctant to move as the igloo
it looked like. But Hyacinth manfully
twisted the key in the frozen
ignition again and again
till the engine, as touchy as Eros,
turned over. We followed a streetcar
which crawled through the paralyzed traffic,
("Let's hope it's the right one!" "It says,
Côte des Neiges"), like King Wenceslas' page
in the tracks of his master. At last
we fetched up in the snow-drifted driveway,
so Hyacinth claimed, of his house,
like so many in Westmount I almost
expected to see as we stood
on the porch looking in for a moment,
another domestic interior.
Hyacinth opened the door
without knocking, I thought, with bravado,
and when we'd divested ourselves
of our overcoats, gloves and galoshes,
(I'd learned my first year in Quebec
to set out on a morning in Autumn
equipped for an evening in Winter),
he ushered me into his father's
redoubtable presence. In front

of a comfortless hearth, ornamental
in view of the tropical heating,
a squat, magisterial personage
waited, irascibly wringing
his hands, which were spotless, as bald
as a baby, and pouting like one.
This was Hyacinth's father, the famous
psychiatrist whom I had often
been told to look up. Introduced,
he inspected me with the professional
eye of a diagnostician.
"How are you?" he asked, not expecting
an answer, though shaking my hand
as if taking my pulse. But his natural
petulance, barely restrained
by politeness, burst forth on his offspring.
"You're late again!" stamping his foot
and displaying his wristwatch, he raged,
"And you know that I haven't yet eaten
since yesterday." Strange, was it not,
that the accents of Rome were so often
Teutonic? "I fast every year
on the Day of Atonement," he begged
to inform me, with something like pride,
"Yom Kippur, as I do on Good Friday."
I nodded; I knew from *The Pillar
of Salt*, which I shrank from acknowledging,
right off the bat, I'd dipped into,
his claim that becoming a Christian
had made him, not less of a Jew,
but incredibly more—not a popular
view in the ghetto, though those,
and not only the Nazis, who swore
that a Catholic Jew was a Jew
nonetheless, might concur. I suspected
however, he viewed his conversion
as rather like entering Graduate
School, a well-earned academic
promotion. "The Holocaust stood
for my own generation," he straddled
the glacial grate with complacency
hardly befitting his narrow
survival, "for what generations
have trod as the Way of the Cross.

I assume you are Catholic? No?"
Not awaiting my doubtful reply,
he expounded his dubious doctrine,
a mixture of Buber and Maritain
topped with a dollop of Freud.
The relation between the Mosaic
(I couldn't help picturing myriad
colourful fragments) and Pauline
or New Dispensation partook,
he averred, of the Oedipal complex,
inevitable, it appeared,
in all dramas of father and son.
Did he always, I wondered, not only
converse like a book but like one
of his own? Indisputably: Hyacinth
who must have heard the whole homespun
paternal megillah a thousand
times, slumped in a chair with a copy
of *Life* on his lap. (For the living-
room doubled as waiting-room serving
the patients of Dr. Immanuel
Star.) "Wouldn't anyone listen
to me for a change?" The explainer
exploded, detecting in me
an unlikely disciple. Naive
as I was in such matters, I viewed
as equivocal, even indecent
his timely defection to enemy
ranks. He would use the same words
without irony less than a dozen
years later at Hyacinth's funeral.

"Dinner, Immanuel, children!"
Charlotte emerged from the kitchen
disguised in an apron as Mutti
and bearing a steaming tureen.
Before sitting, we stood, as we had
at the Priory, bowed if not cowed,
while the head of the household intoned
benedictions in Hebrew and Latin,
"*Baruch...Benedictus...Amen.*"
We were served matzo dumplings in bouillon,
boiled carp and potatoes with horseradish
sauce, and a chocolate torte.

Conversation was general, that
is to say, in the absence of somebody
reading aloud, Dr. Star
dominated the tabletalk. Mutti
(I hadn't the chutzpa to call
her Charlotte, a word as opposed
to a name, that was never pronounced
in that cultured environment) seemed
to spend most of the meal on her feet,
in the kitchen preparing, or clearing
away and presenting the various
courses. Brought up as I was
in the wild, wooly West with its barbarous
manners, I offered to lend
her a hand, but was told, not unkindly,
to stay where I was. In all fairness,
Immanuel Star, while he talked
with his mouth full, unmercifully plied
me with questions—and answers—concerning
Dom Dagobert, Winifred Odin,
Dom Willibrord, Dorothy Day,
not to mention (however, he did)
Verecundia Valentine, all
of which notable Catholics, of course,
I must know? He elicited, too,
my opinion regarding the movement
toward a vernacular liturgy,
prior to giving me his,
and inquired, if he might be forgiven
for touching a personal nerve,
how I felt about celibacy?
He had analyzed many religious
and found underneath their professions
of crises of faith, that the root
of their trouble was normally sexual.
Hyacinth murmured, "There was
a young curate from Ealing...." "What's that?"
my inquisitor snapped. "Just a poem
I learned at Loyola, a limerick."
"Really, is that all the Jesuits
taught you?" "The Irish, at least,"
I attempted a comic diversion.
"Well, how does the rest of it go?"
"I forget." "I have heard of this curate

from Ealing," the doctor displayed
a surprising acquaintance with oral
tradition, "who had, I recall,
'a peculiar feeling'?" I blushed.
"But I see you remember the upshot?"
I quickly denied this, although
it was so, with instinctive hypocrisy,
such a manoeuvre as he,
and his son for that matter, would label
"resistance" no doubt.
                              After dinner
we moved to the sitting-cum-waiting-room
where the whole family tackled
a trio by Mendelssohn, Brahms,
or Dvořák. On 'cello Charlotte
von Dittersdorf-Star's dishpan hands
never faltered, but drew from that gruff,
most maternal of instruments sob
after heartbroken sob, while her husband
belaboured the keyboard, from which
he directed in testy asides,
("One, two three, you come in on the A!"),
disregarded, as far as my fallible
ear could make out, by the others.
That Hyacinth fiddled, ineptly,
exciting his father's recurrent
displeasure ("*Ach, Gott!* Will you practice?")
surprised me, but not very much.
As the urban consumer assumes
that all foodstuffs come frozen or tinned,
I, accustomed to music on phonograph
records, was stunned by the rank,
amateurish raw product, not only
because of the frequent mistakes
which I wasn't musician enough
to detect, but dismayed by its homemade
embarrassing quality: three
human beings in need (I suspected)
of tuning as much as their instruments,
trying to forge an inhuman
perfection of fugitive sound
in the midst of this comfortable room
unfamiliar perhaps in décor,
reassuring in terms of its lamplit

security. Listening to
the impromptu performance was like
watching somebody milking a cow
or performing some other uncouth
agricultural chore, and I marvelled,
so this is how music is made!
The finale, however, resembled
a three-legged race, the contestants
all crossing the finish line moments
apart, with Immanuel Star
in the lead. I applauded belatedly,
one more example of British
Columbian breeding; but Hyacinth's
parents ignored my applause,
(would one clap at the end of a record?),
departing in different directions
as actors withdraw at the end
of a scene in the classical theatre,
she to the kitchen, and he
to his bedroom upstairs, without saying
Goodnight. "It is past father's bedtime
already," grinned Hyacinth. "Doubtless
psychiatrists do their best work
in their sleep." "Mutti's tidying up
for the maid in the morning. I'll give
you a lift to your dorm." But, foreseeing
my evening concluded (or so
I concluded) before it had really
begun, for the first time in ages
I felt it was early, the night
still unbearably young. "I should pay
my respects to—Charlotte," I stalled
like a child at the zoo. "Don't be long."
I suppose it was natural, as her son,
Hyacinth always referred
to his mother as Mutti. My use
of her baptismal name was a strain
which attached me to her generation
but somehow estranged me from his.
At the sink she displayed the same bony
distinction she wore at the loom
or the 'cello; extending a soap-lathered
hand, she dismissed and invited
me back in one kind, economical

gesture. "Consider yourself
in the future like one of the family.
Do not be shy. We shall talk
you and I." If we never in so
many words were to do so, Charlotte,
innate, our complete understanding
was tacit, as was the protection,
just short of approval, you later
extended to shield the particular
friendship of me and your son.
You were always to be on our side,
your complicity sealing our lips.
When you took me next summer to Dorothy
Day's on a visit designed
to repair my irreparable faith,
you said nothing, but showed me the world
at our feet from the 'plane in the shape
of Manhattan, my dizzy first sight
of New York on my very first flight.
As for Dorothy Day, when at last
I encountered that mythical figure,
she sat monumentally silent
as well, like a sibyl with nothing
to say, or, it might be, too much.
You were speechless the last time I saw
you, soon after the "accident," Hyacinth's
suicide, followed by your
suicidal attempt to take flight
from the top of the stairs in pursuit
of him. How can I speak the oration
that's owed you, the Kaddish your renegade
husband neglected to say
at your grave? May the matriarchs, Sarah,
Rebecca and Rachel, receive
you in Israel's tents that eternally
shine on the shores of the biblical
sea! May perpetual light
entertain you, perpetual night
give you rest!
                         I am getting ahead
of my story. Awaiting me, dressed
to go out, in the vestibule, Hyacinth's
likeness, allowing for gender
and age, to his mother, was striking.

I could not foresee how profound
that genetic resemblance would prove,
for he hadn't as yet manifested
the manic-depressive disorder
which she would so floridly flaunt
in such grandiose gestures as whisking
me off to New York, and her scheme
to establish a Catholic Handicraft
Centre on one of the islets
that dot the St. Lawrence. But hearsay
of Hyacinth's hand-me-down mania
shattered me after his death,
when I hadn't begun to display
the same symptoms myself. At the time
I suppose our undiagnosed craziness
forged an unrecognized bond.

While the storm had subsided outside,
an unseasonable chill had descended.
We bundled ourselves into Hyacinth's
bug, where the warmth of our bodies
augmented the car's rudimentary
heater, and headed downtown.
Through the frostily lithographed windshield
an ivory cityscape, etched
by the moon, seemed indifferent save
for the purposes of navigation.
The streets whether empty or not
looked deserted, but Hyacinth had
the preoccupied aspect of one
whom the elements struck as irrelevant.
"What about writing to Mark?"
This suggestion bewildered me, "Where?
Do you have an address, in Morocco
or Paris or Switzerland?" Sooner
or later (but either too soon
or too late) we would write a joint letter
announcing our intimacy
indiscreetly, for like all clandestine
but foolhardy lovers, we had
to tell someone. This innocent, but
not innocuous bombshell pursued
him round Europe from pillar box to
poste restante for some months, till at last

it caught up with its target, both Hyacinth's
playmate and mine, who did what
one should do with a hand grenade, tossing
it back, without comment and under
anonymous cover to Dr.
Immanuel Star the next summer.
That pious psychiatrist, forced
to acknowledge the ongoing hetero-
dox abnormalities happening
virtually under his bed,
had no option but packing us off
to be treated by separate colleagues
of his, in a show of parental
authority somehow extended
to me. My first fling on the couch
was a flop. As in further encounters
with shrinks, my refusal in fact
to be shrunk was accounted resistance.
A single recalcitrant session
comprised my didactic analysis,
teaching me how in obscurantist,
authoritarian hands
the so-called talking cure could become
both pernicious and frankly nonsensical.
Hyacinth's psyche one might
have supposed to be sanforized, following
years of exposure to Freudian
steam, but he went like a lamb
to the cleaners. His cure was complete
in six months, when he learned to relate
to the opposite gender exclusively.
"Dr. Popescu," he murmured
the last time he laid his insomniac
head on my sceptical arm,
"says bisexuals suffer from penis-
fixation, and just have to make
up their minds!" This he did, with disastrous
results: the conformity seized
as a mode of survival would cost
him his life. We lost touch on my taking
French leave from McGill and absconding
to Paris. He married, and fathered
four children before he was 30,
while going through medical school.

Having qualified as a psychiatrist,
Hyacinth's illness eluded
the notice of colleagues and patients
and family, even his father.
He removed himself, leaving no note
but a stack of prescriptions made out
to himself for barbiturates, June
'67. His mother attempted
to follow him, falling downstairs,
and succeeded in breaking her hip.
Four years later she died in a madhouse.
His father complained at her funeral,
so I am told, as at Hyacinth's,
"Nobody listens to me!"

Right across from the Old Presbyterian
College, a wing of the library
called Redpath Hall, which was used
on occasions for large public lectures
and concerts, ablaze with electric
enticement, effused unmistakable
music. "It sounds," I asserted
the obvious, "like a rehearsal
of Handel's *Messiah*." "So soon?
Do you have to go up? You're as bad
as my father." Tonight my devotions
had lost their accustomed appeal.
"Shall we slip in the back?" I objected
to anything underhand; anyway,
wasn't this rather a surfeit
of music, I asked, for one evening?
But "Everything," Hyacinth quoted
that manic enthusiast Schumann,
"is Music." "All right," I prosaically
yielded. Unchallenged we entered
and climbed unobserved to the gallery
empty except for ourselves.

"Get thee up," a contralto exhorted,
"into the high mountains. Arise!"
she encouraged us, "Shine!" in the words
that had wakened me often in childhood.
The hall was unheated; because
of the cold, the musicians had kept

on their coats, the contralto, already
world-famous, her furs, so we listened
in ours. As for shining, I wondered
just when I first noticed that Hyacinth
shone like a son of the morning,
outshining his nice, unexceptional
looks. It is one of the kinder
provisions of providence that
I could not have foreseen how at last
he would shine like the evening star
in the mythical land of the dead.
The command to be comforted (piecemeal
performance befitting rehearsal)
reminded me how unbelievably
bleak and uncomfortable life
in the Church had become, in the light
of this cosy Arminian masterpiece.
"Every valley shall be,"
the heretical tenor exulted,
"exalted, and every mountain
made low." The articulate voice
had a thrilling conviction, a power
to convince with its threat of inverting
the natural order, I missed
in the sedative family trio's
discordant exertions, for most
instrumental performances moved
me to yawn and to squirm, unaffected
by songs without words. Altogether
fed up with the Catholic badlands
on which I had grazed for six months
on a diet of platitudes, flat
as Gregorian chant when compared
to the dizzying choral effects
of the Protestant masters like Bach,
Buxtehude and Handel, I yearned
to return to the free-thinking Rockies.

Of course the *Messiah* is more
than a mere oratorio: millions
have made it an annual rite
and a smug declaration of faith.
Disadvantaged in part by the role
it had played in my youth, when I rudely

asserted myself by refusing
to stand for the last Hallelujah!
I pitied and envied poor Hyacinth
whom it delighted as nearly
a new piece of music. Confined
to a wheelchair, the crippled soprano
who sang of the shepherds abiding
by night in the field with their flocks,
as if airborne, triumphant, surmounted
by means of her glorious voice
tribulation and avoirdupois.
"O rejoice," she invited us, "daughter
of Zion, O daughter," she cried,
"of Jerusalem, shout, for your king
cometh unto thee." Quite a far cry
from *The Catholic Messenger!* Cribbed
from Isaiah, the Authorized Version
libretto appeared to my Protestant
soul—*anima naturaliter
protestans*—all the more wholesome
for being in English, unlike
the vernacular gibberish Vatican
II would unleash on the faithful
in less than a decade: today
the communion of saints makes a noise
like a watered-down Salvation Army
revival. This text, messianic
and personal, promised indefinite
freedoms and joys where the Church
like a faulty contractor perpetually
prated of promises long
since fulfilled. Was the world, I blasphemed,
any better, in fact, for the bleeding
redemption? Was I any happier
having subscribed to that mystery?
Surely the cure had been tried
long enough, and produced no improvement?

"His yoke," so the chorus assured
us, "is easy, his burden is light."
My messiah (for Freud equates Eros
with light) I divined, was to come
and already at hand. This epiphany
hung in the air like a giant

perspicuous mandala, such as
Ezekiel saw in the valley
of bones, whose development opened
the heart as it heartened the ear,
till each note came alive (before drugs
were considered by youths like ourselves
indispensable adjuncts to listening
pleasure), the melody ran
like a messenger through the coordinate
harmony, chords like pilasters
supporting a temple whose heavenly
counterpart owed its existence
to George Frederick Handel, a popular
hack, Tweedledum, as one Philistine
called him, who plagiarized hundreds
of tunes that form part of the permanent
hummable repertoire, turning
out dozens of operas, overtures,
anthems, sonatas, concerti
and music which while incidental
to water and fire, elemental
but not elementary, was hardly
ephemeral. Handel transcribed
like the painstaking drudge that he was
the unspeakable that must be sung
in one language or other. While words
are enough for this world, as belonging
to Caesar's domain, it is music
alone that creates the superior
sphere of duration, which isn't
eternity, yet, but the abstract
enjoyment of time.
                    I awoke
from the revery music induced
just in time to agree with the vocal
quartet, that as man was the author
of death, and the virus of death,
in a nutshell, was sin, the occasion
of sin was the law. The conclusion
seemed painlessly obvious: anomie
guarantees innocence, hence
immortality? Even while blessings
and honour and glory and riches
were sung to the lamb that was slain,

and before the musicians could scrape
back their chairs, or could fold up their scores
like the Stars, a schismatical spirit
induced us to split, to the street
where the snow had resumed, not its first
elemental *allegro con brio*,
but random *andante cantabile*
flakes, and a neighbourly lamppost
made light of another abortive
farewell, as retreating toward
the impressive, ridiculous pile
of the Old Presbyterian College
I tendered my hand in its mitten
with thanks for a memorable day
and an even more memorable evening
I longed to examine in solitude.
"Haven't you time for a drink
at the Shrine?" He referred to a bar
at the gates of McGill, an ill-famed
student hang-out where no one was asked
for I.D., when identity signified
age. Having been there with Mark,
I declined to revisit the scene
of infatuate youth, and protested
as Hyacinth, taking my arm,
without argument marched me across
the marmoreal, snow-covered campus.

We couldn't have heard ourselves think
had we wished, in the beer-swilling, loud
undergraduate crowd at the bar,
but we ordered, or Hyacinth signalled,
a couple of steins which we took
to a table removed from the cheery
mêlée to converse in comparative
privacy. Dazed by the hour
and the setting, my childish but never-
abated amazement at being
exclusively here as opposed
to some vague, theoretical elsewhere,
enhanced by the peripatetic
existence I led in those days
(as if someone who lived all his life
in the place he was born were less subject

to panic?), derived from a permanent
wonder at being, whose requisite
prefix is somewhere. The reader,
in heaven or some Holy Office
on earth, who has followed the story
so far is at liberty, should
he desire, to complete it himself.
Out of multiple possible endings
I seem to have chosen the most
unimaginative for the most
inartistic of reasons, because
it occurred, though reality in
such a business has relative claims.
The creator of fiction alone
can assess the proportion of fact.
If I've tinkered with time, in a tidy
misguided attempt to abide
by the Aristotelian unities,
squeezing the action of several
weeks into one unforgettable
day, I have been topographically
faithful to space.
                I accepted
the cigarette Hyacinth proferred
which, unlike the first, I inhaled
as if toasting our friendship in smoke,
a notorious signal for fire.
It still tasted disgusting; the beer
was no better, though wetter, however
I savoured them both as the flavour
of freedom, as if on parole
I had finished a sentence for once.
I could see there was something that Hyacinth,
wanting to ask, was afraid
to, I couldn't anticipate what,
as he eyed me askance. Curiosity
conquered embarrassment, plain
as the nose on his amiable face.
In a lull of the hearty convivial
uproar around us he muttered
shamefacedly, "Somebody told
me you were. Homosexual." "That
is the clinical label, a hybrid
construction like tele-" I lectured

him, "-vision. I'm sure that our friends
at the bar would say *queer*, and I guess
they are right in my case if they mean
individualistic, peculiar—
who isn't?" He spluttered dissent.
"An American novice at Sweet
Saviour Priory—not such a novice,
perhaps, after all—who conceived
it his duty to naturalize
an outsider like me, once let slip
the arcane, unmistakable homonym,
gay." If this wasn't the first
time he'd heard of this technical sense
of a commonplace adjective, Hyacinth's
open-mouthed puzzlement lied.
It was certainly one of my first
and my few half-ironical uses
of what I dismissed as a nance word,
to which I objected on lexical
grounds. "What a shame, with so many
ambiguous phrases corrupting
the language, to add to their number!"
A lexicographical purist,
in time I would bracket this newfangled
meaning of *gay* with the equally
dubious usage of *hopefully*.
"'Hopefully gay' would describe
either one of us—" Hyacinth scowled—
"though in different indeed complementary
senses. It sheds a new light
on the troubadours whose *Gai Saber*
antecedes Nietzsche's *Fröhliche Wissenschaft.*"
"Isn't it simply a question
of what," —he would never say *we*,
only *you* when we quarrelled, "they want
to be called?" In an era ere negroes
were blacks, this was pretty broad-minded.
"But what if they wanted to call themselves
'niggers' or 'queers'?" I was stalling
again, by my usual verbal
manoeuvres, avoiding the question
implicit in Hyacinth's sheepish
citation of hearsay. "Whatever
you call it, *in posse*; however

not often *in esse*. Last winter
I had a one-sided affair,"
I confessed, "sentimentally speaking:
the physical side was reciprocal."
Hyacinth nodded: he knew
my anonymous lover was one
and the same as his nameless informant.
"Thereafter I thought I'd succeeded
in putting temptation behind
me." "You mean you've been pure, if perverse,
since you entered the Church?" Incredulity
coloured his use of a word
hypothetically Catholic: purity
proved an ideal infrequently
realized. Heterosexuals
married or burnt; homosexuals
lacked the alternative. Standards
like mine, which appeared Jansenistically
strict to a Jesuit-trained
cradle Catholic, merely obeyed
to the letter the rigid instructions
received in Instruction. "At times
are you ready to throw out the water
of life with the bothersome baby
of chastity?"
                    Deaf to this ludicrous
trope, at a neighbouring table
a drunken fraternity brother
reposed pleonastically, slumped
with his head in a puddle of beer.
"Get me straight, I like women," said Hyacinth,
telling the truth. "Well, I've had
no experience, really. Have you?"
So I told him about Theodora.
"The fabled *vagina dentata*!"
he marvelled, "You ought to tell Father.
That's one for the books." "But I've never
told anyone, even my confessor,
not until now." Having told
enough stories to last me a lifetime,
I listened, laid-back, while this heterosexual virgin related
how he was seduced at the age
of fifteen by a schoolfellow into

the pleasures of mutual something
or other, he wasn't precise
and I wasn't prepared for the moment
to press him. How odd our symmetrical
histories ended with each
of us having a single encounter,
a bust, with the opposite sex
to the one we supposed we preferred.

He excused himself, "Care for another?"
Though mine was as good as untouched
I was plastered already, or rather
I felt as if plaster were flaking
away from the mouldering idols
so suddenly smashed in my heart.
In an alcove behind me I heard
(if I didn't hallucinate) what
I could only describe as a voice
from the past: Theodora's, evoked
when I spoke of the devil, emitting
her characteristic *fou rire*
while declaiming, "Racine est un mauvy
poète," and a baritone, also
familiar, but less so, retorted,
"Corneille she is worse." Glancing over
my shoulder, I glimpsed the above-mentioned
blue-stocking dressed fit to kill
in a lethal black sheath, and made up
like a true *femme fatale*, on the lap
of a handsome, profane French-Canadian
type, Jean-Pierre, whom I knew
from the dorm, where he wandered about
in a towel, intoning obscene
variations (or so I assumed)
on *Auprès de ma blonde*. Theodora,
a bottle brunette whom I'd known,
in her cocoa and tea incarnation,
as mousy, was sipping an icky
liqueur, Benedictine or maybe
Chartreuse, while her gallant attempted
to kindle the cigarette stuck
in her plastic, preposterous holder.
These love-birds appeared so oblivious
to their surroundings, I flinched

when I caught Theodora's mascaraed
but beady-eyed stare, magnified
by her new contact lenses. Ungreeted
if recognized, guiltily turning
away, I remembered the line
in *Emaux et Camées* about Pleasure
that laughs in the alcove, and flattered
myself that, discarded, my mistress
was laying my ghost with a giggle.

Unsteadily Hyacinth loomed
at my side. "Shall we vacate this sink
of iniquity? God, you should see
the graffiti downstairs. Some half-cocked
introductory student of Latin
declined the demonstrative pronoun,
you know, *hic, haec, hoc*—you can guess
how it rhymes—in the genitive, dative,
accusative, ablative, vocative
cases; of course the oblique
are the worst." "It sounds more like a queer
conjugation than any declension
I know." "Finish up." "I don't want
any more." "Just a swallow. Let's go."
Shuffling into our coats once again
we abandoned the Shrine to its votaries,
butch Jean-Pierre and that bitch
Theodora, along with a chorus
of Philistine extras, clean-cut
in appearance if scarcely in fact.

After walking me back to Old
Presbyterian College, ostensibly,
Hyacinth stopped by his car.
When he opened the door without further
adieux I got in on the passenger
side. As to where we were going,
I didn't inquire as he drove
through the somnolent crescents and squares
like a drunkard undone by the modern
American weakness for wheels,
but it seemed we'd been driving all day
when not listening to music, which now,
the car radio playing *The Songs*

of a Wayfarer, Hyacinth hummed.
An elopement, no less: what parental
permission were possible, given
the fact that the parties were not
of appropriate, opposite sexes,
their union not only a sin
in the eyes of the Church but a crime
on the books of society? Eros,
the builder of cities, in most
is *persona non grata*. Together
that night we eloped from the world,
destination: each other. The route
that we took to the top of the mountain,
emerging in front of the darkened
casino, which Mark and I used
to frequent, was deserted at this
time of year, though a popular look-out
for lovers on warm summer nights.

Montreal like a great constellation
extended beneath us, outshining
the other extinct and remote
installations above the horizon,
indifferent, silent explosions,
or souls, whose inscrutable motions
control, as mankind has believed
during most of its otherwise meaningless
history, human affairs?
It would take, I observed, as we gazed
at the vast jigsaw puzzle, a trained
astrological eye to make sense,
or implausible nonsense, of such
an apparently random arrangement,
but Hyacinth tried to identify
some of the better-known patterns,
Orion, Callisto and Perseus
named by our mythopoetical
ancestors out of some classical
handbook, all quite arbitrarily.
"Star-gazing star," I recycled
a paranomastical epigram
Plato devoted to one
with a similar name also destined
alas! for disaster, "I wish

that I were the night sky, to observe
you with numberless eyes." I had never,
mirabile dictu, been kissed
by a boy, or a man for that matter,
before, my erotic experience
such as it was—for example,
with Mark—having been unromantic,
hidebound by the schoolboyish code
that condones all perversions but kissing.

Surprised by his sudden embrace,
I surmised it was Hyacinth's habit
(remembering heterosexuals
neck) to make out with his dates
when the time and the place were propitious,
however uncomfortably. Wholly
encompassed while still fully dressed,
a condition his ardour did nothing
to alter, I could not escape,
had I wished, from the vice of his arms,
as we listened to each others' heartbeats
imperfectly muffled by layers
of clothing, including our dufflecoats;
nor, had I wished, could I speak
with his lips over mine, like a lifeguard
attempting my resuscitation,
half-drowned as I lay in the wash
of our mutual wish. I could sense
in his silence and urgency pure
desperation, as if he astonished
himself. The embrace, whose duration
was less than a minute, became
absolute and interminable
till I wondered if afterthought ever
could finish what forethought had never
begun? But before an ambiguous
distance compounded our first
separation, "I had to do something
to," Hyacinth laughed, "shut you up,
with your corny quotations." He stifled
my stupid riposte. At the core
of the sensible multiple wrappings
of wool we were wearing, like sentient
mummies or babies in swaddling-clothes,

both our intelligent bodies
were nervously getting the message.
Ascesis succeeded belief
in the dustbin of personal history
as, simultaneously
wide-awake with excitement and ready
for bed, he relaxed his impetuous
clutch as he reached for the clutch.
"I had better be getting you home."
"Will you drop me?" I asked with regret.
He eventually did, as related
above, as he finally dropped
the pretence and the burden of living;
but dark as the decade ahead
was to prove, it was hardly as dark
as the following hours between midnight
and dawn, to our near-sighted gaze.
"I said home. You can stay overnight,
in the maid's room downstairs. But don't worry:
the maid isn't there." I accepted
this odd invitation without
for the life of me wondering why.

We returned, as if separately,
with no verbal or physical contact
(but none of our movements that evening
made sense until later) to Westmount
where everyone else seemed asleep
save a vigilant light in his parents'
front hall and a critical grandfather
clock on the landing. He sternly
admonished me, "Ssh!" "Is your father
a very light sleeper?" "He swears
that he doesn't, but really he sleeps
like the dead. Let me show you your room."
"And your mother?" "Oh, Mutti won't mind."
At the back of the house, off the kitchen,
in which he had riskily lingered
to finger a lightswitch, he opened
a door. "Here you are!" As if going
along with a harmless charade
I agreed, "Here I am." "Uh, I hope
you'll be comfortable. See you tomorrow."
The clock on the stairway struck one.

"It's already tomorrow." "Today,
then. Good night." We were both of us, all
of a sudden, unspeakably shy,
as if finding ourselves on the threshold
of something unknown, which just might
be a holy of holies. "Good night."
For a moment I thought he was going
to kiss me again, but he turned
and retreated across the immaculate
kitchen and up the back stairs
to his bedroom, without looking back,
a more prudent and scrupulous Orpheus,
leaving me faced with the ultimate
cell, whose ignoble domestic
dimensions contained an exiguous
cast-iron cot, all made up,
and an ironing board with a heap
of clean laundry, no curtains to cover
the blindfolded window, no rug
and no pictures, not even a crucifix,
nothing.
              Alone, I undressed,
for the first time in months without saying
my prayers, and got nude into bed,
which was narrow and cold as the grave.
Half-unconscious already, I slipped
into sleep with the ease of exhaustion
and youth, notwithstanding the strangeness
of all that preceded as well
as my present surroundings. I dreamt
of a featureless, snow-covered plain
about dusk, in the foreground a fence
of barbed wire, and a column of skeletal
figures in rags. In a volley
of incomprehensible orders
in German, my comrade was brutally
torn from my side, separated,
estranged, with no chance for a wordless
farewell, through the ivory gate
of the camp, which the future would prove
to be plastic, not horn. I awoke
God knows when, or was, rather, awakened
by something I had been awaiting
unconsciously, even asleep,

a somnambulic footstep, a hand
on a doorknob, an opening door
and a hoarse, recognizable whisper,
"Goddamn it, I can't get to sleep!"

Like a sleepwalker Hyacinth tiptoed
unerringly straight to the side
of my cot. I extended one hand
and encountered the hem of a flannelette
dressing-gown. "Get into bed!"
I implored, and for once he obeyed
the hypnotic suggestion, discarding
his bathrobe, which fell to the floor
like an obsolete self. In my arms
he lay utterly naked except
for his underpants. "Why?" I objected,
but he, sentimental as well
as naive, hadn't dreamt that it made
any practical difference. "*Totus
in armis et nudus est amor,*"
I garbled a tag from the *Vigil
of Venus*, "But Love, even naked,
is armed head to toe." "It's like going
to bed with a blooming anthology!"
Hyacinth grumbled, not slow
to adopt without shrinking the armour
and language of love. We continued
all night the caresses commenced
in the car, interspersed with involuntary
frequent spasmodic enjoyment,
exploring the pleasures at hand
without sexual sophistry, namely
each other, and falling asleep
in the intervals, murmuring amorous
syllables, principally each
others' names, each so rapt in the other
we felt it redundant to stammer
"I love you," that commonly tawdry
excuse. Although narrow, the bed
was immense for our purposes, clinging
together as both of us did
for dear life; and in Hyacinth's arms
I was coming to grasp what was meant
by the mystical body, at last.

"*Admirabile Veneris idolum
cuius materiae nihil
est frivolum*": words which some monkish
tenth-century Corydon wooed
his elusive Alexis with, wonderfully
sang in my head and my heart
and more wonderfully died on my lips
as I leant on one elbow above
my inert, temporarily sated
beloved, who proved, in the short
run at least, an insatiable lover,
"Adorable image of Love,
nothing common are you fashioned of."
Yet one characteristic of idols
and images tending to be
multiplicity, much as I cherished
the given, my fancy, unfettered,
ran riot imagining further
light-hearted, generic adventures.
I sinned in my heart—is there anywhere
else one can sin?—by mistaking
the end for the means. (A more common
mistake is the opposite.) Open
a door in a wall you believed
was impervious—who could refrain
from a peek, be the opening never
so lovely, the prospect impossibly
vague. My prolonged and unnatural
celibacy overthrown
in a single encounter, my nature
rejoiced in the thought of an infinite
series of possible matches
to come. This was partly the fault
of my failure, which must be called chronic,
to live in the present. How little
I guessed how the yearning one feels
for the past would surpass any faint
curiosity felt for the future!
I think, too, a sad, realistic
suspicion of Hyacinth's needs
as a "normal" or heterosexual
slave to the blind biological
surge that would carry him off

in a matter of months? in a year?
underlay my disloyal, illusory
notion that there would be others.
I counted this frivolous prayer,
which was not to be answered, a blasphemy:
"Make me promiscuous, Lord,
but not yet!" and remorsefully hugged
the unique, irreplaceable other.

Yet Hyacinth wasn't a door
but a window, like that he was posing
in front of, as stark as the wintry
pre-dawn infiltrating the shade
at his back, when I woke. Silhouetted
against the incipient morning,
he looked, with one hand on his hip,
like a figure of Perseus, hovering
over a sleepy Medusa,
averting his eyes from my petrified
gaze (we weren't wearing our glasses),
again fully armed, as if prudence
had given him wings, while the burgeoning
day made his helmet of hair
an aurora. "We ought to be getting
you back to the Old Presbyterian
College, for now," he aroused
me, ignoring my standing appeal
to return to the scene of the crime.
"You don't want to run into my father
at breakfast, though Mutti would not
turn a hair." He withdrew after donning
his robe, which the glimmering twilight
revealed to be indigo, barefoot,
or slipshod in darkness.
                         I dressed
and we met in the driveway. Accustomed
to being abroad before breakfast,
if seldom so early, for Mass,
I expected I might, for the future,
sleep in if I could. "Don't be silly,"
said Hyacinth, as without starting
the engine he put it in the gear,
so we silently coasted downhill
in reverse for a distance for fear

of awaking his parents, "Of course
I'll come up to your room for a while."
In the East, on our right, even now,
notwithstanding the wanly subroseate
flush that was tinting the snow-covered
streets like a scene in so many
old-fashioned Canadian paintings,
behind the eponymous mountain
the definite dawn was not breaking
so much as reluctantly cracking,
while off to the South, straight ahead,
in a region of obdurate darkness,
one planet, unblinking, above
the horizon held sway. "Is that Venus?"
I yawned, astronomically ignorant.
"Isn't it queer that the morning
and evening stars are the same?"

                    FINIS

Daryl Hine was born in 1936 in British Columbia, Canada, and read Classics and Philosophy at McGill University, before going, with the aid of the first of several grants, to live in Paris. He came to this country in 1962, and in 1967 took a Ph.D. in Comparative Literature at the University of Chicago, where he has taught, as well as at Northwestern University and The University of Illinois (Chicago). From 1968 to 1978 he edited *Poetry* magazine. He has published ten collections of verse, including a *Selected Poems,* and verse translations of *The Homeric Hymns,* and *Theocritus: Idylls and Epigrams.*

A NOTE ON THE TYPE

The text of this book was set in Sabon, a type face designed by Jan Tschichold (1902–1974), the well-known German typographer. Because it was designed in Frankfurt, Sabon was named for the famous Frankfurt type founder Jacques Sabon, who died in 1850 while manager of the Egenolff foundry.

Based loosely on the original designs of Claude Garamond (c. 1480–1561), Sabon is unique in that it was explicitly designed for hot-metal composition on both the Monotype and Linotype machines as well as for film composition.

Composition by Graphic Composition, Inc.,
Athens, Georgia
Printed and bound by Fairfield Graphics,
Fairfield, Pennsylvania
Designed by Harry Ford